THE UNVEILING
THE BOOK OF SEVENS

R. JEFF COLLENE

Copyright © 2016 R. Jeff Collene.

All rights reserved. No part of this book may be used or reproduced by any means, graphic, electronic, or mechanical, including photocopying, recording, taping or by any information storage retrieval system without the written permission of the author except in the case of brief quotations embodied in critical articles and reviews.

Scripture quotations taken from the New American Standard Bible®, Copyright © 1960, 1962, 1963, 1968, 1971, 1972, 1973, 1975, 1977, 1995 by The Lockman Foundation. Used by permission. (www.Lockman.org)

Used by permission. www.Lockman.org

WestBow Press books may be ordered through booksellers or by contacting:

WestBow Press
A Division of Thomas Nelson & Zondervan
1663 Liberty Drive
Bloomington, IN 47403
www.westbowpress.com
1 (866) 928-1240

Because of the dynamic nature of the Internet, any web addresses or links contained in this book may have changed since publication and may no longer be valid. The views expressed in this work are solely those of the author and do not necessarily reflect the views of the publisher, and the publisher hereby disclaims any responsibility for them.

Any people depicted in stock imagery provided by Thinkstock are models, and such images are being used for illustrative purposes only.
Certain stock imagery © Thinkstock.

ISBN: 978-1-5127-5702-6 (sc)
ISBN: 978-1-5127-5703-3 (hc)
ISBN: 978-1-5127-5701-9 (e)

Library of Congress Control Number: 2016915160

Print information available on the last page.

WestBow Press rev. date: 10/06/2016

*To my wife,
Barbara,
who has walked with me almost five decades
as we have walked with Him and loved His appearing
while looking for the Blessed Hope.*

CONTENTS

Preface xi
Acknowledgments xiii
Introduction xv

Part 1: Overview 1
    The Step of Faith 3
    The End 17
    These Last Days 29
    The Book of Sevens 35
    Seven Facets 45

Part 2: Seven Keys That Open The Revelation 51
    Key 1: Jesus: The Focus of The Revelation 53
        Loving His Appearing 58
        The Lamb of God 60
        Jesus In The Seven Facets 62

    Key 2: The Church: The Audience of The Revelation 67
        God Has One People 68
        What the Spirit Says to the Churches 75
        Jesus' Message to the Seven Churches 79
        To The Angel of the Church in Ephesus 86
        To The Angel of the Church in Smyrna 89
        To The Angel of the Church in Pergamum 92
        To The Angel of the Church in Thyatira 98
        To The Angel of the Church in Sardis 102
        To The Angel of the Church in Philadelphia 109
        To The Angel of the Church in Laodicea 114
        Conclusion 116

Key 3: Disclosure: The Intent of The Revelation. 119
    A Mystery to be Discovered 120
    The Seven Visions 133

Key 4: Heaven: The Perspective of The Revelation 143
    Creatures of Time 147
    Marking Time 155
    The Challenges of Heaven Time
        Chapter and Verse 158
        Imminent and Transcendent 162
        John's Experience 165
        Past-Present-Future 168

Key 5: Scripture: The Library of The Revelation 173
    Signs and Wonders 181

Key 6: Judgment: The Result of The Revelation 185
    Tribulation 188
    Fellow Companion 194
    The Lord's Day 196
    The Seven Judgment Announcements
    of The Revelation 198
        I.   Revelation in a Sentence: The First
             Announcement of Judgment 198
        II.   Warning to the Seven Churches:
             The Second Announcement of Judgment ... 206
        III. The Seven Seals and Seven Trumpets:
             The Third Announcement of Judgment 208
        IV. The Seven Signs of the War of the
             Seeds: The Fourth Announcement of
             Judgment 229
        V.   The Seven Bowls: The Fifth
             Announcement of Judgment 232
        VI. The Doom of Babylon: The Sixth
             Announcement of Judgment 235

   VII. The Great White Throne:
     The Seventh Announcement of Judgment...237
   Conclusion 239

 Key 7: Restoration: The Promise of The Revelation.......... 243

Part 3: Considerations 253
 Early Church Expectations 255
 History and Impact... 265
 Lenses: Defining Perspectives.............................. 273
 The Rapture of the Church.................................. 291
 Conclusion 299

Notes 303

PREFACE

I became a student of the Bible in the late 1970s after a personal awakening to the reality that God wants us to know Him and that He is self-revealing. I found and continually am surprised by the ways God has shown Himself to us in both general and specific revelation. So I guess I've become a Biblical treasure hunter! The parable of the Kingdom given by Jesus to illustrate the joy of finding the hidden treasure of the Kingdom is descriptive of my personal motive. I have continued to dwell in the Scriptures for decades and became convicted when I realized that I had settled for too little, especially with the challenging Scripture of The Revelation.

I have pursued many mentors over the years through books, sermons, Bible College, and good friends. However, I've never been satisfied with the explanations given for apocalyptic Scriptures. I clearly remember the excitement from the introduction of new possible explanations when each eschatological system was discovered. However, I was soon disillusioned with the results. I felt driven to discern the Big Picture that I was sure existed. With this challenge, and a myriad of lessons learned, I began to see The Revelation with new eyes.

As a pastor and teacher, I need to know what I believe. I, therefore, aim at an intellectual integrity in my explanation that is from my heart and my head. I believe a pastor can be tempted to settle with Biblical explanations in gray areas or with answers defined by others or with no answer at all. I don't want to land there. At the same time, I don't want to become dogmatic—black and white—or arrogant with a form of Gnosticism or self-righteousness. I enjoy the infinite reality of mystery, more specifically, the unveiling of those mysteries.

The Unveiling is an explanation of what I've discovered. My greatest difficulty was realizing and removing the presuppositions that, like fit-over sunglasses, affect all I see. It is my intent and prayer that The Revelation of Jesus Christ would be readable, accessible, and a blessing to all who would avail themselves of His great disclosure, His Unveiling.

ACKNOWLEDGMENTS

Due to my personal process of learning and churning, I must express my gratitude to those closest to me in this life who have endured my ramblings—thinking out loud. First and foremost to my wife, Barbara, who has encouraged me through each topic and chapter, and to my adult children, Jason, Matthew, Bess, and their families for their love and patience. I give special recognition to my daughter, Bess Bonewits (a gifted journalist), for her editing assistance and recommendations. I extend my gratitude to my coworkers, pastors Skip Harris, John Arvin, and Bryce Skaggs, at Cornerstone Community Church in Kansas City, Kansas. These men have stood faithfully by my side for many years and have listened to and reflected on each idea as I fleshed it out at many staff meetings and in personal conversations. It is my hope that we have all grown through this process. Thank you.

INTRODUCTION

The Revelation of Jesus Christ is captivating. I have been drawn to it since my first thorough reading many years ago. Prior to this time, I had been introduced to many ancient images displayed in churches, museums, books, and galleries. I had experienced musical and artistic renditions depicting final judgment. Of course, there are also many modern myths projected in graphic novels and action movies portraying the cataclysmic end of days. However, as a Bible student, each time I approached the book to read and study it, I found it overwhelming. Both its content and the seemingly complicated flow always resulted in frustration leaving too many unanswered questions. This process would repeat year after year. I would regularly give up on trying to follow the revealed narrative and slide into the easy ruts of previously applied meanings taught in numerous sermon series on "The Last Days" or explanations I read in prophetic books and Bible commentaries.

Again, the assigned meanings always seemed to fall short. These explanations came across as a forced application of the Scripture. I would always be puzzled by the arbitrary mixture of described symbols and applied literal contemporary meanings, sometimes in the same sentence. This combination of signs and symbols, and the attempt to literally interpret them and apply them, appeared to lack intellectual integrity as if they were used or interpreted to build a case rather than reveal the truth. These applied interpretive systems or perspectives seemed to fit well in some explanations but did not fit at all in other areas. There was the added confusion of multiple varied and conflicting explanations of godly teachers and commentators, primarily in the past few generations.

Having read many of the known influential books from each perspective, and continuing to absorb as much as I could comprehend and apply, I still was not satisfied. I would love to be able to remember and give credit to the many sources I drew from or credit years of research and language study of my mentors that I have absorbed that have birthed the ideas that have come together to form this book. I have received from many good thinkers and an eclectic pool of teachers. I've heard and can relate to this excellent expression: "I milk a lot of cows, but I churn my own butter." This book is the result of a lot of churning.

At one point, as many other frustrated readers of the Apocalypse, I eventually gave up on expecting a clear understanding and, therefore, lost sight of the obvious—the unveiling of God's truth. I have personally interviewed many Bible students and pastors about their understanding and experience with The Revelation. They, too, expressed the same frustrations. Most had given up on a coherent reading and application of this most important book.

Every other book in the Bible seemed to make sense. Each book appeared to give a clear expression of God's moral character and purpose and our problem and His remedy. All the stories in the Scripture seem to weave together the plight of humanity with the character of God. His moral nature, intentional acts, and overarching purposes are continually opened like the petals of a flower until the beauty of God's love is revealed.

However, when I would arrive at the last book, The Revelation, I would again find myself at a loss as I attempted to assign meaning through historical context and current events. I had experienced this occasionally in previous prophetic books when they also shifted into an apocalyptic mode. As I became more aware of the history of these applications, my uncertainty and frustration increased.

The writer of Hebrews states that the revelation of God is not a mixed bag of puzzling parts. He is not challenging us to piece together a scenario that defines a specific paradigm. Rather, His revelation is clearly seen in Jesus Christ. He is the subject of all Scripture and all Scripture is realized in Him. He is the Word of God, the Word made flesh. The testimony of Jesus is the Spirit of Prophecy. This is The Revelation of Jesus Christ.

> Blessed is he who reads and those who hear the words of the prophecy, and heed the things which are written in it; for the time is near. (Revelation 1:3)

If I read or hear the book of The Revelation of Jesus Christ with a natural mind that is motivated to discern or divine the future, I am as a deaf man attempting to judge music. If I pursue the flow of the seven documented visions with an eye to correlate the described events with recorded history or uncover a cryptic description of contemporary governments, or characters, or modern warfare, I am chasing my tail and will arrive where I began.

None of us has arrived. We are but pilgrims, a moving caravan slowly progressing through the gift of life, this threshold of eternity. I write about The Unveiling as a pilgrim, not an "End Times" expert. I seemed to have come upon a perspective of the seven revealed facets of the seven visions experienced by John that flow together and, to my understanding, correlate with all Scripture, which has begun to make sense to me. This perspective maintains an intellectual and Scriptural integrity that honors God's Word and continues in the stream of a fulfillment theology.

It is my prayer that God's Spirit will open our eyes to see that we might receive His unveiled truth, His great disclosure. I pray that He will give us a spirit of wisdom and revelation. For if He does not do this by His power, we are chasing the wind, trying to capture the elusive eternal and Divine infinite with a mortal and finite mind. God's wisdom and purposes are mysterious and yet discernable for those in relationship with Him. This is not an understanding laying on the surface or a puzzle to be untangled. It is God's greatest message to God's people. It is as the prophet Isaiah proclaims, God's great reveal.

> For from days of old they have not heard or perceived by ear, nor has the eye seen a God besides You, Who acts in behalf of the one who waits for Him. (Isaiah 64:4)

The Revelation of Jesus Christ is boldly introduced and described. His intention is clearly documented from its initial statements. But the ability to receive the truth of His revelation is only spiritually discerned. The natural man is at a loss and will only produce a temporary explanation or a use for the document that will pass away with the era in which it was determined. Therefore, I pray that you will begin in the Spirit. The disciples did not understand Jesus' ministry or His resurrection until their eyes were opened. May God open our eyes to His "Unveiling" of His story. The apostle Paul addressed this reality for us in his letter to the church in Corinth.

> And when I came to you, brethren, I did not come with superiority of speech or of wisdom, proclaiming to you the testimony of God. For I determined to know nothing among you except Jesus Christ, and Him crucified. I was with you in weakness and in fear and in much trembling, and my message and my preaching were not in persuasive words of wisdom, but in demonstration of the Spirit and of power, so that your faith would not rest on the wisdom of men, but on the power of God. Yet we do speak wisdom among those who are mature; a wisdom, however, not of this age nor of the rulers of this age, who are passing away; but we speak God's wisdom in a mystery, the hidden wisdom which God predestined before the ages to our glory; the wisdom which none of the rulers of this age has understood; for if they had understood it they would not have crucified the Lord of glory; but just as it is written, "Things which eye has not seen and ear has not heard, and which have not entered the heart of man, all that God has prepared for those who love Him." For to us God revealed them through the Spirit; for the Spirit searches all things, even the depths of God. For who among men knows the thoughts of a man except the spirit of the man which is in him? Even so the thoughts of God

no one knows except the Spirit of God. Now we have received, not the spirit of the world, but the Spirit who is from God, so that we may know the things freely given to us by God, which things we also speak, not in words taught by human wisdom, but in those taught by the Spirit, combining spiritual thoughts with spiritual words. But a natural man does not accept the things of the Spirit of God, for they are foolishness to him; and he cannot understand them, because they are spiritually appraised. But he who is spiritual appraises all things, yet he himself is appraised by no one. For who has known the mind of the Lord, that he will instruct Him? But we have the mind of Christ. (1 Corinthians 2:1-16)

We live in a time of great doubt and cynicism. The arrogance of man is exposed in his elevation of human reason. This humanistic rationale has been raised to the height of *real* truth. The result is that this arrogance has blinded us to truth Himself. This humanistic redefinition of truth is accepted and promoted by the secular mind, as it can only receive that which is objectively supported by the five senses. The natural man defines reality by what is seen, heard, smelled, tasted, and felt. So the result is concluded that if we don't feel it, it's not real. If we can't prove it with facts that we choose to accept, we doubt its veracity. So this truth, this secular, objective truth, may or may not be the same as the Word of God. This has resulted in a segregation of truth that is defined by that which is something man can justify. We have carved out the meaning of revealed truth and assigned our own. As a result, we have closed the door on God's truth, His Revelation, if we don't receive it in the spirit in which it was given.

Jesus addressed this reality when He was questioned by an earthly judge. This occurred just prior to His willing sacrifice to accomplish His purpose. When He stood before Pilate in the Praetorium under the accusation of the High Priest Caiaphas, Pilate asked what charges He was accused of and was not given an answer. Pilate then proceeded to question Him. His questions were simple and direct. Jesus' response baffled Pilate as if he were merely a pawn in the transaction. When

Pilate asked Him if He was the King of the Jews, Jesus answered with the truth we need to consider if we will receive His Revelation.

> Jesus answered, "Are you saying this on your own initiative, or did others tell you about Me?" Pilate answered, "I am not a Jew, am I? Your own nation and the chief priests delivered You to me; what have You done?" Jesus answered, "My kingdom is not of this world. If My kingdom were of this world, then My servants would be fighting so that I would not be handed over to the Jews; but as it is, My kingdom is not of this realm." Therefore Pilate said to Him, "So You are a king?" Jesus answered, "You say correctly that I am a king. For this I have been born, and for this I have come into the world, to testify to the truth. Everyone who is of the truth hears My voice." (John 18:34–37)

Jesus stated His purpose in revealing Himself to us. He is the point of decision. He is the truth. He came to testify to the truth! It is only by hearing His voice that we can have access to the truth. It will be accessible through no other avenue. Our option is to be "of the truth."

Revelation consists only of the thoughts of God. The five senses will be disoriented in any attempt to gain a natural traction in this last book of the New Testament. It was given as visions and realized as an experience by John to communicate a truth greater than man's reason and directed to God's people. It is supernatural. Even John's documentation displays his disorientation, and he is continually reminded by the angel to write down what he saw and heard. He is overwhelmed in the experience and by the truth he is seeing, experiencing, and comprehending. This is also the experience of anyone who approaches this book in the Spirit and wisdom of God. The opening to the reality of the spiritual dimension is all-consuming and overwhelming.

Our five senses give us a handle on reality within the minimal existence of our four dimensions. We can comprehend height, width, depth, and a measure of time. However, our access to the fifth dimension of spiritual reality is only accessed by faith. We do not walk by sight but by faith (2

Corinthians 5:7). Jesus responded to this test of reality by quoting truth revealed millennia before that "Man does not live by bread alone but on every word that proceeds out of the mouth of God" (Matthew 4:4).

May we discern God's wisdom in His mystery, the hidden wisdom that God predestined before the ages to our glory.

> Finally, brethren, whatever is true, whatever is honorable, whatever is right, whatever is pure, whatever is lovely, whatever is of good repute, if there is any excellence and if anything worthy of praise, dwell on these things. (Philippians 4:8)

PART 1

OVERVIEW

THE STEP OF FAITH

> If a man will begin with certainties, he shall
> end in doubts, but if he will be content to begin
> with doubts, he shall end in certainties.
> —Francis Bacon, *The Advancement of Learning*

> The beginning of wisdom is the fear of the Lord and knowledge
> of the holy one is understanding.
> —Proverbs 9:10

Writing on The Revelation of Jesus Christ is not just a daunting challenge but a humbling experience. The Scriptures are clear that there is nothing new under the sun, and I do not think my efforts are so unique as having not been considered before now. But I do hope to reintroduce The Revelation of Jesus Christ and this reality of a fresh and possibly renewed perspective into the conversation. My motive is to bring God's amazing Disclosure back into the Christian conversation devotionally and practically. I don't want to just make a point. I want to make a difference.

I am continually rehearsing my own spiritual and Biblical trek through these past six decades that have resulted in excitement, confusion, disillusionment, and resignation, not necessarily in that order. However, I have come to the wonderful place of daily expectation. I really believe, and have experienced, God disclosing Himself to me in many ways, primarily through His Word and His Church. I am amazed, though I do understand, that many pastors and serious Bible students no longer study or teach The Revelation of Jesus Christ. It has been relegated to the category of historical morality or futuristic imagination. This has resulted in confusion and disillusionment. The fruit of poor Bible teaching is misuse and abuse leading to no use!

There seem to be two developing camps concerning the explanation and application of The Revelation. One camp considers the book simply explained from past history while the other camp sees its unfolding contents imminently realized. Generally, the study of eschatology has suffered from one of two attitudes: neglect or overemphasis. The result has been a discounting reaction of those in the first camp that can result in treating The Revelation as an appendix to their theological systems. At the same time, the second camp has become fully absorbed, even obsessed, with an ongoing search for the next sign that will indicate the coming doom or their escape.

The contention of these two camps and their resulting confusion has led many to just choose to ignore the book. Some have resigned themselves to the fact that there is no possibility of making sense of the radical and discomforting consummation of the prophecies. Also, since much of eschatology has a focus on events that have not yet occurred, many Christians have ignored it. Another fruit of this confusion is the resulting separation of eschatology from the rest of Christian life and doctrine. My contention is that we, the Church, have lived in "these last days" since Christ's first coming, and the big picture of the conclusion of the two Biblical ages (BC and AD) are more relevant to the main themes of Christian activity and thought than many realize. The cross is the hinge of human history that delineates these ages, and we are now recipients and students of the first age and participants in the second.

I have come full circle in my personal considerations. I have increasingly gained a sense of expectation and a measure of certainty since I began to pursue God's intention with His Revelation. I realize that there are a number of schools of thought that dominate the interpretation and application of this book. My frustration at trying to justify any of them with clarity was further complicated with an inability to read the Scripture without being influenced by their presuppositions. That is, hearing what was said *about* the Word rather than a face value reading *of* the Word. Instead, I began pursuing clarity about the worldviews and systems of interpretation and then considering how their imposed perspectives affected my devotional reading of the Revelation. With this awareness, I am now attempting to push the door of the Revelation back open for myself and, as a pastor, encourage those who want to include it in their regular devotions again. Blessed is he who reads The Revelation!

The Revelation should not be discounted. It certainly should not be discarded into the dustbin of ancient documents relegated to superstition or myths for modern entertainment. Some have even tried to simplify the meaning and purpose of The Revelation by relegating it to a dualistic diatribe of exaggerated symbols of cartoonish proportions. The mystery of apocalyptic literature has escaped the comprehension of many of today's literary intellectuals who measure all truth and wisdom by a stunted rule of human understanding and scientism or the imposition of a contemporary literal interpretation. Some also approach the ancient disclosure with an antagonistic hubris that closes the door of comprehension in their own face.

This is why attempting to write anything about The Revelation of Jesus Christ is a daunting challenge and a humbling experience. The more I learn through prayer and study, and the more I *think* I know, the more I realize that I don't know. There is a wisdom in realizing that our humble reaction and amazement experienced at the seemingly infinite proportions to the acquisition of knowledge is that the ever lengthening diameter of knowledge only reveals the circumference of that which we do not know.

> "As our circle of knowledge expands, so does the circumference of darkness surrounding it." —Albert Einstein[1]

So this study begins as a mystery to be unveiled, a truth hidden but opened in relationship with the Source. The historical fact of the survival and inclusion of this apocalyptic document in the New Testament should initiate both the curiosity and humility of the reader, especially of the students that attempt to "master" the book. I believe that The Revelation of Jesus Christ is readable and applicable. It is the Author's intent that we receive His unveiled testimony.

> **I believe that The Revelation of Jesus Christ is readable and applicable! It is the Author's intent that we receive His unveiled testimony.**

Francis Bacon in his 1605 book, *The Advancement of Learning*, said, "If a man will begin with certainties, he shall end in doubts, but if he will be content to begin with doubts, he shall end in certainties." I am content to begin with doubt, but I am doing so in faith. Faith is not the absence of doubt but the overcoming of doubt. I love the process of discovery in the ever-opening mysteries of God. The seemingly incomprehensible realities and the infinite truths are made available to the finite mind. This then sets the stage for a challenging set of revelations that intend to bridge that gap between the two.

Faith is expressed in many ways. The most basic of these is our creed, the "I believe" statements of faith that define where our faith lays: belief. I remember memorizing the ancient creed of the apostles as a child.

> I believe in God, the Father almighty, creator of heaven and earth.
>
> I believe in Jesus Christ, God's only Son, our Lord, who was conceived by the Holy Spirit, born of the Virgin Mary, suffered under Pontius Pilate, was crucified, died, and was buried; He descended into hell. On the third day He rose again; He ascended into heaven, He is seated at the right hand of the Father, and He will come to judge the living and the dead.
>
> I believe in the Holy Spirit, the holy catholic and apostolic church, the communion of saints, the forgiveness of sins, the resurrection of the body, and the life everlasting. Amen.

This creed is defining and introductory; however, faith lived out is expressed relationally. We must live in the "I trust" reality of the interaction of a finite creature with an infinite God. We are like the child in the car seat of his mother's car, strapped down, facing the wrong direction in a machine beyond comprehension, headed to an unknown destination. But all is well when you are with Mom!

> **Faith is expressed in our creed with "I believe."**
> **Faith is expressed in our relationship with "I trust."**
> **Faith is expressed in love with "I obey."**

The reality of faith is expressed in action, in love, with "I obey." Jesus said if you love Him, you will obey Him.

> Jesus answered and said to him, "If anyone loves Me, he will keep My word; and My Father will love him, and We will come to him and make Our abode with him. He who does not love Me does not keep My words; and the word which you hear is not Mine, but the Father's who sent Me." (John 14:23–24)

This is the reality of a life of faith that truly believes and trusts. So I am content to begin with doubt, but I am doing so in faith.

We have a curious nature. Every parent is aware of the incessant flow of questions from their toddlers in the early years. Initially, our insatiable appetite is easily satisfied with the answers we receive about every recognized aspect of our lives. However, as we get older, the questions become more complicated and many are unanswerable. The "why" questions begin to overcome the "what" questions. The satisfyingly simple answers and dogmatic certainties expressed in the early years lead to the doubtful and arrogant years when we think we've figured things out, that we have all the answers we need in life, or believe that we have access to them. The current postmodern approach has gone so far as to discount and discard the wisdom of the past, carving out all meaning, so a so-called relevant meaning can be assigned.

Hopefully, life's maturing process leads us to realize that we really don't have all the answers, as the big questions of life loom over us with greater and greater weight. Someone once said that we can live a few minutes without air, a few days without water, and a few weeks without food. But we can live forever without answers. I know this is a true statement in this life, but I don't believe it is a necessary conclusion. Besides, while our curiosity is still at work, we wonder.

> **All Christian language about the future is a set of signposts pointing into a mist.**
> —N. T. Wright

N. T. Wright in *Surprised by Hope* states a revealing proposition: "All Christian language about the future is a set of signposts pointing into a mist." The branch of metaphysics dealing with the nature of being, ontology, describes the pursuit of answers to the big questions of life: Why am I here? What is my purpose for being? What happens after this life? Is this all there is? Why is there something rather than nothing? The reality of these inherent human questions, I believe, is God's purpose for His Revelation, to answer these life questions. We are not those who live without hope. As the apostle Paul proclaims,

> Therefore, having been justified by faith, we have peace with God through our Lord Jesus Christ, through whom also we have obtained our *introduction by faith* into this grace in which we stand; and we exult in hope of the glory of God. And not only this, but we also exult in our tribulations, knowing that tribulation brings about perseverance; and perseverance, proven character; and proven character, hope; and hope does not disappoint, because the love of God has been poured out within our hearts through the Holy Spirit who was given to us. (Romans 5:1–5, emphasis added)

THE UNVEILING

I hope to convince the reader of a simple truth that I have discovered. This truth is that The Revelation of Jesus Christ is readable, purposeful, and applicable. I have come to know that God is good; He is self-revealing. In fact, we know nothing of Him except that which He has revealed to us! It is my conclusion that the title of the last book of the New Testament is not only named because of the first word of the book but also to express the intent of the writer.

Therefore, I continue to read *The Apocalypse*, Greek for The Revelation, the unveiling of Jesus Christ, with this expectation, to discern the mysteries of God and to learn of His plan and His purpose. I read it with an expectation to see His intentions revealed and unfolded for His glory and our benefit. I hope to be a faithful steward of His mysteries (1 Corinthians 4:1).

In light of the incomprehensible series of wars and catastrophes of the past centuries and the resulting blossoming of contemporary progressive thinking of the modern mind apart from the mind of God, many peculiar and creative ideas have been introduced in man's ontology, his reason for being. It appears that the majority of people find the current answers unsatisfactory. The relative nature of modern reasoning is so filled with a bent of philosophical presentism, which makes everything about now and about us. This uncritical adherence to present-day attitudes has a tendency to interpret past events in terms of modern values and concepts. These thoughts and attitudes arrogantly dismiss the wisdom of the ages and the testimony of God's people through those ages. The church and her ministries have been dismissed as institutional intrusions and cultural impositions. A result is that The Revelation has also been cast on the refuse pile of history. The result is that we approach the ideas of our existence and our end, our eschatology, in light of current thought with little wisdom or spiritual insight.

Concerning those who look to God and His Word, however, I assume most serious students of Scripture wrestle with apocalyptic literature and the conflicting perspectives of its teachers. I have also come to the conclusion that everyone is still curious. If they have not been jaded by false teachers or disappointed by wrong conclusions, they are interested in a truly coherent reading of the Book of Revelation. Unfortunately, many seekers and Christians have been led astray and come to ungodly and unscriptural conclusions as a result. Many others have wearied and lost interest in its pursuit due to the fearful pronouncements and dire expectations. Some have given up on comprehending the complicated, confusing, and conflicting narrations by well-intentioned teachers who seemed to have formed an explanation and drawn a following.

I also have pursued an explanation and continue to accumulate and teach on "These Last Days" with a desire to help those who follow Jesus Christ and His way of life to see Him and His big story in a clearer light. This book is an introduction to the foundational, if not simplistic, truths that open the greater reality.

First, I have discovered and will introduce seven keys that I believe unlock or open Biblical apocalyptic literature. Second, using these keys as an overview, I am continuing to produce a commentary of The Revelation. Finally, for the past number of years, I have been accumulating a historical overview of "These Last Days," the period of time between Jesus' first coming until His second coming. It is my desire to apprehend and comprehend the applications of The Revelation through the past two millennia as these applications have led to many of today's conclusions.

Again, it is my belief that the *Apocalypse*, the Revelation of Jesus Christ, is readable and applicable in every age. It is my hope that the reader will pick up The Revelation again and read it with new eyes. This book is written from the presupposition that the Scriptures, the Old and New Testaments, are the inspired Word of God. They are true and reliable and, I believe, comprehendible in that God has revealed Himself to us through both general and special revelation.

It is His intention to make Himself known, and therefore, His Word is to be understood by the help of His Holy Spirit for that purpose. It is my contention that God's revelation is simple enough for a child to grasp its initial and primary meaning, yet so deep that we will spend eternity plumbing its depths. God intends to reveal Himself to His people. He is a self-revealing God! The Scriptures are intended for everyone. The Author has not written for scholars but for the hungry, those interested in receiving the revelation of God. I so appreciate that God's Word is aimed at the heart rather than the head. If our receipt of God's revelation were dependent on our intellect, well, the majority of us would have no hope. In Locke's "Notes On Ephesians 1:10," he states that "an impartial search into the true meaning of the sacred Scripture is the best employment of all the time they have." Yes, we are to apply ourselves with the resources we have at our disposal.

> Be diligent to present yourself approved to God as a workman who does not need to be ashamed, accurately handling the word of truth. (2 Timothy 2:15)

At the conclusion of Jesus' earthly ministry recorded toward the end of Matthew's gospel, Matthew documents a unique and historical event that occurred at the point of Jesus' death. The symbolic significance of this event is the display of the vision of this book.

> And Jesus cried out again with a loud voice, and yielded up His spirit. And behold, the veil of the temple was torn in two from top to bottom; and the earth shook and the rocks were split. (Matthew 27:50–51)

He describes the physical reaction of God's creation to this momentous event. It is recorded as a localized earthquake with a Divine purpose. The temple of Jerusalem represented the physical place on Earth where God's presence dwelled with His people, regardless of the fact that the Ark of the Covenant had not been mentioned and probably had been removed centuries prior to Jesus day. This, along with the absence of the *Shekinah*, the shining manifestation of the presence of God, the temple still held the holy sense of Divine presence. The reconstructed temple of the Idumean, Herod the Great, with the inner sanctuary and Holy of Holies, was empty of the original holy artifacts. However, the veil of the

Holy of Holies continued to represent the separation in the sacrificial system between a holy God and a sinful man. This was a symbol of the temporary gulf that God bridged through the sacrificial system giving humanity access to Him in prayer and worship within His prescribed calendar and the Feasts of the Lord and their sacrifices.

It is assumed that the politically assigned High Priest of the first century continued his charade of entering the Holy place before the missing Ark of God. Once a year during the Fall Feast, on the Day of Atonement (Yom Kippur), the High Priest was to sprinkle innocent blood on the mercy seat for the sin of the people, but it was not there! The last mention of the Ark was hundreds of years prior at the celebrations of Passover by the last godly king Josiah in 2 Chronicles 35, before Babylon destroyed and sacked Jerusalem the first time.

So the veil of the temple still represented a provisional separation between God and His people. But at the conclusion of Jesus' work on the cross, this veil was violently and publically violated, torn from top to bottom, exposing human hypocrisy and revealing a permanent change in man's access to this holy place. God was no longer out of reach. Access to the presence of God was no longer limited to one man from one tribe one day a year. He now invites and exhorts His people through the writer of Hebrews to take advantage of the access He provides.

> Therefore let us draw near with confidence to the throne of grace, so that we may receive mercy and find grace to help in time of need. (Hebrews 4:16)

Jesus' earthly ministry of fulfillment was the beginning of the end of this sacrificial age. The Revelation then introduces us to its final consummation in the realization of Jesus' prophecy on the Mount of Olives. The torn veil of the temple at Jesus' death on the cross, the cutting off of Messiah, was the first phase of Daniel's seventieth week and the end of the Old Covenant. These two tracks of the consummation of the ages are the subject of *The Unveiling*.

THE UNVEILING

The Bible is the most central book in the history of the world. It has been—and will continue to be—discounted by many. Abraham Heschel, the Jewish theologian and scholar, critically addressed Christian scholars with this observation:

> It has seemed puzzling to me how greatly attached to the Bible you seem to be and yet how much like pagans you handle it. The great challenge to those of us who wish to take the Bible seriously is to let it teach us its own essential categories; and then for us to think with them, instead of just about them. (J. Richard Middleton, *The Liberating Image*)

Christianity is a revealed religion. God has spoken! This book is my attempt to set aside conflicting thoughts and assigned meanings that have been applied through the centuries with a desire to see the essential categories of The Revelation come to the surface and then think with them instead of just about them. It is my desire to experience the seven visions of The Revelation with John and see and experience what he saw and documented for our benefit.

Given such a wealth of revelation stirs up a responsibility in the heart to both pursue and attempt to understand the words and their meaning. Due to the complex integration of the common English language, a dictionary is a required tool—both the original and the revised versions. If at all possible, it is very helpful to understand what the words meant to the original hearers. This challenge is realized by study and is assisted by the Holy Spirit through His inspired teaching gifts that Jesus gave His church. The understanding gained should give us instruction in life. In other words, we attempt to understand, first, what the words say. Then, establish a context in what the words meant to the original hearers. And, finally, "What do they mean to me or how can I apply them in and to my life?"

Regardless of our comprehension, we are to consume the Word as food for thought, for action, for being. Revelation is central to Christianity. Truth is knowable, and God's Word is knowable and must be central.

Jesus said "He who has My commandments and keeps them is the one who loves Me; and he who loves Me will be loved by My Father, and I will love him and will disclose Myself to him." (John 14:21)

So as we pursue Him, listen to Him, and obey Him, He reveals Himself to us. This includes His plans and purpose and our understanding in life. As the writer of Proverbs concludes,

> The beginning of wisdom is the fear of the Lord and knowledge of the holy one is understanding. (Proverbs 9:10)

Jesus is the Holy One. Wisdom is the speaking voice of God. This voice resonates in and through His creation and speaks into our lives. He spoke all things into being—He holds all things together by the Word of His power—His wisdom is available to those who ask for it. The Scripture is not a book of religion but a narrative, a unique interpretation of universal history, of creation and the human race—His story.

The Scripture is not a book of religion but a narrative, a unique interpretation of universal history, of creation and the human race. His story.

Again, The Revelation of Jesus Christ reveals a series of seven visions experienced and documented by John (seven being the number of completion, fullness, and rest). These visions are not only interrelated and overlapping, but they also reveal different aspects of similar events and truths. It gives multiple narrations of God's interaction with a fallen world, the history and revelation of His ever-releasing judgment, and its ultimate consummation. We are to read the whole text; it is the grand narrative from God's perspective. We are not to divide it up to fit into our lives or make it all about us and all about now. Jesus is revealed. He is the center of the story. He brings meaning to the story from beginning to end. We are to find our place in His story. As the Apostle Paul exhorts the church in Rome:

> Therefore I urge you, brethren, by the mercies of God, to present your bodies a living and holy sacrifice, acceptable to

THE UNVEILING

God, which is your spiritual service of worship. And do not be conformed to this world, but be transformed by the renewing of your mind, so that you may prove what the will of God is, that which is good and acceptable and perfect. (Romans 12:1–2)

The motivation for our pursuit of His Word is not to master a rational explanation that will divine our future but a transformation of our own hearts in the light of His revelation. Our deep channels of thought that compose our mind are to be formed by His wisdom. Therefore, Scripture is a unique interpretation of the human person as a responsible actor in His story. The Bible is not a book about me but about God!

It seems that man's frustrations with God's Word are continually expressed by those who approach His Word with an intellectual and self-gratifying motive rather than from a humble reception of the intended revelation given. Remember, Jesus' words always aim at the heart rather than the head. His intention is to sow words of life into the soil of our hearts so we might be changed from the inside out. So in frustration of an intellectual mastering of His Word, many give up and quit the pursuit. As a result, they are fasting their required spiritual food.

This is illustrated in a story of which I wish I could give credit, for it is a powerful lesson. It is the story of a grandfather and his visiting grandson at his place in the mountains. Each morning, Grandpa would get up early and sit at the kitchen table reading from his old dog-eared Bible. His grandson, who wanted to be just like him, tried to imitate him in any way he could. However, the grandson found it very difficult to develop a habit of reading his Bible.

One day, the grandson announced, "Grandpa, I try to read the Bible just like you. But I just don't get it, and what I do seem to understand I forget as soon as I close the book. What good does reading the Bible do? I feel like I'm just wasting my time."

The grandfather quietly turned from putting some coal in the stove and asked, "Would you take this old wicker coal basket down to the river and bring me back a basket of water?"

The boy gave his grandfather a puzzled look and did as he was told. However, all the water drained out before he could get back to the house. The grandfather smiled and said, "That's all right. Just go and get me another basket of water."

This time the boy ran faster, hoping to retain some water, but again the old wicker basket was empty before he returned home. Out of breath, he told his grandfather that it was impossible to carry water in a basket and that he was not going to be able to do as he had asked. The grandfather said, "You are doing well, but would you get just one more basket of water?" He then went to the door to watch the boy try again.

At this point, the boy knew it was impossible, but he wanted to show his grandfather that even if he ran as fast as he could, the water would leak out before he got far at all. The boy scooped the water from the river and ran hard, but when he reached his grandfather, the basket was again empty. Out of breath, he said, "See, Grandpa? It's useless. I'm just wasting my time!"

"So you think it is useless?" Grandpa said. "Look at the basket." The boy looked at the basket, and for the first time, he realized that the basket had changed. It looked different. Instead of a dirty old wicker coal basket, it was clean.

"Son, that's what happens when you read the Bible. You might not understand it all or remember everything, but when you read it, it will change you from the inside out."

This is the truth of God's Word. We are invited to read and promised a blessing if we do so. The Revelation begins with this exhortation, "Blessed is he who reads and those who hear the words of the prophecy, and heed the things which are written in it; for the time is near" (Revelation 1:3). I want to help make Revelation readable so that it will be read. I want God's revelation to change me, cleanse me, and have its way with me. I pray the same for the readers of this book.

THE END

God has never been reactive, but He is always revealing!

In the days of the voice of the seventh angel, when he is about to sound, then *the mystery of God is finished*, as He preached to His servants the prophets.
—Revelation 10:7, emphasis added

God will invade. But I wonder whether people who ask God to interfere openly and directly in our world quite realize what it will be like when He does. When that happens, it is the end of the world. When the author walks onto the stage the play is over. God is going to invade, all right: but what is the good of saying you are on His side then, when you see the whole natural universe melting away like a dream and something else - something it never entered your head to conceive - comes crashing in; something so beautiful to some of us and so terrible to others that none of us will have any choice left? For this time it will be God without disguise; something so overwhelming that it will strike either irresistible love or irresistible horror into every creature. It will be too late then to choose your side. There is no use saying you choose to lie down when it has become impossible to stand up. That will not be the time for choosing; it will be the time when we discover which side we really have chosen, whether we realized it before or not. Now, today, this moment, is our chance to choose the right side. God is holding back to give us that chance. It will not last forever. We must take it or leave it.
—C. S. Lewis, *Mere Christianity*

The Revelation is more than *The End*; it is the whole story. However, it is the end with which we are most concerned. Evidently, God intends that we come to know the whole story, not just our conclusion. As an act of mercy and a demonstration of our inclusion, the Creator God has pulled back the curtain of His Story, our history and our future. He has revealed His plan and the process for His purpose to have a people of His own possession who love Him by choice and enjoy Him and His creation. His descriptions are mind-blowing, frightening, and exciting, and His symbols are both ancient and foundational as He unfolds His story in The Revelation. The Revelation is multifaceted and complete—heaven oriented—event filled—and all-consuming. This is The Revelation of Jesus Christ, which God gave Him to show us, His servants by inclusive choice.

His descriptions are mind-blowing, frightening, and exciting. His symbols are both ancient and foundational as He unfolds His story in The Revelation.

His message and original intent are stated at the onset by His recorder, the apostle John. John includes his own participation and understanding in the opening chapter. He identifies himself as a fellow brother and companion "in the tribulation and kingdom and patience of Jesus Christ" (Revelation 1:9). This reference is the earliest indication of the primary purpose for giving this disclosure to the reader: it is an exhortation for perseverance. We are to be faithful to the end as God reveals His promise and that end.

There are some who are critical of the assumption that accepts John the Apostle as the author. The evidence for this assumption is built into the language of the book itself. First, John simply introduces himself with his first name. He would have been well known to the churches of the first century and especially to the immediate audience, the churches of Asia. The Gospel of John further develops language included in The Revelation with key thoughts that identify Jesus as the Word of God (Revelation 19:13; John 1:1, 14) and the True Witness (Revelation

THE UNVEILING

2:13; 3:14; John 5:31–47; 8:14–18). The John of The Revelation is also acknowledged by some of the early church fathers as the disciple of the Lord, His apostle. There are many scholarly works of explanation for authorship. I choose to simply flow with the historical assumption of the authenticity of John the Apostle.

There is another reason that the authorship of Revelation is a point of contention. The argument for or against the apostle John is a component of the case that is built for an early or late date of The Revelation being penned. That determination then serves as a key component of a promoted eschatological system (their assumed system of relating to the end of the world or the events associated with it). There are many crucial conclusions that ultimately reflect or substantiate the perspective of the commentator. These will be introduced in a later chapter of considerations entitled "Lenses."

Refocusing on the purpose of The Revelation, we are exhorted to hang in there! We need hope to live. Those who live with hope do so because someone planted the seed in their lives through a promise. This promise is built into the language and traditions of humanity's cultures, but most fall short. Someone needs to impart a hope that is true, a confident expectation in a dying world. Many today live without this kind of hope, and, as Christians, this is our mandate and a primary motivation to spread the Good News.

From ancient times, all who had looked forward in a faith based on the protoprophecy, the first and foremost promise of God's remedy in Genesis 3:15, looked for a provision shrouded in mystery. Their only clarity lie in the reality of a Divine provision and the expectation of that provision through the "seed of the woman." This also sheds light on the Old Testament emphasis on the value of a woman in Israel's culture and the curse of a barren womb. This is expressed by Mary's relative, Elizabeth, at the realization of her pregnancy. The Scripture records,

> When Elizabeth heard Mary's greeting, the baby leaped in her womb; and Elizabeth was filled with the Holy Spirit. And she

cried out with a loud voice and said, "Blessed are you among women, and blessed is the fruit of your womb! (Luke 1:41–42)

This is a hope of restoration, a promise of God to His people. We are now those who look back and realize that this was fulfilled in Jesus the Messiah—His life, death, burial, and resurrection. All who looked forward in hope or have looked back in faith to Jesus the Christ for that provision have found their answer in the cross, the hinge of history.

God's promise of judgment on the deceiver has given the confidence of justice to all who trust in Him. This is His provision for hope, for redemption, and for purpose. Since He clearly proclaimed His intention to provide the remedy to mankind through the eternal blood of the Lamb, humanity has continued to live either in that hope or in an ignorance of that provision.

Now for millennia, all those who have walked the earth with this hope and in this faith have ultimately come to their end in this life, as all mankind does. "It is appointed for men to die once and after this comes judgment" (Hebrews 9:27). Our eschatology, our end, was announced in a warning and realized in the consequences of Adam's choice: "You shall surely die" (Genesis 2:17). This is the personal and experiential reality of our own realized eschatology and our continued study of end things.

As introduced in the Genesis protoprophecy, all eschatology includes the three basic components of a judgment of the wicked, a reward for the righteous, and an ultimate restoration. Regardless of the era of our service in the Kingdom of God on earth, we are serving as His "called-out ones" in the world. We are all to persevere until the end, our end, while expecting an ultimate end. This is a challenge for us to live our lives in a broken world yearning for restoration in bodies destined to die yet looking for the resurrection. The old maxim is our motivation in life: "I will live as if this is my last day on earth but work like I have a hundred years."

The protoprophecy is God's provision.

> And I will put enmity between you and the woman, and between your seed and her seed; He shall bruise you on the head, and you shall bruise him on the heel. (Genesis 3:15)

God proclaims His intention for the initiation of His plan for man's redemption and the restoration of all things. God has never been reactive, but He is always revealing. His proactive plan of faith, hope, and love was present in His heart before the first Word of His creation was spoken. Jesus is the Lamb of God slain from the foundation of the world; as the writer of Hebrews states, "The works were finished from the foundation of the world" (Hebrews 4:3). God knew what it would cost Him before He began the process. He is the wise master builder who counted the cost and deemed it worthy to have a people of His own possession who chose Him in love. He created us in His image with a purpose in mind: companionship, creativity, and co-ruling as a kingdom of priests in His creation.

> And He has made us to be a kingdom, priests to His God and Father—to Him be the glory and the dominion forever and ever. Amen. (Revelation 1:6)

And again,

> You have made them to be a kingdom and priests to our God; and they will reign upon the earth. (Revelation 5:10)

Remember, God does not react, but He does reveal. All that we know is a result of His revelation, His expressed desire to dwell with man, to make Himself known, to expose His heart and His nature so we might choose Him and love Him in return. God is self-revealing, and we are blessed to be stewards of His mysteries.

God does not react, but He does reveal.

My desire is simple. I want to help Jesus followers receive the blessing of Jesus' Revelation by making it readable. I believe that His Word is eternal and His intended application of The Revelation is not limited to the first-century church or the third-millennium saints. I hope to simplify the multiple facets of The Revelation by clarifying the sequence and relationship of the seven visions that John experienced. I also hope to point out the unintended consequences of chapter and verse divisions, as these complicate rather than elucidate and infer an assumed flow of the visions. Finally, I hope to use these keys to The Revelation to peel away some of the layers of historical and presumptive interpretations and applications that cloud our view from what I believe was originally intended. My purpose is practical: that the church may read and be blessed as introduced with this promise in The Revelation of Jesus Christ,

> Blessed is he who reads and those who hear the words of the prophecy, and heed the things which are written in it; for the time is near. (Revelation 1:3)

The opening verses of chapter one reveal Jesus as the source of the unveiling. John is the witness to the Word of God and the testimony, "even to all that he saw." The opening verse also states the consequence of the reading.

This revelation was not intended as a form of divination for uniquely gifted teachers to unravel their angle and sequence of the prophetic puzzle as their view of the future or their explanation of the past. Fear motivates a need for control, and man's attempt to divine the future is a vain attempt to reinforce that sense of control. God's intention is for His people to find their security in Him and to be blessed by their inclusion in His plan and the awareness of His purpose. This is the truth of the often stated reminder of this comfort that we do not know what the future holds but we know Who holds the future.

The Revelation concludes in the same fashion of exhortation, blessing those that read and heed.

> Behold, I am coming quickly! Blessed is he who keeps the words of the prophecy of this book. (Revelation 22:7)

THE UNVEILING

We naturally develop a system of thinking, a worldview based on our culture, education, and experiences, whether we realize it or not. It is important to become aware of this bent and try to comprehend the effect it has on our interpretations of life. This influence is pervasive when we consider apocalyptic pronouncements. It is my desire to pursue a Biblically revealed explanation and application of The Revelation. So becoming aware of the influencing factors, the lenses we look through, is very eye-opening. If we look at the world through rose-colored glasses, all will look rosy. If we are aware of these lenses and remove them for an untainted view, our perception changes. This is difficult to accomplish! The same is true for The Revelation.

The Revelation is the unveiling of Jesus Christ to His saints for His purpose of exhortation and encouragement. If we become aware of and can expose the reality and impact of our natural bent, our perspectives and the paradigms of our religious cultures, then we might realize the ideas that tend to influence our understanding and interpretation of The Revelation.

The blessing of our Christian heritage is rich and deep, but it can also cloud our perception, applying a presupposition of the applications of Scripture. It is sometimes difficult to gain the intent of the Scripture because of what we have been told the Scripture says. This can ring louder in our ears than the actual reading of the words. We have accumulated great insight and, at the same time, quite a load of baggage through the years. This baggage, for many different reasons, can make it almost impossible to simply read the Scripture.

We need to become aware that we have developed a worldview and, for many, a Scriptural perspective and interpretive system. As a result, we see the world as through a lens by which we view the Scripture and its application. Armed with this knowledge, we can then begin to open our minds and forge fresh and deep channels of thought that give the light we need to persevere. I hope to bring a fresh look. I have observed some basic keys that may be obvious to some readers, and they open

The Revelation and simplify a perspective. These are the topics of "The Seven Keys That Open The Revelation" in Part Two.

My intent is to begin with the end in mind. This is the second habit of *The Seven Habits of Highly Effective People* taught by Stephen Covey in his book by that name. At the beginning of 2011, I began a Sunday morning series for Cornerstone Community Church in Kansas City, Kansas, on the book of Revelation. I had not taught through the book to my church before this time. In fact, I realized that I had not studied through the book or outlined it since Bible College. This teaching discipline has been my habit for regular study of books and topics for many years. I enjoy the clarity that comes with systematic study and pursued application. I have done this with a number of other books and topics that are available in the resources on my church website, www.onthecornerstone.org. Like many pastors, I had shied away from a systematic teaching of The Revelation. Too much confusion, too many charlatans, too many disappointments, too little understanding. This misuse and abuse led to my "no use" for the book. Yes, I regularly read Revelation in my annual Bible reading, and I referred to familiar Scriptures from the book in my teaching, but I had not attempted to gain a clear overview since those Bible College days decades ago. Prior to this teaching series I had been led to read and reread The Revelation over and over again for over a year. I had a desire to saturate my mind and heart in this book, to meditate on God's Word.

The pastoral problem with teaching The Revelation to a conclusion is comparable to the contemporary political reactions to imposed legislation in Washington. The volume of pages of new laws and regulations are so complicated and corrupt that statesmen and lobbyists alike condemn and cast insults. They swear to cast them out as soon as they have the power to do so but offer no replacement for the original problem addressed. I found myself in this conundrum by rejecting the popular explanations and applications of The Revelation but unable to offer another coherent explanation. This book is an introduction to some of my thoughts and discoveries as I have pursued that pastoral application and those Biblical explanations.

Like my fit-over sunglasses, I had to intentionally remove inherited and applied perspectives to begin to see without their influence and my presuppositions. It is difficult to do, but it is possible. When The Revelation is read without bias, it explodes with even more impact, and God's perspective is made known. The mysteries and depth of its visions will capture the imagination. Again, it is difficult but very rewarding. This difficulty has resulted in many either ignoring the book or obsessing about it. I believe it is to be read as God's Word, His revelation to us for our benefit. When it is read, it produces transformation and we gain insight into the nature of God and the nature of man. As we read, we will become more aware of the spiritual reality of the dominant spiritual dimension.

> For our struggle is not against flesh and blood, but against the rulers, against the powers, against the world forces of this darkness, against the spiritual forces of wickedness in the heavenly places. (Ephesians 6:12)

After reading the book of Revelation through many times, a number of keys became apparent. These keys are so obvious as to seem unnecessary to note. However, I will proceed with their introduction and expand each one in Part Two.

The *first key*, and most obvious, is that Jesus is the focus of The Revelation. This first key brings an overruling reality of peace and order in a violent and chaotic description of judgment. He is glorious and victorious throughout the documented visions. The Revelation begins with Him, centers on Him, reveals His mercy and power, and ends with Him.

The *second key* needs to be stated, as simple as this might seem, in that God's people are His audience. The Revelation is not written to an unbelieving world but to a believing people. I will elaborate on the perspective required to define, include, and speak to God's people. This key addresses the consideration of two audiences, Israel and the Church, and clarifies the Biblical application and disclosed inclusion.

The *third key* is as important as the introductory phrase of the book. This is that disclosure is the intent of The Revelation. God's motive is clear from the first sentence. The title is more than the first words of the book; it is the very nature of God: self-revealing. He has unveiled His plan and purpose to His people.

The *fourth key* is transformative. This is the unique approach that has allowed me to see with new eyes, and I hope it serves you just as well. This is the overwhelming view that heaven, the spiritual dimension, is the perspective of The Revelation. A Divine paradigm is needed to see all that God reveals to His people. Our limited view can serve us poorly. As the illustration of the penny held close to the eye can block the view of an entire mountain, so our finite chronological view can blind us to the heavenly perspective being opened to us.

The *fifth key* is foundational in this: what God has already revealed is not in conflict with what He is revealing. Rather, the Old and New Testaments are the library of introduction for The Revelation and the literary model for interpretation. Commentators have reported that there are over four hundred references to the Old Testament in The Revelation. I have not counted them myself, but I do not doubt their study. The Biblical practice of noting and studying the first mention of words, types, and symbols, especially in Genesis but throughout Scripture, is the foundation for seeing the additional truths and the mysteries opened to us.

The *sixth key* is the dominant theme of unfolding judgment as the purpose of The Revelation. Throughout Scripture, the "Day of the Lord" describes His judgment on His people and His intervention in human history. The seven separate visions of the book reveal God's judgment on a sinful people and a sinful world. It is my opinion that the seven separate descriptions of announced judgments are a kaleidoscopic view of His fulfilled Word on these pronouncements throughout Scripture rather than a linear sequence of events. Both the realized judgment on humanity's sin and on Israel, the temple and the sacrificial system, as well as the ultimate global consummation of the age are realized in the visions of the released judgments, sometimes simultaneously.

The *seventh key* is the most encouraging realization of the promise of restoration. "Behold, I am making all things new" (Revelation 21:5). This hope is revealed in the glorious Christ in the beginning of the book and concludes with the victorious Christ united with His people in the full restoration with a new heaven and a new earth.

THESE LAST DAYS

It is God who has the last word on the last days.

God, after He spoke long ago to the fathers in the prophets in many portions and in many ways, in these last days has spoken to us in His Son.
—Hebrews 1:1–2

The study of eschatology, or "these last days," includes much more than the close of the age. In other words, we are an eschatological people, also referred to as living an inaugurated eschatology. Our personal paths all lead to the same end, and we are curious as to how this plays out. The writer of Hebrews states this boldly and without exclusion:

> And inasmuch as it is appointed for men to die once and after this comes judgment. (Hebrews 9:27)

The New Testament references to the descriptive phrase "these last days" open our understanding to a greater inclusion of God's overall time frame. The promised coming of the Messiah and His finished work is the fulfillment of the Old Covenant, the cross of Christ being the very hinge of human history. The Scriptural value and detail of the human channel by which God enters the human race through the portal of the godly seed is realized in the nation of Israel. It has been clarified and codified in the Judean and Davidic lineage lists of Matthew and Luke's gospels. Matthew's kingly lineage leading to Joseph and Luke's ethnic lineage leading to Mary both reveal a prophetic parentage and a Divine hand in the fulfillment of the Genesis 3:15 proclamation to provide man's remedy for sin and separation. There are many other Scriptures fulfilled by this fact.

The apostle Paul boldly proclaims this gospel and states that *it* is the power of God for salvation to everyone who believes, to the Jew first and also to the Greek (Romans 1:16). So this flow of blessing is through His portal to His people. As the gardener waters the garden, the life-giving water flows to the water hose first and then to the flowers. God's blessing has come through His provided seed and has been made known to the world, to the Jew first and then to the Gentile.

We live in a time that seems to discount the past, to devalue tradition and heritage. There appears to be an intentional goal to carve out and repurpose meaning and history. The modern mind is even recapturing the empty rhetoric of the ancient past with the notion that time continually and interminably repeats itself. The pagan primordial Babylonian religious beliefs of the unending cycle are reiterated in many of the contemporary humanistic views of evolution and progression based on the unending natural cycle of the big bang.

As a person of faith, I have come to acknowledge that God is the God of history and Scripture is the iteration of that history from His perspective and for His purpose. The Revelation is His unveiling of that story to His creation.

These last days include the days from Christ's first coming until His second coming.

The Apostle Peter referenced this continuity and this particular phrase in his "Day of Pentecost" message to the early church in the book of Acts.

> But Peter, taking his stand with the eleven, raised his voice and declared to them: "Men of Judea and all you who live in Jerusalem, let this be known to you and give heed to my words. For these men are not drunk, as you suppose, for it is only the third hour of the day; but this is what was spoken of through

the prophet Joel: 'And it shall be *in the last days*,' God says, 'That I will pour forth of My Spirit on all mankind; And your sons and your daughters shall prophesy, And your young men shall see visions, And your old men shall dream dreams; Even on My bondslaves, both men and women, I will in those days pour forth of My spirit and they shall prophesy. And I will grant wonders in the sky above and signs on the earth below, blood, and fire, and vapor of smoke. The sun will be turned into darkness and the moon into blood, before the great and glorious day of the Lord shall come. And it shall be that everyone who calls on the name of the Lord will be saved.'" (Acts 2:17–21, emphasis added)

Also the writer of Hebrews begins in the same fashion reminding the readers that

God, after He spoke long ago to the fathers in the prophets in many portions and in many ways, *in these last days* has spoken to us in His Son, whom He appointed heir of all things, through whom also He made the world. And He is the radiance of His glory and the exact representation of His nature, and upholds all things by the word of His power. When He had made purification of sins, He sat down at the right hand of the Majesty on high. (Hebrews 1:1–3, emphasis added)

Then the apostle Paul clarifies this in his final and fatherly letter to his successor, Timothy.

But realize this, that *in the last days* difficult times will come. For men will be lovers of self, lovers of money, boastful, arrogant, revilers, disobedient to parents, ungrateful, unholy, unloving, irreconcilable, malicious gossips, without self-control, brutal, haters of good, treacherous, reckless, conceited, lovers of pleasure rather than lovers of God, holding to a form of godliness, although they have denied its power; avoid such men as these. (2 Timothy 3:1–5, emphasis added)

Finally, the book of James also notes the same relevance.

> Come now, you rich, weep and howl for your miseries which are coming upon you. Your riches have rotted and your garments have become moth-eaten. Your gold and your silver have rusted; and their rust will be a witness against you and will consume your flesh like fire. *It is in the last days* that you have stored up your treasure! (James 5:1–3, emphasis added)

In fulfillment of the prophecies of Isaiah and Daniel we hear the same echoes.

> The word which Isaiah the son of Amoz saw concerning Judah and Jerusalem. Now it will come about that *in the last days* the mountain of the house of the LORD will be established as the chief of the mountains, and will be raised above the hills; and all the nations will stream to it. And many peoples will come and say, "Come, let us go up to the mountain of the LORD, to the house of the God of Jacob; that He may teach us concerning His ways and that we may walk in His paths." For the law will go forth from Zion and the word of the LORD from Jerusalem. (Isaiah 2:1–3, emphasis added)

It is God who has the last word on the last days. His revealed truth includes more than the contemporary ideas of the end of the age. If we find our understanding, definitions, and speculation at odds with what God has revealed about the last days in His Scriptures, we have some things to consider. The fact that much of what is said about the last days today is very much at odds with what God has said about this period of time. As we continue to proceed into the twenty-first century, it becomes obvious that we are indeed living in *these last days*. However, when the Bible uses the phrase "these last days," it is more inclusive than the contemporary pronouncements. Today the phrase is used to incorporate and describe the final months or years leading to the consummation of the age.

The Bible uses the term *last days* to refer to the end of an era and, more radically, the end of an age. This phrase then includes the fulfillment of the prophecies concerning judgment on Israel, the destruction of the temple, the end of the sacrificial system, *and* the consummation of all things. These overlapping ideas are introduced by Daniel the prophet in his description of the seventy weeks of judgment. These conclude with the sixty-ninth week prophecy that includes Christ's crucifixion, "Messiah will be cut off," and the seventieth week, including the final judgment on the "city and the sanctuary" (Daniel 9:26). The Revelation includes this final week along with the consummation of the ages. These two ages include the ages of waiting and fulfillment. First, the age of waiting from the fall of man until the first coming of Messiah; second, the age of God's Spirit-empowered church in the earth. Both have their "last days" and their dramatic conclusions.

There are a multitude of topics to consider and pursue in the discussion of "These Last Days." How we consider this topic and its related subjects affects how we live, how we receive the revelation of God's ever-increasing kingdom, and God's original prophetic message fulfilling the protoprophecy of His intention and the following prophets and their prophecies.

We have the privilege and resources to observe centuries of eschatological history. Motives are revealed and explanations are made for the ever-changing interpretations and applications of the book of Revelation. There are also a number of contemporary views, interpretations, and developed eschatological systems that now dominate the body of teaching concerning "These Last Days." I will again refer you to the chapter entitled "Lenses" toward the conclusion of this book that details the four dominant systems of interpretation that include the historicist, preterist, idealist, and futurist perspectives.

Many other topics have been fleshed out in recent generations, including Adventism, Dispensationalism, a secret rapture, the Day of the Lord and the Lord's Day, the fall of Jerusalem, the man of sin and the Antichrist, the Great Tribulation, and numerous millennial views. This has developed into quite a complicated and detailed body of study of contrasting views of the explanations of Revelation and the consummation of the ages.

Since eschatology is the study of things expected to occur at the end of the age, the end of history, there are many projections and interpretations applied to this scenario. Traditionally, the study of eschatology has suffered from two opposite attitudes: neglect and overemphasis. Some consider it a distraction to living out a life that reflects the gospel of forgiveness, love, and service. Others see it as the motivating factor that touches our reality and makes the gospel relevant.

The Biblical factor of eschatological relevance is important regardless of your approach to living out the gospel of Jesus Christ. A proper understanding of The Revelation provides an exhortation and a motivation for persevering until the end as a faithful witness. So while some Christians ignore The Revelation and even treat it as an appendix to the Biblical message and others seem obsessed with current events and deal with little else, the apostle James exhorts us with these words:

> Therefore be patient, brethren, until the coming of the Lord. The farmer waits for the precious produce of the soil, being patient about it, until it gets the early and late rains. You too be patient; strengthen your hearts, *for the coming of the Lord is near.* Do not complain, brethren, against one another, so that you yourselves may not be judged; behold, the Judge is standing right at the door. As an example, brethren, of suffering and patience, take the prophets who spoke in the name of the Lord. We count those blessed who endured. You have heard of the endurance of Job and have seen the outcome of the Lord's dealings, that the Lord is full of compassion and is merciful. (James 5:7–11, emphasis added)

THE BOOK OF SEVENS

> "Seven" is the theme of The Revelation of Jesus Christ as He reveals the ultimate "Seven," or Shabbat, the conclusion of judgment and of this age.

> Therefore, let us fear if, while a promise remains of entering His rest, any one of you may seem to have come short of it.
> —Hebrews 4:1

God has relentlessly revealed truth to humanity with His symbols, as they, like a picture, are worth a thousand words. The Apostle Paul reveals the clarity of understanding in his revelation that the Old Testament itself is symbolic in allegory. It is not just a mental symbol; it is the truth in reality and history. The reading of the Old Testament gives the impression in our mind of God's truth dwelling within the stories, containing an ongoing undercurrent in the history and events that are passed on to us through His testimony in His people. This greater truth is amplified in this final book of Revelation, as it is the consummation of His revealed will, His history.

A number is an abstract entity used to describe quantity or to ascribe position or relevance. It is a symbol, a sign, by which something is inferred. Numbers have always been used as a reflection of reality in a quantitative form. The first writings of many languages have been found to be representations of numbers that indicated the count and transfer of products or animals in the ancient economy.

The Revelation is a book of *sevens*. The inferred reflection of the introduction of the Biblical meaning from the Book of Beginnings—Genesis—is carried through the entire canon of Scripture. The first use of this number described the *seven* days of creation. It is a sweeping and defined reference to God's intended and finished work resulting in rest and is carried through, inferred, and referenced throughout Scripture denoting completion, fullness, and rest.

The final, complete, and full Word of God's covenant story is revealed in this last book of the New Testament. The naming of Biblical books has historically been derived from the initial word or words in the document resulting in its descriptive name. "Apocalypse" is an English transliteration of the original Greek word. "The Revelation," a translation of this word, is the title given to the last book of the New Testament. It is God's last word, His full disclosure leading to His promised rest.

The completion, the fulfillment of all things, does not end in judgment but restoration.

This title, The Apocalypse, has been, through its contemporary and fearful conclusions, come to be identified with the great judgment at the consummation of this age. Though this is near the conclusion of the book, it is not the conclusion. The completion, the fulfillment of all things, does not end in judgment but restoration. It is my intention to expose that the reality of the judgments described in The Revelation are inclusive of all judgment prophesied from the beginning, including all the consequences of human sin. This begins at the original sin of Adam in the garden of Eden and the judgment of that sin on him and his children to the judgment that has been more fully realized by humanity throughout our history of sin. The resulting fall of man and the consequence of that fall is the judgment that was forewarned (Genesis 2:17). This judgment is detailed in The Revelation to its full and complete final judgments at the consummation of both ages, BC and AD.

THE UNVEILING

The warning of judgment on God's people and their access to Him through the fulfillment of the Law is intertwined with the judgment at the end of the age. This dual reality, like a two-sided coin, is so blended in the seven visions that they have puzzled many for centuries. The current dislocation of the church from the truth of her Hebrew roots has added to the confusion of this application. It has become clear that without the revelation of God's judgment and His plan of redemption from the fall of man to the first coming of Christ, and without this library of our Hebrew roots of covenant and the nature of God to draw from, we are only left to assign meaning to the visions and symbols. So the opposite is true, and to our benefit, if we will draw from revealed truth.

This book describes the revelation of Jesus Christ as the unfolding and ultimate fulfillment of God's prophetic warning and promise to Adam in the garden. The judgments revealed are all inclusive and complete. The Revelation gives *seven* different vantage points, or perspectives, of the released judgments of God. Again, the dominant idea of unfolding judgment with the ultimate restoration is repeated *seven* times, the Biblical number representing a perfect completion and fullness, leading to rest.

Numerology is the study of the mystical relationships between numbers and things. This is a highly subjective area of consideration. However, as in mathematics, numbers assist us in grasping greater realities. This understanding is utilized throughout Scripture for this purpose as we see in the first thirty-four verses of Genesis. The number *seven* is introduced as God's indication of completion and rest. These verses are intended to introduce us to the God of creation and His intimate involvement in His creation, especially the formation of humanity. When we turn this into a mathematical formula and attempt to apply a sequence of events in a literal fashion, we begin to lose the depth of God's intended revelation in the following few verses of description:

> Thus the heavens and the earth were completed, and all their hosts. By the seventh day God completed His work which He

had done, and He rested on the seventh day from all His work which He had done. (Genesis 2:1–2)

This same number creates the thread of a dominant theme throughout Scripture and is the dominant symbol concluded in The Revelation. It is continually repeated throughout Scripture as a symbol of completion and rest in the *"seventh,"* or the Sabbath, also the *Shemitah*, or sabbatical year. In The Revelation, the number *seven* is referenced or repeated over *seven times seven*, indicating completeness and conclusion of all things.

In the letter to the Hebrew Christians, the writer states,

> Therefore, let us fear if, while a promise remains of entering His rest (*His Sabbath*), any one of you may seem to have come short of it. (Hebrews 4:1 emphasis added)

And again, rest in

> Seeing then that we have a great High Priest who has passed through the heavens, Jesus the Son of God, let us hold fast our confession. For we do not have a High Priest who cannot sympathize with our weaknesses, but was in all points tempted as we are, yet without sin. Let us therefore come boldly to the throne of grace, that we may obtain mercy and find grace to help in time of need. (Hebrews 4:14–16)

He introduces the Sabbath year, even a Jubilee of *seven sevens*! A reconciled relationship, a true Shabbat, His rest.

Throughout the Old Testament we see the introduction and command for God's Great Gatherings, the *seven* Feasts of the Lord. Moses' documentation in Leviticus 23:1–4 reveals God's Divine calendar denoting His appointment schedule with His people. The three Hebrew words used to introduce these assigned moments defining these celebrations are *chag*, which is translated "appointed by God," an appointment; *miqra*, translated as a "holy convocation;" and finally, *mowed*, which translates as "festival" (a Holy Ghost party!).

So the combined definition of these terms can be phrased as the *seven feasts of the Lord* assigned as special times, appointed by God where the covenant people of God come together for a time of spiritual renewal and celebration in God, with the *seven*, or Sabbath, being the foundation and theme of all the feasts.

Jesus is our Passover.

After the *seven sevens* of days following that first Passover, on that fiftieth day, the Law was given and the nation of Israel was birthed on the first *Shavuot* (Hebrew), or *Pentecost* (Greek). The tragedy of unbelief and disobedience resulted in three thousand slain. This feast is realized in the New Testament after Jesus' fulfillment of the Passover that on that fiftieth day the Pentecost of the church was celebrated with the outpouring of the Holy Spirit as grace was realized and the church was born with three thousand swept into the Kingdom of God. We now look forward to the fulfillment of the Fall Feasts of Booths (*Sukkot*) in the *seventh* month when the great ingathering of God's harvest is realized. This begins with the Feast of Trumpets followed by a remembrance of God's provision in His atoning work. The Revelation details this Great Ingathering at the end of the age.

We read in Genesis 2:1-3 that the day begins at sundown, so Sabbath is celebrated from sundown on the sixth day (our Friday) to sundown on the *seventh* day (our Saturday). God's work was done! This Shabbat was to continue from that point forward. However, man's sin destroyed the original true Shabbat. When man broke Sabbath, God began His work of redemption. He introduced His remedy with the protoprophecy of Genesis 3:15 and followed His Word with His action in Genesis 4:21 by killing an animal, shedding its blood, and covering the nakedness of Adam and Eve.

Since the entire Old Testament is an allegory declaring God's message of hope, I would presume that the animal sacrificed in the garden of Eden that day was a lamb, a type and symbol of God's provision. This is due to the completed revelation of the Lamb of God that takes away the sin of the world (John 1:29).

So the theme of God's rest—His redemptive plan—is not an optional day off but a day of remembrance and celebration in relationship with the Creator God. Moses documents in Exodus 20:3–11 the means by which our living pattern imitates God's moral character and intention. Some think Sunday is the Christian Sabbath, or "New Shabbat." Some think it is kept because of the law (if so, we must work six days☺) (Exodus 20:6). However, work is followed by rest. This idea is expressed by the Hebrew word for Sabbath, which means "cessation."

The Revelation is God's disclosure of the complete work of redemption in His creation and the conclusion of His work. The result is rest at the end of the age and a cessation of judgment and man's strife in a broken world in bodies destined to die. So Sabbath rest is also a time for God's people to consider and enjoy what God has accomplished.

The word *Shabbat* is related to the Hebrew word *shevet*, which means to dwell or to abide. This is the source of Jesus' invitation to "Come unto me all who are weary and heavy-laden, and I will give you rest" (Matthew 11:28). God's intention is to dwell, to tabernacle, with His creation—His Temple in His rest. Genesis 3:8–9 states the original and innocent relationship between God and man and reports that He walked with them in the garden in the cool of the day. He has revealed His plan to restore that relationship.

God started His work in a garden, the Garden of Eden, and restarted again in the Garden of Gethsemane, but He will complete His work in a city, the New Jerusalem that contains a life-giving garden.

We could say that God started His work in a garden, the Garden of Eden, and restarted again in the Garden of Gethsemane, but He will complete His work in a city, the New Jerusalem that contains a life-giving and eternal garden.

> Then he showed me a river of the water of life, clear as crystal, coming from the throne of God and of the Lamb, in the middle of its street. On either side of the river was the tree of life, bearing twelve kinds of fruit, yielding its fruit every month; and the leaves of the tree were for the healing of the nations. (Revelation 22:1–2)

God's intention is to relate to us. Shabbat is a day "Unto the Lord our God," first as His creation in relation with Him and, second, in His redemption. The Shabbat was commanded so that man would relate to God.

> You shall remember that you were a slave in the land of Egypt, and the LORD your God brought you out of there by a mighty hand and by an outstretched arm; therefore the LORD your God commanded you to observe the Sabbath day. (Deuteronomy 5:15)

God's rest, Shabbat, is the only ritual mentioned in the Ten Commandments. Biblical rituals and traditions have been established to build and strengthen our relationship with God and each other. The feasts of the Pentateuch and then both ordinances of the church, the Eucharist (or Communion) and water baptism, accomplish this. We have established many other traditions to remember and celebrate godly encounters throughout history, from the Feast of Dedication, Hanukkah, the Feast of Purim, All Saints Day to Christmas.

> The author of the Pentateuch writes "but the seventh day is the Sabbath of the Lord your God. In it you shall do no work: you, nor your son, nor your daughter, nor your male servant, nor your female servant, nor your ox, nor your donkey, nor any of your cattle, nor your stranger who is within your gates, that your male servant and your female servant may rest as well as you." (Deuteronomy 5:14)

So the Sabbath is an ordinance that relates redemption directly to God's Story—His Story—"History." God's story concludes in The Revelation with the sabbatical conclusion of judgments and restoration. God's people are directed to keep the Sabbath because God has delivered and redeemed His people as signified in their deliverance from bondage in Egypt.

> And I will put enmity between you and the woman, and between your seed and her seed; He shall bruise you on the head, and you shall bruise him on the heel. (Genesis 3:15)

And again He concludes,

> Therefore, let us fear if, while a promise remains of entering His rest, any one of you may seem to have come short of it. (Hebrews 4:1)

The Sabbath rest holds promise of the ultimate salvation that God will accomplish for His people. As certainly as He delivered them from Egypt through Moses, so He has delivered His people from sin through the Great Redeemer, and this will be realized at the end of the age.

The protoprophecy of Genesis 3:15 follows creation and the initial innocence and the fall of man. God's very next work was bloody sacrifice, the slaughter of the innocent animal to cover their nakedness (Genesis 3:21). This work was completed at Golgotha when Messiah declared, "It is Finished!" (John 19:30)

Moses clarifies in Leviticus 23:3 and Exodus 31:13,

> But as for you, speak to the sons of Israel, saying, "You shall surely observe My Sabbaths; for this is a sign between Me and you throughout your generations, that you may know that I am the LORD who sanctifies you."

Ezekiel 20:12 records,

THE UNVEILING

> Also I gave them My Sabbaths to be a sign between Me and them, that they might know that I am the LORD who sanctifies them.

Finally, *"Seven,"* or the Sabbath, includes the idea and practice of celebrating rest, conclusion, or salvation. "For the Son of Man is Lord even of the Sabbath" (Matthew 12:8). So the purpose of Shabbat was a reminder to rest in Him. This is a sign of being "set apart for God" (holiness), as mankind senses an inadequacy in his existence. This inadequacy and insecurity is a by-product of sin alienating us from God. We can't rest in our finished works but in His. Therefore, on the Sabbath, we renew our relationship with God and reinforce our faith. It is a sanctifying sign like the wedding ring between a husband and wife, a circle that has no end. The Sabbath is a holy convocation for the "set apart ones," the saints of God. Sabbath reorients our lives toward God by reprioritizing our relationship with God. It is a prospective reminder, a sign of a life relating to God. It is as a road sign that warns, "Eternity Ahead: A Hopeless End or an Endless Hope!" for us to observe and respond to.

Moses records and clarifies for God's people,

> So the sons of Israel shall observe the sabbath, to celebrate the sabbath throughout their generations as *a perpetual covenant*. It is a sign between Me and the sons of Israel forever; for in six days the LORD made heaven and earth, but on the *seventh* day He ceased from labor, and was refreshed. (Exodus 31:16–17 emphasis added)

It is a perpetual sign of a future perfect rest yet to come. The psalmist in 95:11 and the writer of Hebrews 4 calls it "My Rest." Sabbath is a foretaste of the world to come. This age is like the eve of Sabbath; the next age *is* Sabbath. Shabbat was meant to be a picture of the eternal rest we have in the Messiah, realized in Jesus. Therefore, it is appropriate that the number *seven* is the theme of The Revelation of Jesus Christ as He reveals the ultimate *"seven,"* or Shabbat, the conclusion of judgment and of this age in a series of revealing *sevens*.

SEVEN FACETS

A simple reading of The Revelation reveals a long list of *sevens* consummating the Shabbat of God. The number *seven* and the references to *seven* are repeated over fifty times. This list begins with the *seven* churches, the *seven* Spirits before the throne, the *seven* golden lamp stands, the *seven* stars, and the *seven* angels.

In the heavenly scene, we see the *seven* lamps of fire, the *seven* Spirits of God, the *seven* seals on the book of judgment, the *seven* horns, the *seven* eyes, and again the *seven* Spirits of God followed by *seven* ascribed honors to the Lamb.

From the *seventh* seal flow the *seven* angels with the *seven* trumpets and the *seven* thunders. The *seven* signs are illustrated with the *seven* horns, *seven* heads, *seven* plagues and *seven* more angels with the *seven* bowls of judgment. These are followed by the *seven* mountains and the *seven* kings.

The number *seven* is referenced as a dominant theme with respect to completion in The Revelation. There are *seven* distinct visions experienced and documented by John. Each vision is a unique facet of God's revelation. With the instruction of the angel, John is introduced to yet another facet of Jesus' revelation and is startled by the brilliance of its illumination. Though there are *seven* facets, there is only one story. Jesus' provision and victory are the dominant theme.

This is illustrated by the story of the seminary students who took a break from their studies in Revelation to play some basketball. When they entered the gym, they saw the custodian eating lunch and reading his Bible. They asked him what he was reading and he answered,

"Revelation," to which they immediately asked him if he understood what he was reading. He responded, "Sure. Jesus wins. End of story!"

Considering these *seven* unique facets that make up The Revelation, we must consider each one in light of the others. It is not a single, continuous historical narrative but rather a series of compact and interrelated visions. The Revelation includes historical narrative like the book of Daniel, and some interrelated events are mentioned in both books. But we need to be aware that the chapter and verse organization was a documenting tool that was not intended to interpret the flow. Now that we have that tool, we can assume that everything follows literally and historically, and we try to puzzle out the events to fill in the sequence in a chronological narrative.

The *seven* Visions of The Revelation are listed here, and a detailed outline is found in the third Key, Disclosure: The Intent of The Revelation.

First, the vision of the glorified Christ with the *seven* stars and the *seven* lampstands addressing the *seven* churches. This introduction in chapters one through three gives us a full and complete picture of the plan and purpose of God. The revealer, Jesus, is introduced in all His glory by the recorder, John. The audience is immediately addressed, and the purpose of the following visions is clearly stated: simply to persevere until the end. The overview of the plan and purpose are detailed in the *seventh* verse of the first chapter, including all of time, past, present, and future, by the One who is the Alpha and the Omega.

The *seven* components of each letter to the churches include 1) an introduction, 2) Jesus' introductory attribute, 3) His description of their deeds, 4) His commendation, 5) an exhortation, or encouragement, 6) His instructions, and 7) His promise.

Second, the heavenly vision of the throne room of God and the attending audience of His people and the heavenly hosts. The Lamb of God with the scroll with the *seven* seals that are released at His discretion throughout the history of man and concluding with the *seven* trumpets. This second vision covers all of human history as judgment is released by the only One worthy to break the seals. Chapters four through eleven detail the impact of God's judgment on the world and, specifically, on the old system replaced by Jesus fulfillment of the Law. This judgment continues until the end of "these last days."

Third is the vision of the *seven* signs. These signs represent the dominant characters in the war of the seeds introduced in Geneses 3. Chapters twelve through fourteen reveal the heavenly perspective with earthly symbols and are descriptive of the ongoing battle initiated by the fallen Lucifer and carried on through the history of man.

First, the woman as prophesied in Genesis.

Second, the dragon of old, introduced in Genesis, the snake that intrudes and inspires the fall.

Third, the child that is promised and given birth and then escapes destruction to the right hand of God. The Holy Seed promised in Genesis. Jesus, the promised Messiah, the Lamb of God, slain from the foundation of the world now seated with the Father.

Fourth, the angel of God. Spiritual warfare represented by Michael ("Who is like God?") as he battles with the dragon, which is thrown down to earth.

Fifth, the beast from the sea. This sign is later revealed as the great harlot that represents the demonically inspired systems of the earth. These include the consummation of judgment on Jerusalem and perseverance of the saints.

Sixth, the beast from the earth. This sign represents the historical characters that rise up in Earth's corrupted systems, both in the concluding judgment on Jerusalem and the ongoing persecution of the saints. These characters are satanically inspired and empowered in counterfeit signs and wonders to bring destruction to humanity generally and to God's people specifically.

Seventh, the Lamb and the hosts of heaven. This vision is concluded with the seven angels that serve God's purpose in His creation.

Fourth, the vision of the *seven* bowls of God's wrath released at His command by seven angels as seen in chapters 15 and 16 as a picture of the final and conclusive release of the wrath of God (Revelation 15:1).

Fifth, the vision of the doom of Babylon and God's destruction of the demonically inspired systems of control and power in the earth. These are the satanically inspired systems that were offered to Jesus at His testing in the wilderness to rule the earth. These are the temporary systems that enslave the people of the earth based on money, sex, and power. Chapters 17 and 18 detail the judgment of these systems embodied in the great harlot with the name of "Babylon the Great, the mother of harlots and of the abominations of the earth" (Revelation 17:5).

Sixth, the vision of the four Hallelujahs. Chapters 19 and 20 reveal the introduction of the marriage supper of the Lamb, the victorious King of Kings and Lord of Lords, the binding of Satan, and the White Throne judgment with the final judgment, the second death.

Seventh, the closing vision of chapters 21 and 22 detail the new heaven and the new earth, the bride of Christ and the New Jerusalem, and the presence of God in her midst.

THE UNVEILING

The *seven* judgments are similarly aligned, but as mentioned earlier, beginning with the *seventh* verse of The Revelation:

> Behold, He is coming with the clouds, and every eye will see Him, even those who pierced Him; and all the tribes of the earth will mourn over Him. So it is to be. Amen. (1:7)

This verse serves as an overview of the revelation of God to His people in the totality of time and the totality of His judgment on the age of the temple sacrifice and the end of the age. This "Revelation in a sentence" will be opened in the sixth key, Judgment: The Result of Revelation.

This then will be followed by the second set of judgments pronounced on the disobedient church in the first vision. Third is the judgments on all of mankind that are released by the only One worthy, the Lamb, and the sealed scroll, as unveiled in the second vision. The fourth judgment is revealed through God's story of the *seven* signs and the *seven* angels in the third vision. The fifth judgment falls as the conclusive *seven* vials of wrath in the fourth vision. The sixth judgment narrative is released on the great harlot, Babylon, in the fifth vision. And the *seventh* and final judgment is the great White Throne of Christ in the sixth vision. The judgment announcements of The Revelation are offset by the seven blessings or beatitudes of The Revelation (1:3, 14:3, 16:15, 19:9, 20:6, 22).

In keeping with this theme, I have defined *seven* keys that unlock, or open, the book of Revelation. These keys are intended to open a perspective to gain a vantage point on the whole book so we may more clearly see what John saw, experienced, and documented of these *seven* revealing visions. So as these keys are used throughout the reading of The Revelation, we will see that the book maintains a cohesive flow and context. As the precept states, a text out of context is a pretext.

The **seven** keys that will be introduced in the next part are as follows:

1. Jesus: The Focus of The Revelation
2. The Church: The Audience of The Revelation

3. Disclosure: The Intent of The Revelation
4. Heaven: The Perspective of The Revelation
5. Scripture: The Library of The Revelation
6. Judgment: The Result of The Revelation
7. Restoration: The Promise of The Revelation

PART 2

SEVEN KEYS THAT OPEN THE REVELATION

Key #1
JESUS: THE FOCUS OF THE REVELATION

Revelation is focused on Jesus, the Messiah! It's all about Jesus, His ministry, His victory over sin, Satan, and death, His finality. The Kingdom of our Lord and His Christ has been established!

And I looked, and behold, in the midst of the throne and of the four living creatures, and in the midst of the elders, stood a Lamb as though it had been slain, having seven horns and seven eyes, which are the seven Spirits of God sent out into all the earth.
—Revelation 5:6

A living, holy, majestic, omniscient, authoritative, powerful Christ stands in the midst of the churches, holds their destiny in His hand and says: "Stop fearing. I was dead. I am alive forever more. More than that, I hold in My hand the keys to death and the grave. You should not fear to go to any place to which I hold the key. You may be persecuted to death but I am still your king."
—Ray Summers, *Worthy Is The Lamb*

The most obvious key is the most crucial. Humanity is center to God's plan, and our eternal destinies are bound to His will and purpose, but The Revelation is of "His will and purpose." It is The Revelation *of* Jesus Christ! Man has a tendency to make everything about himself and, therefore, everything about now. Fear of the unknown and a desire to control the future become a consuming passion in this dizzying time of profusion. We seem to be racing toward some unseen pinnacle of ultimate consummation that continues to evade our grasp. So we gasp for another breath and leap to another conclusion. This is why Jesus begins with His encouragement and His command in Revelation 1:17b-18 saying, "Do not be afraid; I am the first and the last, and the living One; and I was dead, and behold, I am alive forevermore, and I have the keys of death and of Hades.

The Revelation is the revelation is *of* Jesus Christ. He is the Alpha and the Omega, the beginning and the end. He is the initiator, the creator, the firstborn of all creation. He spoke all things into being and holds all things together by the Word of His power. From the opening verse to the closing prayer, Jesus is the focus. Jesus is the revelation.

A defining announcement is made at the end of The Revelation: "For the testimony of Jesus is the spirit of prophecy" (19:10). This verse proclaims that all God has to say to us is said in His Son. He has nothing else to say to us. The writer of Hebrews introduces his epistle with this clarification:

> God, after He spoke long ago to the fathers in the prophets in many portions and in many ways, in these last days has spoken to us in His Son, whom He appointed heir of all things, through whom also He made the world. And He is the radiance of His glory and the exact representation of His nature, and upholds all things by the word of His power. (Hebrews 1:1–3)

So that which witnesses to Jesus, that which glorifies and reveals Him, is the very heart of God's pronouncement to man, the spirit of prophecy. Prophecy is the utterance of the voice of God; the receipt of that Word is His wisdom, His speaking voice in His creation. Man is graced by God's Spirit to prophetically forth-tell (proclaim) the will of God or to foretell (predict) the purpose of God. Regardless of the intention of the Spirit, the purpose remains the same: to testify of Jesus.

THE UNVEILING

The Revelation discloses the reality that Jesus reigns from the "right hand of the Father." It reveals Jesus' authority to release judgment with His ultimate intentions and His plans of consummation. In the opening verses, He is referenced as the source and the subject of the words that follow:

> The *Revelation of Jesus Christ*, which God gave *Him* to show *His* servants—things which must shortly take place. And *He* sent and signified it by *His* angel to *His* servant John, who bore witness to the word of God, and to *the testimony of Jesus Christ*, to all things that he saw. (Revelation 1:1–2, emphasis added)

In the first three chapters, He reveals Himself with powerfully descriptive adjectives and attributes. These attributes are described for the benefit of His church as she fulfills her purpose in this age. As the head of the church, each attribute reveals His quality, His power, and His authority in her oversight and chastisement. He announces, "I am the Alpha and the Omega," says the Lord God, "who is and who was and who is to come, the Almighty" (Revelation 1:8). He leaves no question as to the source or the focus of The Revelation.

He is the One Who addresses His church and expresses His omniscience with a bold introduction of each oracle stating, "I know your works." He is omniscient and imminent. He knows all things. He is able to judge, and He is in our midst. He is the One Who is at work in His church as He walks among the seven candlesticks and the seven stars are in His hand. He is also the One who expresses His desire and concludes each letter with the same plea, "He who has an ear, let him hear what the Spirit says to the churches." This is His invitation and His request for those who will listen and receive from Him, the Head of the Church.

Jesus' descriptive title in each epistle is taken from the introduction in Revelation 1:12–16, and each description reflects the nature of His address to the church. He reveals His attributes that provide for the very need of the church addressed with the revelation that will empower them to respond to His exhortation. His Name is a strong tower! He is the focus of The Revelation!

Following the first vision of the glorified Christ revealed in the opening verses, we are invited to ascend to a heavenly place to catch a glimpse of Jesus before the throne, the second vision. The symbolic portrayal of Jesus reflects all that has been disclosed in Scripture through man's history.

> And I looked, and behold, in the midst of the throne and of the four living creatures, and in the midst of the elders, stood a Lamb as though it had been slain, having seven horns and seven eyes, which are the seven Spirits of God sent out into all the earth. (Revelation 5:6)

Jesus is the center of the heavenly scene. This vision flows from the very nature of Jesus as God's Mediator in His creation. The vision John reports describes the only true and worthy sacrifice of God for His creation.

> "Worthy is the Lamb who was slain to receive power and riches and wisdom, and strength and honor and glory and blessing!" And every creature which is in heaven and on the earth and under the earth and such as are in the sea, and all that are in them, I heard saying: "Blessing and honor and glory and power Be to Him who sits on the throne, And to the Lamb, forever and ever!" Then the four living creatures said, "Amen!" And the twenty-four elders fell down and worshiped Him who lives forever and ever. (Revelation 5:12–14)

He is revealed as the only Being worthy to break the seals that restrain the full judgment of God. As the worthy Lamb, the voluntary substitutionary sacrifice for man's sin, He is the only one qualified to release the judgment that falls on a sinful humanity and the cursed creation, this very judgment as announced by God to Adam that he "would surely die" (Genesis 2:17). Following the merciful and sequential breaking of the seals releasing the judgment, we are reminded, "Salvation belongs to our God who sits on the throne, and to the Lamb!" (Revelation 7:10). Jesus is the willing Lamb of God in the face of the consequences of man's sin, resulting in judgment. The apostle Paul proclaims the reality of this unfolding wrath to the Roman Church:

> For the wrath of God is revealed from heaven against all ungodliness and unrighteousness of men who suppress the truth in unrighteousness, because that which is known about God is evident within them; for God made it evident to them. For since the creation of the world His invisible attributes, His eternal power and divine nature, have been clearly seen, being understood through what has been made, so that they are without excuse. (Roman 1:18-20)

God's mercy is evident by His provision in the face of the consequences of man's choices. He announces, "For the Lamb who is in the midst of the throne will shepherd them and lead them to living fountains of waters. And God will wipe away every tear from their eyes" (Revelation 7:17) He is called the "Lamb slain from the foundation of the world" (Revelation 13:8). This title reveals His eternal purpose. As the writer of Hebrews states, "The works were finished from the foundation of the world" (Chapter 4:3). God is showing His hand of mercy as intended from the beginning. He knew the price of love and was willing to pay our debt. His children are those who choose Him; this is not a last resort, but His love. God wants children who choose to love Him. He is capable of creating beings without a free will, without an option, but He chose the expensive way, the way of love. Man was created in the image of God, a creature of volition.

Revelation is focused on Jesus, the Messiah! It's all about Him, His ministry, His victory over sin, Satan, and death, His finality.

The Revelation announces the wonderful celebration awaiting those who receive the Lamb. The apostle John writes,

Then he said to me, "Write: 'Blessed are those who are called to the marriage supper of the Lamb!'" And he said to me, "These are the true sayings of God." (Revelation 19:9)

The Revelation concludes,

> And he showed me a pure river of water of life, clear as crystal, proceeding from the throne of God and of the Lamb. In the middle of its street, and on either side of the river, was the tree of life, which bore twelve fruits, each tree yielding its fruit every month. The leaves of the tree were for the healing of the nations. And there shall be no more curse, but the throne of God and of the Lamb shall be in it, and His servants shall serve Him. (Revelation 22:1–3)

Revelation is focused on Jesus, the Messiah! It's all about Him, His ministry, His victory over sin, Satan, and death, His finality. The Kingdom of our Lord and His Christ has been established through His incarnation, His death by crucifixion, and His resurrection! This is not a future hope but a realized fulfillment of the plan of God.

Jesus announces Himself at the outset, "I am the Alpha and the Omega, the Beginning and the End," says the Lord, "who is and who was and who is to come, the Almighty" (Revelation 1:8). He should be our focus! We are not to live fearfully but obediently and in holiness. We are not to be "of the world" but of the King and His Kingdom. Therefore, we are to "Worship God! For the testimony of Jesus is the spirit of prophecy" (Revelation 19:10b).

Loving His Appearing

The apostle Paul reminds Timothy to keep the end in mind and that there is a special reward for all those who "love His appearing." This anticipation of the people of faith is an outward expression of the hope that fills our hearts and motivates our lives. Paul was obviously

THE UNVEILING

motivated in this way too. He considers this transition and reminds Timothy of his hope.

> Finally, there is laid up for me the crown of righteousness, which the Lord, the righteous Judge, will give to me on that Day, and not to me only but also to all who have loved His appearing. (2 Timothy 4:8)

The Greek word *epiphaneia* is transliterated "epiphany," which means "appearing." This refers to both the first and second advent of Christ, depending on the context. Again, Paul states in his letter to Titus his expectation.

> He is ... looking for the blessed hope and glorious appearing of our great God and Savior Jesus Christ. (Titus 2:13)

The follower of Jesus Christ believes His announcement that His Kingdom is not of this realm. And like Abraham, our father of faith,

> He was looking for the city which has foundations, whose architect and builder is God ... But as it is, they desire a better country, that is, a heavenly one. Therefore God is not ashamed to be called their God; for He has prepared a city for them. (Hebrews 11:10, 16)

For we have this confidence, as he wrote Timothy in his final letter, "But has now been revealed by the appearing of our Savior Jesus Christ, who has abolished death and brought life and immortality to light through the gospel" (2 Timothy 1:10).

> For if by the one man's offense death reigned through the one, much more those who receive abundance of grace and of the gift of righteousness will reign in life through the One, Jesus Christ. (Romans 5:17)

This gift has resulted in our great benefit as he describes in the second letter to the Corinthians that by His grace we are "made the righteousness of God in him" (2 Corinthians 5:21). John adds in his first epistle: "And now, little children, abide in Him, that when He appears, we may have confidence and not be ashamed before Him at His coming" (1 John 2:28). He gives us this challenge and hope:

> Beloved, now we are children of God; and it has not yet been revealed what we shall be, but we know that when He is revealed, we shall be like Him, for we shall see Him as He is. And everyone who has this hope in Him purifies himself, just as He is pure. (1 John 3:2–3)

Jesus is the "Lamb of God that takes away the sin of the world." (John 1:29)

The Lamb of God

In the most obvious key to Revelation we must consider the most repeated image and description of Jesus as the focus of Revelation. He is described as the Lamb with twenty-eight references (*seven* times *four*), *Seven* is the key number, and *four* is the number of universality in creation. The Lamb is the key figure in the breaking of the seals, the heavenly descriptions of the signs, and in the conclusive and victorious marriage supper. He is referenced in the conclusion of God's unveiling with these descriptive visions:

> Then he said to me, "Write: 'Blessed are those who are called to the marriage supper of the Lamb!'" And he said to me, "These are the true sayings of God." (Revelation 19:9)

> And he showed me a pure river of water of life, clear as crystal, proceeding from the throne of God and of the Lamb. In the middle of its street, and on either side of the river, was the tree of life, which bore twelve fruits, each tree yielding its fruit every month. The leaves of the tree were for the healing of the nations. And there shall be no more curse, but the throne of God and

of the Lamb shall be in it, and His servants shall serve Him. (Revelation 22:1–3)

Jesus is the "Lamb of God that takes away the sin of the world" (John 1:29). The Lamb is the presumed animal sacrificed by God in Eden to cover the nakedness of Adam and Eve. In Genesis 4, a lamb is Abel's acceptable sacrifice in contrast to Cain's corrupted produce from the ground that had come under the curse of sin. So as God reveals His moral nature to His creation, He reveals Himself as a lamb. He is the lamb slain from the foundation of the world. This revelation discloses God's original intention. He knew the price that would be paid before He spoke the first molecule into creation. He is the wise master builder who has counted the cost and was willing to pay the price for those who would choose Him, those that would love Him.

> And I looked, and behold, in the midst of the throne and of the four living creatures, and in the midst of the elders, stood a Lamb as though it had been slain, having seven horns and seven eyes, which are the seven Spirits of God sent out into all the earth. (Revelation 5:6)

> "Worthy is the Lamb who was slain to receive power and riches and wisdom, and strength and honor and glory and blessing!" (*Seven*) And every creature which is in heaven and on the earth and under the earth and such as are in the sea, and all that are in them, I heard saying: "Blessing and honor and glory and power (*Four*) Be to Him who sits on the throne, And to the Lamb, forever and ever!" Then the four living creatures said, "Amen!" And the twenty-four elders fell down and worshiped Him who lives forever and ever. (Revelation 5:12–14 emphasis added)

> Salvation belongs to our God who sits on the throne, and to the Lamb! (Revelation 7:10)

> For the Lamb who is in the midst of the throne will shepherd them and lead them to living fountains of waters. And God will wipe away every tear from their eyes. (Revelation 7:17)

> All who dwell on the earth will worship him, whose names have not been written in the Book of Life of the Lamb slain from the foundation of the world. (Revelation 13:8)

Jesus In The Seven Facets

In the first vision, He is the "Son of Man" among the seven lampstands.

> And in the middle of the lampstands I saw one like a son of man, clothed in a robe reaching to the feet, and girded across His chest with a golden sash. His head and His hair were white like white wool, like snow; and His eyes were like a flame of fire. His feet were like burnished bronze, when it has been made to glow in a furnace, and His voice was like the sound of many waters. (Revelation 1:13–15)

To the churches, He is

> The One who holds the seven stars in His right hand, the One who walks among the seven golden lampstands (Revelation 2:1b).

> The first and the last who was dead and has come to life (Revelation 2:8b).

> The One who has the sharp, two-edged sword (Revelation 2:12b).

> The Son of God, who has eyes like a flame of fire and His feet are like burnished bronze (Revelation 2:18b).

THE UNVEILING

> He who has the seven Spirits of God and the seven stars (Revelation 3:1b).
>
> He who is holy, who is true, who has the key of David, who opens and no one will shut, and who shuts and no one opens (Revelation 3:7b).
>
> The Amen, the faithful and true Witness, the Beginning of the creation of God (Revelation 3:14b).

In the second vision, He is

> Behold, the Lion that is from the tribe of Judah, the Root of David, has overcome so as to open the book and its seven seals. (Revelation 5:5b)
>
> And I saw between the throne (with the four living creatures) and the elders a Lamb standing, as if slain, having seven horns and seven eyes, which are the seven Spirits of God, sent out into all the earth. (Revelation 5:6b)
>
> "Worthy is the Lamb that was slain to receive power and riches and wisdom and might and honor and glory and blessing." And every created thing which is in heaven and on the earth and under the earth and on the sea, and all things in them, I heard saying, "To Him who sits on the throne, and to the Lamb, be blessing and honor and glory and dominion forever and ever." And the four living creatures kept saying, "Amen." And the elders fell down and worshiped. (Revelation 5:12–14)

In the third vision, He is the male child:

> And she gave birth to a son, a male child, who is to rule all the nations with a rod of iron; and her child was caught up to God and to His throne. (Revelation 12:5)

Also in Revelation 12, He is the victorious Christ of God in verse 10, the Lamb slain in verse 11, the male Child again in verse 13, and the Lord the saints testify of in verse 17. In Revelation 13:8, He is author of the slain Lamb's Book of Life.

In the conclusion of the third vision, He is the seventh sign, the Lamb. He is standing with those who rule with Him in the governing symbol of the twelve tribes that are separated unto Him. He is gloriously described by John and those who surround the Lamb as follows:

> Then I looked, and behold, a white cloud, and sitting on the cloud was one like a son of man, having a golden crown on His head and a sharp sickle in His hand. (Revelation 14:14)

In the fourth vision, He is the encourager of the saints:

> Behold, I am coming like a thief. Blessed is the one who stays awake and keeps his clothes, so that he will not walk about naked and men will not see his shame. (Revelation 16:15)

In the fifth vision, He is the proclaimed victor:

> These will wage war against the Lamb, and the Lamb will overcome them, because He is Lord of lords and King of kings, and those who are with Him are the called and chosen and faithful. (Revelation 17:14)

In the sixth vision, He is the worshipped King, the Lamb that hosts the marriage supper, and the spirit of prophecy. He is called "Faithful and True" as the rider of the white horse of victory. He is the Judge on His great white throne. He is the King of Kings and the Lord of lords.

> And I saw heaven opened, and behold, a white horse, and He who sat on it is called Faithful and True, and in righteousness He judges and wages war. His eyes are a flame of fire, and on His head are many diadems; and He has a name written on Him which no one

knows except Himself. He is clothed with a robe dipped in blood, and His name is called The Word of God. (Revelation 19:11-13)

In the final and seventh vision, He is revealed as in the introduction: He is the restorer of all things.

> And He who sits on the throne said, "Behold, I am making all things new." And He said, "Write, for these words are faithful and true." Then He said to me, "It is done. I am the Alpha and the Omega, the beginning and the end. I will give to the one who thirsts from the spring of the water of life without cost." (Revelation 21:5-6)

In conclusion, the first key is the most important key, as The Revelation concludes with the exhortation, "Worship God! For the testimony of Jesus is the spirit of prophecy" (Revelation 19:10).

Just as in Jesus day of earthly ministry, the contemporary church with her self-absorbed eschatology is in danger of missing its Messiah, as did the Pharisees. Many of the interpretations and applications of The Revelation in the Western church are driven by fear and can produce an elitist following for those who "know the signs" and are prepared for their escape. We need to be very careful to discern the spirit of the message given. If the motive or results are based on fear or an expression of vengeance, these motivations must be exposed as false teaching. The Gospel of Jesus Christ is a Gospel of the King and His Kingdom. His rule of love and holiness is preceded by His own ministry and example to those who "take up their cross and follow Him" (Matthew 16:24).

The Revelation is focused on Jesus, the Messiah! It's all about Jesus, His ministry, His victory over sin, Satan, and death, His finality. The Kingdom of our Lord and His Christ has been established! It is not going to be established; it is finished! He accomplished this through His incarnation, His earthly life and ministry, His death by crucifixion and burial, and His resurrection! This is "The Revelation of Jesus Christ" as stated in the first verse of the Apocalypse:

From Jesus Christ, the faithful witness, the firstborn from the dead, and the ruler over the kings of the earth. To Him who loved us and washed us from our sins in His own blood, and has made us kings and priests to His God and Father, to Him be glory and dominion forever and ever. Amen. (Revelation 1:5–6)

He has entitled Himself: "'I am the Alpha and the Omega, the Beginning and the End,' says the Lord, 'who is and who was and who is to come, the Almighty'" (Revelation 1:8).

He is our focus! "He who testifies to these things says, 'Yes, I am coming quickly.' Amen. Come, Lord Jesus" (Revelation 22:20).

Key #2

THE CHURCH: THE AUDIENCE OF THE REVELATION

*God has one people,
one covenant family of faith.*

> He who has an ear, let him hear what
> the Spirit says to the churches.
> —Revelation 2:7

If the church could be aroused to a deeper sense of glory that awaits her, she would enter with a warmer spirit into the struggles that are before her. Hope would inspire ardour. She would even now arise from the dust, and like an eagle, plume her pinions for loftier flights than she has yet taken. What she wants, and what every individual Christian wants, is faith—faith in her sublime vocation, in her Divine resources, in the presence and efficacy of the Spirit that dwells in her—faith in the truth, faith in Jesus, and faith in God. With such faith there would be no need to speculate about the future. That would speedily reveal itself. It is our unfaithfulness, our negligence and unbelief, our low and carnal aims, that retard the chariot of the Redeemer. The Bridegroom cannot come until the Bride has made herself ready. Let the Church be in earnest after greater holiness in her own members, and in faith and love undertake the conquest

of the world, and she will soon settle the question whether her resources are competent to change the face of the earth.
—Ian Murphy, *The Puritan Hope*, Collected Writings, 1872 vol. 2, 48

God Has One People

The second key is as obvious as the first, though it needs to be stated and remembered throughout the seven visions that John has documented for us. It is clear that the introduction of The Revelation is addressed to Jesus' bond servants, His servants bound to Him for life: "The Revelation of Jesus Christ, which God gave Him to show to His bond-servants" (Revelation 1:1a).

Holding this simple key helps the reader stay focused on the *intimacy* intended in God's disclosure. It is not a warning to the Gentile world or the unbelieving Jews, but a revelation, an unveiling, a disclosure to His bond servants. The Church is the audience of The Revelation. This key addresses the confusion introduced by some commentators. Some introduce The Revelation of Jesus Christ as His ultimatum on a disobedient humanity. Some assume two audiences for The Revelation: Israel and the Church. This key clarifies, by the introductory verse, the Biblical application and disclosed inclusion.

The designation of a bond servant is a title introduced in the Book of Exodus. It describes a slave, a person that is totally responsible to and dependent upon another person, who chooses to remain a slave due to the love for his master and his desire to be bound to him.

> But if the slave plainly says, "I love my master, my wife and my children; I will not go out as a free man," then his master shall bring him to God, then he shall bring him to the door or the doorpost. And his master shall pierce his ear with an awl; and he shall serve him permanently. (Exodus 21:5–6)

Addressing The Revelation to His bond slaves immediately clarifies that God is revealing His will to His people, those who have chosen

Him. The apostle Paul powerfully proclaims this choice in his letter to the Galatian church.

> I have been crucified with Christ; and it is no longer I who live, but Christ lives in me; and the life which I now live in the flesh I live by faith in the Son of God, who loved me and gave Himself up for me. (Galatians 2:20)

A bond slave is one that, like the apostle Paul, chooses to break from his independence and to surrender to the Son of God. No one can do this for you; you must do it yourself. This is the passion of my relationship with Jesus. I deliberately choose to set my rights aside and become a bond slave of Jesus Christ. Jesus chooses to disclose Himself to His bond slaves.

Jesus personally addresses His connection to His Body as He reveals Himself as being in their midst. He is the glorified Christ walking among the seven lampstands with the messengers represented as the seven stars in His hand. The stars, or messengers, translated "angels," are the key representatives, or interlocutors, of the local church. The seven golden lampstands represent the completeness of the church as light in a dark world. He is reminding them that He is the head of the Body, aware of and at work among His church, walking among its distributed light.

> Light is sown like seed for the righteous and gladness for the upright in heart. (Psalm 97:11)

All seven epistles to the seven churches begin with "I know your works." Jesus says the same to us today: "I know your works, your service, your obedience and even more." His intimacy and omniscience is reiterated in each letter, He knows and He is present. He is in the midst of them.

Each letter ends with "He who has an ear, let him hear what the Spirit says to the churches." This also is for our exhortation. Do we have ears to hear? Will we receive Jesus' counsel, His instruction and exhortation? Jesus' title in each epistle is taken from, and even expanded upon, His introduction and reflects the nature of His address to the church: "His Name is a strong tower!" (Proverbs 18:10).

> Then I turned to see the voice that was speaking with me. And having turned I saw seven golden lampstands; and in the middle of the lampstands I saw one like a son of man, clothed in a robe reaching to the feet, and girded across His chest with a golden sash. His head and His hair were white like white wool, like snow; and His eyes were like a flame of fire. His feet were like burnished bronze, when it has been made to glow in a furnace, and His voice was like the sound of many waters. In His right hand He held seven stars, and out of His mouth came a sharp two-edged sword; and His face was like the sun shining in its strength. (Revelation 1:12–16)

The apostle John specifies the audience even further in verse four by directing his letter to the seven churches that are in Asia. The simplicity of this introduction eliminates any confusion as to whom the disclosure is made. To be clear, it is not addressed to an unregenerate world, nor is it directed to a Hebrew ethnic minority. It is directed to the church, the *ecclesia*—the "called-out ones" of God in the earth.

His direct addresses to these seven churches are a specific revelation not unlike other New Testament epistles. They are, first, specific and relevant to the addressed church and, second, true for all His people in His church throughout this age. As stated before, the church includes all those in all time who make up the universal church, the Body of Christ, of which Jesus is the Head. Only God knows the heart of man, and He is the true and ultimate Judge. He knows and identifies His own as His bond servants, as the apostle Paul clarifies in his letter to the Roman church.

> For the wrath of God is revealed from heaven against all ungodliness and unrighteousness of men who suppress the truth in unrighteousness, because that which is known about God is evident within them; for God made it evident to them.

> For since the creation of the world His invisible attributes, His eternal power and divine nature, have been clearly seen, being understood through what has been made, so that they are without excuse. For even though they knew God, they did not honor Him as God or give thanks, but they became futile in their speculations, and their foolish heart was darkened. (Romans 1:18–21)

The apostle Paul introduces these two specific witnesses of creation and conscience that have been set before man. God determines our faith in Him by a reaction of "awe" in His creation and a response of "ought" in light of our guilty conscience before the God of creation. God has one people, one family of faith. In Jesus Christ, God has become one with us and has opened the door for us to become one with Him. This simple truth has been threaded through all God's revelation given through the millennia of this age.

It is a grave misunderstanding of Scripture that results in the false deduction that the God of the Old Testament is different than the God of the New Testament. A similar misunderstanding arrives at a false deduction that the people of God are limited to the ethnic Hebrews in the Old Testament. They are His people chosen to accomplish His purpose, but His love is not limited nor His grace restrained. This assigned limitation of ethnicity, a misunderstanding of God's people, has been carried over and assigned in this new age with the delineation of two separate people of God: Israel and the church. The promises of God in the Old Covenant find their fulfillment in Jesus Christ. So the promises made to the nation of Israel are not limited in Him. The result of this delineation concludes that God deals differently with ethnic Israel than He does with His church. The result is a superimposed application of The Revelation on two different audiences.

The apostle Paul, an ethnic Jew of the tribe of Benjamin, is very clear in his letter to the Roman church how he relates to his brethren, his kinsmen, according to the flesh. He is grieved about their rejection of God's provision in Jesus Christ. He is hopeful in their receiving this revelation and their Messiah. His deduction is consistent with previous Scripture in that God has always had a remnant of believers within the nation of Israel and a scattering of believers throughout the nations. However, this nation has always been a covenantal people from the mixed multitude. We can see that the plan and purpose of God was realized in the lineage of Messiah in fulfillment of His promise in Genesis 3:15 leading to the ultimate redemption and restoration of His finished work.

For example, when the people of Israel were delivered out of Egypt as described in Exodus 12, they were called a "mixed multitude." This infers a covenant community rather than an ethnic commonality. In the New Testament, these believers were called "God fearing Gentiles" (Acts 13:26). This reality is reinforced by God's clarification to Moses that only those foreigners who enter into the covenantal relationship of blood by circumcision are allowed to observe the Passover of God (Genesis 17:12–13; Exodus 12:43–49).

A covenant community rather than an ethnic commonality!

This inclusion is reinforced later by the acceptance of Caleb as God's representative for the tribe of Judah. Caleb is listed in Numbers 13:6 as being associated with the tribe of Judah and further defined in chapter 32 as a descendant of Jephunneh, a Kenezite. So Caleb was not a descendant of Jacob but of Kenaz, a Kenezite of the tribes of Edom descended from Jacob's twin brother, Esau.

> These then are the records of the generations of Esau the father of the Edomites in the hill country of Seir. These are the names of Esau's sons: Eliphaz the son of Esau's wife Adah, Reuel the son of Esau's wife Basemath. The sons of Eliphaz were Teman, Omar, Zepho and Gatam and *Kenaz*. (Genesis 36:9–11)

God's bond servants are His covenantal people. Israel is the name given by God to Jacob with the meaning of "one who strives with God"

(Genesis 32:28). Judah is a name given by God to describe a worshiper (Genesis 29:35). The people of God are true worshippers who strive with God. The Apostle Paul stated this again to the Roman church in light of his heritage.

> For he is not a Jew who is one outwardly, nor is circumcision that which is outward in the flesh. But he is a Jew who is one inwardly; and circumcision is that which is of the heart, by the Spirit, not by the letter; and his praise is not from men, but from God. (Romans 2:28–29)

The apostle Paul also clarified the relationship of God's people to ethnic Israel in the same letter. This understanding is in concert with Jesus' exhortation to the Pharisees.

> But it is not as though the word of God has failed. For they are not all Israel who are descended from Israel; nor are they all children because they are Abraham's descendants, but: "Through Isaac your descendants will be named." That is, it is not the children of the flesh who are children of God, but the children of the promise are regarded as descendants. (Romans 9:6–8)

> Therefore bear fruit in keeping with repentance; and do not suppose that you can say to yourselves, "We have Abraham for our father"; for I say to you that from these stones God is able to raise up children to Abraham. (Matthew 3:8–9)

God's covenant community consists of God's people, children of promise by faith. Doctrines have developed in the church in the absence of her Hebrew roots resulting in assigned meanings that are not rooted in the Old Testament. Those who are unaware of these Hebrew roots have, consequently, introduced confusion in the identity of the people of God. The idea that God has two people, ethnic Jews and the church, has developed into a contemporary argument that divides His disciples into two camps, theologically, historically, and, now, politically. These notions have produced some unique ideas in Bible interpretation and in regard to the state of ethnic (or national) Israel. Today's political landscape is colored by both Jewish and Christian Zionism as well as global multiculturalism. The current Progressive position promotes a humanistic approach that defies history and faith. For many Christians, it appears that the foundation of their concerns for the land of Israel and the city of Jerusalem are a reflection of their prophetic expectations, their apocalyptic perspectives. These expectations can trump a concern for social justice, and as a result, their political sympathies are tied into their apocalyptic scenarios.

Some insist that ethnic Jews are no longer of any consequence in the plan of God because the church has replaced them in His ultimate plan and purpose in the consummation of the ages. This "Replacement Theology" is birthed out of a misunderstanding of the grace of God in His dealings with ethnic Israel. On the other side of the argument, some in the church have established an elevation of ethnic Jews and their developed traditions enhanced while in exile. These rituals are then carried over and even imposed on the church as the truest expression of Christian faith.

God's blessing on these chosen people to accomplish His will and establish His portal into humanity has resulted in some radical responses from those on the outside. The demonically inspired anti-Semitism that has manifested throughout history is also mirrored by a contemporary Philo-Semitism that has developed in the church resulting in a new form of Judaizing dogma. Paul expressed the favor of God in his inclusion to the Roman church.

> For I could wish that I myself were accursed, separated from Christ for the sake of my brethren, my kinsmen according to the flesh, who are Israelites, to whom belongs the adoption as sons, and the glory and the covenants and the giving of the Law and the temple service and the promises, whose are the fathers, and from whom is the Christ according to the flesh, who is over all, God blessed forever. Amen. (Romans 9:3–5)

We should not assume that the Scriptures teach a "Replacement Theology." Nor should we attain to a "Messianic Jewish" aristocracy and theology. Rather, we need to see and celebrate the prophetic "Fulfillment Theology" of Jesus' ministry. Jesus is recorded in proclaiming this in Matthew's gospel with clarity.

> Do not think that I came to abolish the Law or the Prophets; I did not come to abolish but to fulfill. For truly I say to you, until heaven and earth pass away, not the smallest letter or stroke shall pass from the Law until all is accomplished. (Matthew 5:18–19)

The apostle Paul announces to the Roman church:

> For I am not ashamed of the gospel, for it is the power of God for salvation to everyone who believes, to the Jew first and also to the Greek. For in it the righteousness of God is revealed from faith to faith; as it is written, "But the righteous man shall live by faith." (Romans 1:16–17)

The intention of God with the Jewish people is analogous to watering your garden with a water hose. The life-giving water is to the hose first and then to the garden. The hose is the vehicle for the purposed water. Israel is God's vehicle for His purpose in the earth, His human portal for His purpose in His creation to provide His remedy for His people. This is the audience of God's unveiling of His plan and purpose in His creation and the consummation of the age.

What the Spirit Says to the Churches

The Revelation of Jesus Christ was given and documented a few decades after His ascension to the right hand of the Father. There are scholarly discussions debating the date it was written with two primary deductions resulting in the two general dates. The early writing is considered to be in the third decade after Jesus' ascension and the late writing in the sixth decade. Both dates presume influence on the interpretation of The Revelation in relation to the Roman destruction of Jerusalem.

Academics also note that an earlier writing assumes John's writing skills were not as precise as the latter writing. This is said to account for the writing style difference in his gospel and epistles in comparison with the grammar and style of The Revelation. This is a topic of consideration in the fifth key that recognizes Scripture as the library and literature of The Revelation. It is important to remember that John's apocalypse was written by the command of the angel in the midst of an overwhelming experience. This also should be considered as having some influence on the unique writing style of all apocalyptic literature, most specifically in The Revelation. Consider the dozen commanded instructions by the angel to John to "write this down." The consuming experience continually distracted him from his task.

Concerning the author of the book, some commentators quote the church fathers for their assumptions and others quote later writers and historians. There is a specific reference in the second century attributing The Revelation to the apostle John; others deduce that it was written by another disciple named John.

The assumption of the earlier date led some to unpack the message of The Revelation for the early church and the destruction of Jerusalem, the temple, the sacrificial system, and ultimately the Roman Empire. Their perspective, defined as preterist in nature, that is, already fulfilled, concludes that The Revelation is completely fulfilled in the visions given for that era. There are radical and moderate views of this perspective that force the prophetic understanding into a past fulfillment.

The assumption of the latter writing, AD 90s, generally assumes a futuristic fulfillment of The Revelation and its cataclysmic judgments with the exclusion of the Roman destruction of Jerusalem and the destruction of the temple. This assumption leaves a gaping question concerning the writer's exclusion of Jesus' most dramatic prophetic word, the destruction of the temple with "not one stone left upon another" (Matthew 24:2; Mark 13:2). This view then presumes the building of yet another earthly temple and the reinstitution of blood sacrifice prior to the consummation of the age.

So the dating of this documents feeds into the interpretive perspectives of commentators for a past or future fulfillment. I have given an introductory explanation of the four primary views of apocalyptic literature in a closing chapter of Part 3 entitled "Lenses."

Regardless, John's introductory comment is very clearly addressed in Revelation 1:4: "John to the seven churches that are in Asia." There were many other churches in that region. These churches were birthed out of the missionary activities of the early church. These were churches that John identifies with a clear assumption of authority. John's authority comes first from the instruction of Jesus Himself and second from inferred relationship as their archbishop addressing the bishops or messengers of these churches in an apostolic manner.

There are also some historical considerations that shed light on their inclusion for the selection of these churches. The letter was not sent to the church in Jerusalem, though all churches are impacted and included in the New Testament epistles to the churches. Again, the dating of the letter is unknown; if it was written after the fall of Jerusalem, the church of Jerusalem had been dispersed prior to AD 70. So the church, though Jewish in its origination, would now be increasingly Gentile.

The churches of Revelation are addressed "the church" in the Gentile Asia Minor. The focal point of the church was moving west. However, it is most peculiar that none of the epistles of the New Testament make note of this tragically conclusive event in the history of Israel: the destruction of the Temple and the city of Jerusalem. The most dynamic prophecy Jesus made about Jerusalem is not referenced in any of the books except The Revelation. These references will be covered in detail in the Sixth Key—Judgment, The Result of The Revelation. The parallel consummations of judgment are realized in the judgment of Jerusalem prophesied throughout Israel's history and detailed in the conclusion of that judgment in Jesus' great reveal. These two fulfilled judgments are the conclusion of the mystery of God.

> Behold, He is coming with the clouds, and every eye will see Him, even those who pierced Him; and all the tribes of the earth will mourn over Him. So it is to be. Amen. (Revelation 1:7)

> But in the days of the voice of the seventh angel, when he is about to sound, then the mystery of God is finished, as He preached to His servants the prophets. (Revelation 10:7)

THE UNVEILING

Jesus' Message to the Seven Churches

The seven Churches of Asia Minor addressed are named and titled as follows:

Revelation 2:1-7 Ephesus — The Loveless Church

(<Greek> *ephesos*, meaning "permitted")

Revelation 2:8–11 Smyrna — The Persecuted Church

(<Greek> *smyrna* from myrrh, a burial ointment)

Revelation 2:12-17 Pergamos — The Compromising Church

(<Greek> *pergamos*, meaning "elevation" or "height")

Revelation 2:18–29 Thyatira — The Corrupt Church

(<Greek> *thyatira* from a sacrifice of labor)

Revelation 3:1–6 Sardis — The Dead Church

(<Greek> *sardis*, meaning "Prince of Joy")

Revelation 3:7–13 Philadelphia — The Faithful Church

(<Greek> *philadelphia* meaning "brotherly love")

Revelation 3:14–22 Laodicea — The Lukewarm Church

(<Greek> *laodicea* meaning "rule of the people")

The seven churches mentioned were geographically located in a small circle of cities on the western edge of Asia Minor. The growth and distribution of the early church followed the major cities and the established synagogues of the diaspora. The churches were established in very influential cities, geographically and historically important areas in the first century. The tight circle of churches listed in the first three chapters of The Revelation are contemporaries, and their associated exposés, challenges, and failures relate to all churches throughout this age.

It is important to see that Jesus' messages to His churches are sandwiched between the vision of the glorified Christ and the vision of the Glorified Church. These letters reveal that even though the issues each faced are challenging and the test is hard, each church is commanded to overcome its obstacles and persevere until He comes.

Our hope and confidence are buoyed by these unfolding revelations. First, we are introduced to the victorious glorified Christ in chapter one. Following these seven letters, we are invited to consider the heavenly scene in chapter four. Then in chapter seven, we see the conclusion before the throne.

> After these things I looked, and behold, a great multitude which no one could number, of all nations, tribes, peoples, and tongues, standing before the throne and before the Lamb, clothed with white robes, with palm branches in their hands, and crying out with a loud voice, saying, "Salvation belongs to our God who sits on the throne, and to the Lamb!" (Revelation 7:9–10)

Jesus commands John and states clearly that the church is His audience.

> I, John, your brother and fellow partaker in the tribulation and kingdom and perseverance which are in Jesus, was on the island called Patmos because of the word of God and the testimony of Jesus. I was in the Spirit on the Lord's day, and I heard behind me a loud voice like the sound of a trumpet, saying, "Write in a book what you see, and send it to the seven churches: to Ephesus

and to Smyrna and to Pergamum and to Thyatira and to Sardis and to Philadelphia and to Laodicea." (Revelation 1:9-11)

The book itself was written by John from Patmos, modern Patino, a small, rocky island (ten miles by six miles) in the Aegean Sea located about thirty-seven miles southwest of Miletus in Asia Minor (modern-day Turkey). This island is very near the seven churches he addressed. Due to its isolation, it is recorded as being used by the Romans as a place of isolation and occasional exile for political malcontents or criminals. John's mention of the island in Revelation 1:9 probably means that he was such a prisoner, having been sent there for preaching the gospel.

Dating The Revelation is influenced by Eusebius in the fourth century. He is known as a Roman historian and exegete, one who provides an explanation or draws out the meaning of a text. He was a Christian polemicist, one who engages in controversy, of Greek descent. He is also recognized as an early church father and the bishop of Caesarea Maritima about AD 314. He is noted as the key reference for the later date, as he came to believe that John was sent to Patmos by Emperor Domitian in AD 95 and released after one and one half years.

However, the internal evidence of The Revelation presumes an earlier date for the book. It includes the lack of any reference to the fulfillment of Jesus' great prophecy of the destruction of the temple except in the concluding judgments as mentioned. It does, however, contain the last mention of the earthly temple and a description of the holy city in the first fourteen verses of chapter eleven. This parenthetical description follows the completion of the seventh-seal judgment in chapter ten with a clear directive to John to take this word down for all to hear, as it describes the final judgment on Jerusalem.

As a church member, John identifies with the churches and their difficulties and challenges.

> I, John, your brother and fellow partaker in the tribulation and kingdom and perseverance which are in Jesus. (Revelation 1:9)

Again, the primary practical purpose of The Revelation is to prepare the church for persecution and to persevere until the end, not to divine the future or tickle our ears. Jesus did not discount or soft sell the life of a believer in a broken world.

> These things I have spoken to you, that in Me you may have peace. *In the world you will have tribulation*; but be of good cheer, I have overcome the world. (John 16:33, emphasis added)

Jesus' message to His church of two thousand years ago, and every year since, has been the same: receive His peace in His world and overcome the challenges faced enduring until the end.

So The Revelation of Jesus Christ was given to John "to show his servants what . . . things which must shortly take place" (Revelation 1:1). They were occurring then and are occurring now. Some events were about to take place and other events were in the future. The visions disclose great events that cover all of this current age with references to previous ages and ages to come.

A general observation sets the stage for the recipients of The Revelation. As with the rest of the New Testament canon, the epistles to the seven churches of Asia Minor, where John had presumed to have served as an apostle, were instructions that addressed their specific situation and were to be received by all the churches. Even though there were many dozens of churches in this region, it appears that these churches were chosen for the common challenges and the lessons they provide for all churches throughout "these last days."

The New Testament reveals that the era known as "these last days" generally covers the period of time from Jesus' first coming until His second coming. So the issues raised for each church, the commendations given, and the problems exposed are specific to each church addressed and yet are representative of all churches until His return. In His letters to these seven churches, Jesus reveals His very personal regard and evaluation. He gives greater revelation of Himself and His warning and/or reward for each church.

THE UNVEILING

Each letter contains the four key components of commendation, exhortation, instruction, and a promise. It is difficult to process the gift of exhortation in light of our natural responses and cultural influences, but it is like a two-sided coin that reflects either correction or encouragement. Jesus understands human nature and the need we have for affirmation, but He does not withhold the clear and merciful correction to discipline those He loves. In keeping with the theme of completion and closure, He includes a seven-step process of address that includes the following:

1. An introduction
2. Jesus' introductory attribute
3. His description of their deeds
4. His commendation
5. An exhortation and/or encouragement
6. His instructions
7. His promise

These seven churches serve as "types" for us to reflect on and to learn from. The characteristics of these churches shine a spotlight on the many different challenges of all churches and reveal warnings to the church today. Jesus then gives us greater revelation in the consummation of our salvation, our relationship with God and its intimacy, and the hope of the restoration of all things with the church serving Him as kings and priests to rule with Him on the earth forever!

> He who has an ear, let him hear what the Spirit says to the churches. To him who overcomes I will give to eat from the tree of life, which is in the midst of the Paradise of God. (Revelation 2:7)

The victorious title that Jesus introduces to His disciples in Caesarea Philippi describes a conclusive victory in life and in conclusion. Seated at the base of the massive Mount Hermon and the mouth of the cave of the Greek goddess Pan, Jesus set the stage with this powerful imagery. Tradition states that Alexander the Great had a Greek temple built at this location to solemnize the pagan worship of blood sacrifice at the mouth of Hades, this place of the dead. The base of this mountain served as a quarry for the building project of Caesarea Philippi and was probably littered in gravel. The gravel (Peter from *petra*, meaning "rock") was in contrast to the stone face of Hermon (this rock). In the assumed context of this geographic location, Jesus affirms Peter's proclamation with this affirming contrast.

> And I also say to you that you are Peter, and on this rock I will build My church, and the gates of Hades shall not prevail against it. And I will give you the keys of the kingdom of heaven, and whatever you bind on earth will be bound in heaven, and whatever you loose on earth will be loosed in heaven. (Matthew 16:18–19)

Jesus is building His church, the *ecclesia*, the "called-out ones," God's assembly. The Revelation opens us to the heavenly scene of its consummation.

> After these things I looked, and behold, a great multitude which no one could number, of all nations, tribes, peoples, and tongues, standing before the throne and before the Lamb, clothed with white robes, with palm branches in their hands, and crying out with a loud voice, saying, "Salvation belongs to our God who sits on the throne, and to the Lamb!" (Revelation 7:9–10)

The practical and historical considerations for the selection of these seven churches shed more light on their message and reach. The letter was not sent to the church in Jerusalem, though all churches are impacted and included in the epistles to the churches. As previously stated, the dating of the letter is unknown. If it was written after the fall of Jerusalem, the church of Jerusalem had been dispersed prior to AD 70. This dispersion and the blessing on the Jewish culture in the Roman world would have yielded large populations of Jews throughout this area. The church, though Jewish in its origination, would now be increasingly Gentile. So The Revelation is addressed to "the church"

THE UNVEILING

in the Gentile Asia Minor of a mixed ethnicity. The focal point of the church was moving west.

These epistles reveal the unchanging nature of God in Jesus Christ to His church. The lessons, promises, and warnings given to these churches apply not only to the seven churches of The Revelation but to all churches in this age. These churches serve as types for us to reflect on and learn from. The blended characteristics of these churches present the many different local churches and their challenges throughout history as well as their warnings. Through these letters, Jesus also gives us greater revelation in the consummation of our salvation, our relationship with God, and the intimacy we enjoy. He concludes each letter with the reality of the hope of the restoration of all things with the church serving Him as kings and priests to rule with Him on the earth forever.

Jesus promises great blessings to the overcomers, the morally victorious, for those who do not compromise with the temptations that this temporary world offers. Chapters two and three of Revelation state,

> To Ephesus: They will be granted to eat of the Tree of Life in the paradise of God.

> To Smyrna: They are promised that they will not to be hurt by the second death.

> To Pergamos: They are blessed to receive some hidden manna, a white stone, and a new name.

> To Thyatira: They will be given authority over the nations and the morning star.

> To Sardis: They shall be clothed in white garments and their names written in the Book of Life and confessed before God and the angels.

To Philadelphia: God will make them a pillar in the temple of God and He will write His Name upon them.

To Laodicea: They will sit down with Jesus on His throne.

"To the angel of the church in Ephesus write:" (Revelation 2:1)

The first letter is to the church of Ephesus, the same church that the apostle Paul addressed in his New Testament epistle. The revelation Paul opens to them is amazing. He reminds them that they have been blessed with every spiritual blessing in heavenly places in Christ. They have been chosen in Him before the foundation of the world so they would be holy and blameless before Him (Ephesians 1:3–4). The promises of God opened to them and for us reveals a church that should need no exhortation, yet this is the first church addressed by Jesus.

The city of Ephesus was the largest and most important trading port in the Roman province of Asia, situated at the mouth of the Cayster River on the shore of the Aegean. At the time of the early church, it was in a state of decline due to the silting of its harbor and its control of trade in the region had diminished. The apostle Paul had lived there for over two years during his third missionary journey, making it central to the evangelization of the entire province. The famous temple of Artemis was built at a sacred site of an ancient Anatolian fertility goddess located about one and a half miles northeast of the city. This magnificent structure was ranked as one of the seven wonders of the ancient world. It was widely represented on Roman coins and was reputed to be four times the size of the Roman Parthenon. The great theater in Ephesus, into which the rioting mob carried Paul's traveling companions, had a capacity of about twenty-four thousand. It remains largely intact to this day at the end of the impressive marble boulevard that led from Mount Pion to the ancient harbor, now several miles inland.

THE UNVEILING

Jesus commended the church at Ephesus for its works of rejecting evil, its perseverance, and its sound orthodoxy. However, "it left its first love." Jesus' reference here, and to the church of Pergamum regarding the "Nicolaitans," presumes that this identifying title was common in the first century. It is somewhat cryptic to the church two millennia after the fact. There are a couple of descriptive explanations of the name. The first is seen as a definition of the two Greek words in the name, the word *nicao*, meaning "to conquer," and *laos*, meaning "the people." Therefore, some apply this adjective as an accusation against a clergy class that "rule over the people." Additionally, there is a reference to Nicolas of Antioch who began a sect teaching a separate priesthood. The distant reference is acknowledged by a few ancient texts.

An insightful explanation is referenced by Irenaeus, an early church father of the second century. He writes that the Nicolaitans themselves claimed Nicolas of Jerusalem as their founder. Nicolas is mentioned in the book of Acts (6:5) as a native of Antioch and a proselyte (convert to Judaism) and then a follower of the way of Christ. Immediately following the birth of the Church in Jerusalem, he was chosen by the whole multitude of the disciples to be one of the first seven deacons and was ordained by the apostles.

There are conflicting stories of the deacon Nicolas that attempt to explain the libertine Gnostic sect and the unrestrained special liberties of their followers, the Nicolaitans. Another church father, Epiphanius, bishop of Salamis, Cyprus, at the end of the fourth century, relates his understanding of some of the details of the life of Nicolas the deacon. He describes him as having descended into the grossest impurity and became the originator of the Nicolaitans as well as other libertine Gnostic sects. He records that Nicolas had an attractive wife, and he had refrained from intercourse as though in imitation of those whom he saw to be devoted to God. He endured this for a while but in the end could not bear to control his incontinence. But because he was ashamed of his defeat and suspected that he had been found out, he ventured to say, "Unless one copulates every day, he cannot have eternal life" (Epiphanius, Panarion, 25, 1).

There are other accounts that protect Nicolas's reputation but still attribute the libertine sect as associated with his comments and in response to his personal struggles. In the second century, Clement of Alexandria gives a different account. He states that Nicolas led a chaste life and brought up his children in purity. And on a certain occasion, having been sharply reproved by the apostles as a jealous husband, he repelled the charge by offering to allow his wife to become the wife of any other person. It is reported that he was in the habit of repeating a saying that is ascribed to the apostle Matthias also: "It is our duty to fight against the flesh and to abuse it." I suggest that his words were perversely interpreted by the Nicolaitans as authority for their immoral practices.

Regardless of the origination of the name, it is clear that Jesus' exhortation points to the lives of unrestrained indulgence of some in the churches of Ephesus and Pergamum. The criticism Jesus levels at Ephesus is that their love for Christ is no longer fervent. He instructs them to do the works they did at first with a promise of the Tree of Life.

Nicolaitan: Regardless of the origination of the name, it is clear that Jesus' exhortation points to the lives of unrestrained indulgence of some in the churches of Ephesus and Pergamum.

The primary lesson for the church of all ages is for caution to be taken when religious liturgy and good works replace a living, loving relationship with Jesus. He implores them to open the door of their hearts again so the intimacy of their relationship might be rekindled. He warns against the deception that creeps into the life of a weary saint, one so busy about the work of the church that he or she begins to justify things in his or her life that would have no place if he or she were intimate with Jesus.

Like the Ephesian church, "blessed with every spiritual blessing," all Christians have the potential of the temptation to get so caught up in the work of the ministry, the "good deeds," so as to become "weary in well doing" and lose our "first love." Our busyness can lead to a cynical stubbornness that works out of our natural abilities, experiences, and strengths rather than depending on the Holy Spirit. This is a result of turning from Jesus and His grace, His enablement. We can then become tempted in our weariness to justify the sin of self-pity and self-indulgence, resulting in the pursuit of false comforts that can be defined as Nicolaitanism and result in not finishing well. The Ephesians are challenged to finish well, as are we!

Jesus words are spoken openly to all His church: "He who has an ear, let him hear what the Spirit says to the churches" (Revelation 2:7, 11, 17, 29; 3:6, 13, 22).

"And to the angel of the church in Smyrna write:" (Revelation 2:8)

Smyrna is addressed by Jesus and He introduces Himself as "The first and the last, who was dead, and has come to life." He reveals His power over the great threat that they face: persecution unto death! In just four verses, Jesus speaks to His own in direct and encouraging words for those facing the greatest difficulty.

This epistle is directed to the messenger of the church of Smyrna but addresses all those who suffer persecution. The churches of the first century endured the Judaizers and Emperor Nero's persecution, which was amplified in the following years by his successor, Diocletian. During the ongoing persecution of the first and second centuries, this letter became even more applicable to the dispersed Christians in the Roman Empire and the church throughout the ages.

The persecution of the early church began in Jerusalem and spread throughout the Roman Empire by the initiation of the Caesar Nero Imperial cult and the Judaizers of each city. The early church grew in influence and numbers, but their prospects were ever darkening.

Polycarp, known as a disciple of the apostle John and the second-century bishop of Smyrna, is an example of this persecution. According to the ancient scroll of the Martyrdom of Polycarp as documented by the church fathers of the first centuries of the church, he died a martyr, bound and burned at the stake and then stabbed when the fire failed to touch him.

The report that has been given of Polycarp, considered by some as another angel or messenger of the church at Smyrna, is a detailed record of his martyrdom. This record beautifully illustrates the prophecy, the charge, and the promise of this letter. Regardless of the questions of dating in the second century, this report is well worth our consideration. The stories that were handed down reveal the history of persecution, the epistle to the church of Smyrna, and the bishop that wears the martyr's crown.

> In the year of our Lord 167 a cruel persecution broke out against the Christians of Asia Minor. Polycarp would have awaited at his post the fate which threatened him, but his people compelled him to shelter himself in a quiet retreat, where he might, it was thought, safely hide. And for a while he remained undiscovered, and busied himself, so we are told, in prayers and intercessions for the persecuted Church.
>
> At last his enemies seized on a child, and, by torture, compelled him to make known where he was. Satisfied now that his hour was come, he refused further flight, saying, "The will of God be done." He came from the upper story of the house to meet his captors and ordered them as much refreshment as they might desire, and only asked of them this favor, that they would grant him yet one hour of undisturbed prayer. The fullness of his heart carried him on for two hours, and even the heathen, we are told, were touched by the sight of the old man's devotion. He was then conveyed back to the city, to Smyrna. The officer before whom he was brought tried to persuade him to yield to

the small demand made upon him. "What harm," he asked, "can it do you to offer sacrifice to the emperor?

This was the test which was commonly applied to those accused of Christianity. But not for one moment would the venerable Polycarp consent.

Rougher measures were then tried, and he was flung from the carriage in which he was being conveyed. When he appeared in the Amphitheatre, the magistrate said to him, "Swear, curse Christ, and I will set thee free."

But the old man answered, "Eighty and six years have I served Christ, and he has never done me wrong: how, then, can I curse him, my King and my Savior?"

In vain was he threatened with being thrown to the wild beasts or burned alive; and at last the fatal proclamation is made, that "Polycarp confessed himself a Christian." This was the death-warrant. He was condemned to be burnt alive. Jews and Gentiles, the whole "synagogue of Satan," here described, alike, hastened in rage and fury to collect wood from the baths workshops for the funeral pile.

The old man laid aside his garments, and took his place in the midst of the fuel. When they would have nailed him to the stake, he said to them, "Leave me thus, I pray, unfastened; he who has enabled me to brave the fire will give me strength also to endure its fierceness." He then uttered this brief prayer: "O Lord, Almighty God, the Father of thy beloved Son Jesus Christ, through whom we have received a knowledge of thee, God of the angels and of the whole creation, of the whole race of man, and of the saints who live before thy presence; I thank thee that thou hast thought me worthy, this day and this hour, to share the cup of thy Christ among the number of thy witnesses!"

The fire was kindled; but a high wind drove the flame to one side, and prolonged his sufferings; at last the executioner dispatched him with a sword.

So did one of Christ's poor saints at Smyrna die, "faithful unto death," and winner of "the crown of life," and never to "be hurt of the second death." (Henry Wace, Dictionary of Christian Biography and Literature to the End of the Sixth Century A.D., with an Account of the Principal Sects and Heresies, s.v. "Polycarpus, bishop of Smyrna")

The lesson of the church of Smyrna is the primary purpose of The Revelation of Jesus Christ. This is Jesus' exhortation to persevere until the end, even your end, or until He comes. Jesus commands the church of Smyrna and us, "Do not fear."

Jesus words are spoken openly to all His church: "He who has an ear, let him hear what the Spirit says to the churches" (Revelation 2:7, 11, 17, 29; 3:6, 13, 22).

The lesson of the church of Smyrna is the primary purpose of The Revelation of Jesus Christ.

"And to the angel of the church in Pergamum write:" (Revelation 2:12)

Jesus describes Himself as the One with the two-edged sword that proceeds from His mouth. This is a graphic picture of His readiness and authority to bring judgment. He alone is worthy to break the seals releasing the restrained judgment on humanity's sin.

And I saw heaven opened, and behold, a white horse, and He who sat on it is called Faithful and True, and in righteousness He judges and wages war. His eyes are a flame of fire, and on His head are many diadems; and He has a name written on

Him which no one knows except Himself. He is clothed with a robe dipped in blood, and His name is called The Word of God. And the armies which are in heaven, clothed in fine linen, white and clean, were following Him on white horses. From His mouth comes a sharp sword, so that with it He may strike down the nations, and He will rule them with a rod of iron; and He treads the wine press of the fierce wrath of God, the Almighty. And on His robe and on His thigh He has a name written, "KING OF KINGS AND LORD OF LORDS." (Revelation 19:11–16)

Jesus' words are a two-edged sword that convict and expose and ultimately bring final judgment.

For the word of God is living and active and sharper than any two-edged sword, and piercing as far as the division of soul and spirit, of both joints and marrow, and able to judge the thoughts and intentions of the heart. And there is no creature hidden from His sight, but all things are open and laid bare to the eyes of Him with whom we have to do. (Hebrews 4:12–13)

Jesus knows the temptations and discouragements that we face right where we live. He referenced the demonic stronghold of that pagan city to Satan's throne. Pergamum (modern-day Bergamum in western Turkey) had served as the capitol of Attulus a century earlier and was considered by some as the Roman capital of Roman Asia or Asia Minor. It was a throne city for ancient mythical gods with saving attributes assigned to Caesar for worship in the Imperial cult.

This city was very influential in the region and boasted having the largest library in the world, second only to Alexandria, Egypt. It was also unique in the production of parchment, which receives its name from the Pergamena charter, as this material was discovered here for book purposes. At the time, they were also in competition with the papyrus of Alexandria, Egypt.

The physical appearance of the ancient city adds to this descriptive title of "where Satan's throne is." The city is built on an elevated plateau, situated now to the west of modern Bergamum. The Greek word *pergamos* is translated as "height" or "elevation" and references a fortified city. It also had the appearance of a great throne when approaching from the west.

Jesus refers to Sardis as "Satan's throne" for more spiritual reasons. The city had been described as a sophisticated hub of development with a laborers guild, or union. Sardis was considered a pagan-cathedral city, a center of academia, and therefore had many royal residences. It was a center of worship for Dionysius, Zeus, and Asclepius (the guardian of health). This third Roman god probably wielded the greatest influence in the death of Antipas, the bishop of the city and possibly the messenger addressed in this letter.

The ancient church tradition states that Antipas was a healer and was also set in as the bishop of Pergamum by John the Apostle. There are conflicting stories of his martyrdom. However, it is reported that he was placed in a large brass bull, the symbol of worship of the gods, and the bull was placed over a fire until red hot. This grotesque sacrifice was also known as "the blood sprayer." The victims were placed in the brass bull as an oven for a living sacrifice. This sacrifice was considered acceptable when the resulting explosion of blood burst from its nostrils. Christians became the target of this persecution from the pressure of the Judaizers, the guilds of the pagan temples, and the increasing threat of the Imperial cult.

The Judaizers accused Christians of the sin of Balaam, referencing the story told by Moses (Numbers 31:16). Balaam was a prophet who counseled the Moabites through their king Balak with a means to deceive the Israelites that would compromise and result in their defeat. He lured them into the carnal justification of immorality with a misappropriation of the promises of God. So the reference to Balaam in this letter exposes the dangerous compromise in the church of these failures. This compromise allowed the social life of pagan worship, an overindulging party spirit that involved drinking the wine of pagan libations and eating the meat of pagan offerings ultimately leading to even greater licentiousness.

Corrupt doctrines and corrupt worship often lead to a corrupt way of life. The issue of Gentile believers eating meat offered to idols was addressed in the first council in Jerusalem. The Jewish believers were offended by the Gentiles who lived with them. They were instructed to abstain from that which offends the Jews for sake of its offensiveness. The sacrifice itself was without meaning to a follower of Jesus. The prophet Isaiah announced God's satirical illustration to Israel concerning a man and his idol as he casts down a cedar for his purpose:

> Then it becomes *something* for a man to burn, so he takes one of them and warms himself; he also makes a fire to bake bread. He also makes a god and worships it; he makes it a graven image and falls down before it. Half of it he burns in the fire; over *this* half he eats meat as he roasts a roast and is satisfied. He also warms himself and says, "Aha! I am warm, I have seen the fire." But the rest of it he makes into a god, his graven image. He falls down before it and worships; he also prays to it and says, "Deliver me, for you are my god." They do not know, nor do they understand, for He has smeared over their eyes so that they cannot see and their hearts so that they cannot comprehend. No one recalls, nor is there knowledge or understanding to say, "I have burned half of it in the fire and also have baked bread over its coals. I roast meat and eat *it*. Then I make the rest of it into an abomination, I fall down before a block of wood!" He feeds on ashes; a deceived heart has turned him aside. And he cannot deliver himself, nor say, "Is there not a lie in my right hand?" (Isaiah 44:15–20)

The apostle Paul also addressed this issue with the Corinthian church in response to questions of legalism and of bringing an offense to a weaker Christian. However, Jesus is exposing the motive of the licentious behavior, not just the act.

Corrupt doctrines and corrupt worship often lead to a corrupt way of life.

The church at Pergamum dealt with a social culture of appeasement, compromise, and self-justification that resulted in a practical recantation of their faith. This is similar to the "practical atheism" found in the secularized church today. This is the acknowledgment that God exists, but not in any way that matters. The church of the first century that participated in the social life of the city was then realized as a formal recognition of false worship. In times of persecution, tasting the wine of libations (drink offerings) or meat offered to idols (blood sacrifices) was understood to signify a recantation of Christianity. There was also the satanic parody of the Imperial cult: Nero demanded to be called "Lord and God" and "Savior of the world."

The church at Pergamum dealt with a social culture of appeasement, compromise and self-justification that resulted in a practical recantation of their faith.

The Nicolaitan warning is given to this church also. The compromise of self-justifying sin that was warned and hated in Ephesus was *tolerated* in Pergamum. The accusation referenced the Old Testament character of Balaam and the contemporary heresy of Nicolaitanism. Remember, Nicolas was a deacon of the early church who expressed a radical separation from sin to the point of throwing himself on the grace of God. Lawless Christians who wanted to justify their sin and depend on the limitless grace of God became even worldlier than they were before. As Zig Ziglar so simply warned, "Be careful not to compromise what you want *most* for what you want *now*."

During the past generation, while Christians have temporarily gained political ground, there has been a loss of ground in terms of our uniqueness as Christians. In the book *Twilight of a Great Civilization*, Carl Henry observes,

> We are so steeped in the anti-Christ philosophy—namely, that success consists in embracing not the values of the Sermon on the Mount but an infinity of material things, of sex and status—that we little sense how much of what passes for practical Christianity is really an apostate compromise with the spirit of the age.

The whole church is called to repent of Nicolaitanism. When compromise is allowed in the church, it is a leaven that leavens the whole lump. The Nicolaitan influence in the early church was a threat to the godly living and faithful witness of the whole church by the justification of licentiousness and compromise. Jesus warns of our enmity with God that is the foolishness of warring against Him.

> **We are not diplomats but prophets, and our message is not a compromise but an ultimatum.**
> **—A. W. Tozer**

Jesus also references an item of the Holy of Holies, the hidden manna, as an invitation to the intimacy that He offers those who are His. In this context, He is promising those who are currently compromised that if they will repent and return, the promise of true intimacy and acceptance is received. Manna was the heavenly food of the Israelites while in the wilderness. Jesus is called it the "Bread of Life" and the "Manna which comes down from heaven" (John 6:48–50). He invites us to receive from Him in a personal relationship rather than partaking of the godless libations of the culture of the world.

> Do not love the world nor the things in the world. If anyone loves the world, the love of the Father is not in him. For all that is in the world, the lust of the flesh and the lust of the eyes and the boastful pride of life, is not from the Father, but is from the world. The world is passing away, and also its lusts; but the one who does the will of God lives forever. (1 John 2:15–17)

He also offers a white stone and a new name written on it, referencing the reality of forgiveness, acceptance, and a fresh start. Receiving the white stone represented absolution. Some Old Testament commentators conjecture that the stones of the high priest's vest with the urim and thumin, which mean "light and perfections" or "revelation and truth," were of diamond, the white stone. So there is the added sense of God's open revelation to those who receive Him. Their new name represents their adoption into the family of God. Jesus commands them to repent.

"And to the angel of the church in Thyatira write:" (Revelation 2:18)

Jesus' letter to Thyatira is the longest, and He gives the harshest correction to a growing church that has been exposed to bad teaching, a corrupt doctrine that corrupts the whole church. The word *thyatira*, translated from Greek, means "an odor of affliction." This is an appropriate name for the result of their corruption. So Jesus reminds them of the dark period in Israel's history with a wicked king, Ahab, in the northern lost kingdom and his pagan wife, Jezebel, an odor of affliction for the people of God.

Jesus' penetrating gaze is described as One Who has eyes like a flame of fire. The judgment in His address is amplified by the stand He takes before them with feet like burnished bronze, the metal of judgment throughout Scripture. Jesus stands in judgment of a corrupted church. He is God's Son, His eyes are pouring a fiery blaze, and He is standing on feet of furnace-fired bronze. The church is totally exposed before her Lord. She is being corrupted by a false prophet and will not escape Jesus' judgment.

Historical documents and archeological digs show Thyatira was a quickly developing city-state that was flourishing in the developing trades of the area. The city of Thyatira is mentioned in the introduction of Lydia, a seller of purple from that city (Acts 16:14). The historical records have revealed the growing economy of this area was due to the

Roman military garrison placed there, as the supply of military needs demanded that the city produce uniforms, arms, etc.

Church growth teachers and some church planters have realized that churches that are intentionally planted in a booming, upwardly mobile area have a greater potential to grow quickly with the local economy. These same churches can struggle with the challenge to grow in depth as well as to width. Their fast growth can be a result of the momentum of the crowd and, as a result, lack the discipline required for maturity. This kind of growth can produce the appearance of success but lack the deepened character required to face the temptations of hypocrisy. Pastors have complained that the fast-growth churches are a mile wide but only an inch deep.

This kind of growth can produce the appearance of success but lack the deepened character required to face the temptations of hypocrisy.

The environment the church of Thyatira faced was a dominant pressure to get along with the guilds. Guilds were established for order, consistency, economy, and control. The association of artisans or merchants controlled the practice of their crafts in a particular town. This was a very political but necessary association. The city of Thyatira was known for her guilds of metallurgy (an early and developing source of bronze), bakers, potters, dyers, tanners, uniform fabrication, masonry, etc. These were similar to contemporary unions and fraternal organizations but were geographically localized. The politics of the day required that the guilds would be supportive of the Imperial cult that had developed under Caesar Nero, a developing pagan system of worship. As a result, the church was instructed to yield its concerns for the sake of business and survival, as the city wanted the favor of Rome.

So Jesus reveals, again, that He is Lord and Judge. He knows their struggle, but they are a church of love and faith and service and perseverance. He acknowledges the increase in their testing and the pressure they are under. The church has always faced resistance by the natural and carnal world. There is an enemy with a clear and consistent mode of operation to kill, steal, and destroy (John 10:10). Even today, a demonically inspired secularization of thought in the modern world undermines the church as she wavers in her uncertainty. The cultural pressures of tolerance and political correctness press an ignorant and deceived church into the mold of the world. Many become intimidated and even cast away their faith and question the Word of God.

Even today, a demonically inspired secularization of thought in the modern world undermines the church as she wavers in her uncertainty.

So the true Christian who follows Jesus as a person of faith is marked by an idolatrous culture as intolerant, narrow and ignorant. Much of the church has been goaded into changing the meaning of words, the value of life, the sanctity of the marriage bed, the wonder of procreation, even to the acceptance of all forms of excuses for sexual confusion and selfish gratification. Jesus exhorts His church to continue in the faith!

Jesus accuses this church of tolerating the one who represents the demonically inspired religion of the world. He draws on the image of the historical queen embodied in the "woman Jezebel." who attempted to thwart God's people and pervert her leaders. She is a self-described prophetess—demonically inspired to lead God's bond servants astray. This is the source of corruption and the influence is destructive. They were charged with "tolerating" this continued corruption of the church. This toleration is more than enduring; it is accepting the unacceptable!

Some of the language used in this letter intimates that this was more than a spiritual influence but also a direct relational influence in the church. The woman called Jezebel had been inferred by early historians as possibly the wife of the bishop of the church of Thyatira. The evidence is not conclusive but this may give more understanding to the confusion and to her corrupting influence in the church. She is a charged as being a self-proclaimed, unrepentant prophetess, even a teacher and therefore a leader. She has no will to repent and therefore has no recourse but God's judgment.

There is a specific warning of an immediate judgment on this source of adulterous and idolatrous influence in the church and on all who would join her: "a bed of sickness." Again, Jesus is a righteous judge, and He alone stands as the only One worthy to break the seals of judgment on all humanity. The "bed of pleasure" becomes the "bed of pain." The perversion of idolatry and immorality that is produced is also judged. The apostle Paul reveals that sexual sin is self-destructive: "The immoral man sins against his own body."

> All things are lawful for me, but not all things are profitable. All things are lawful for me, but I will not be mastered by anything. Food is for the stomach and the stomach is for food, but God will do away with both of them. Yet the body is not for immorality, but for the Lord, and the Lord is for the body. Now God has not only raised the Lord, but will also raise us up through His power. Do you not know that your bodies are members of Christ? Shall I then take away the members of Christ and make them members of a prostitute? May it never be! Or do you not know that the one who joins himself to a prostitute is one body with her? For He says, "The two shall become one flesh." But the one who joins himself to the Lord is one spirit with Him. Flee immorality. Every other sin that a man commits is outside the body, but the immoral man sins against his own body. Or do you not know that your body is a temple of the Holy Spirit who is in you, whom you have from God, and that you are not your own? For you have been bought with a price: therefore glorify God in your body. (1 Corinthians 6:12–20)

The early church, like the church today, was plagued with false teaching. This teaching proclaimed special knowledge (Gnosticism) leading to elitism and the justification of sin. Jesus judged these lies as the "deep things of Satan." These are the demonically inspired thoughts of man that deter them from the truth of God's Word with a motive to elevate a man. James 3:13-18 clarifies that the sources of our thoughts and these Gnostic ideas would be of demonic origin and produce the devilish result of loss and death. Such lawlessness, the sin first exposed in Genesis 3, is still manifested today. The church of Thyatira had become corrupted by these lies and the motivation of wanting to get along, of fitting in, of justifying sin.

> **Be careful not to compromise what you want most for what you want now.**
>
> —Zig Ziglar

Jesus exhorts His church to overcome this temptation even until the end. When we feel trapped, victimized, and helpless, we are to remember His promise. Persevere until the end and you will end up with Him, the King of kings, the Lord of lords, the One Who sits at the right hand of the Father and rules over all! All the potter has made that does not measure up to His intention will be shattered and broken to pieces. Our greatest reward is the "morning star" Himself!

"And to the angel of the church in Sardis write:" (Revelation 3:1)

Sardis was once a great city, an ancient city at the location of modern Sart in Turkey's Manisa Province. Sardis was the influential capital of the ancient kingdom of Lydia (under King Croesus), one of the important cities of the Persian Empire. It was the seat of a proconsul under the Roman Empire and the metropolis of the province Lydia in later Roman and Byzantine times. Geographically, it was situated on an important highway leading from the interior to the Aegean coast, allowing it to command the wide and fertile plain of the Hermus. Once great, now inconsequential. Once alive, now dead. Like so many things of this world, passing away. This comparison does not need to be reflected in the life cycle of a local church, but it has become prevalent.

Jesus' primary message to this dead church was to *remember and return*. They needed to be won back to true godliness. Jesus reminds her that He has the full measure of the Spirit of God and a full investment and involvement in the local church. In Him and from Him is all-sufficient grace that is inexhaustible and unsearchable for all His people.

The very description of the church is an oxymoron: a "dead church"! They have the title of the "called-out ones" (*ecclesia*)—the church—those alive to God! One of the archaeological findings of this ancient city is the marble throne of the bishop of Sardis. This is a blatant expression of the focus on the church, which is dead. Rather than a living sacrifice on the altar of the will in worship, the dead church builds a throne to men of earthly value.

Jesus is reminding the dead church then and now that He has the Spirit in full, and when the Spirit of God is joined with the spirit of man, life flows. There is the breath of God that brings revelation and regeneration; the breath of God produces the inspiration of man. The Holy Spirit will illuminate the mind of man with the thoughts of God and set his heart on fire, fully alive in Him. When the wind of the Spirit fills the sails of a Christian's life, he is moved along in the center of God's will. Then the church will be alive to God and empowered by the Spirit to accomplish the work of service that honors God and brings His Kingdom. So He exhorts them to *"Wake up."*

The apostle Paul warned the church of Ephesus of this potential problem.

> Therefore be imitators of God, as beloved children; and walk in love, just as Christ also loved you and gave Himself up for us, an offering and a sacrifice to God as a fragrant aroma. But immorality or any impurity or greed must not even be named among you, as is proper among saints; and *there must be no filthiness and silly talk, or coarse jesting, which are not fitting, but rather giving of thanks. For this you know with certainty, that no immoral or impure person or covetous man, who is an idolater, has an inheritance in the kingdom of Christ and God.*

Let no one deceive you with empty words, for because of these things the wrath of God comes upon the sons of disobedience. Therefore do not be partakers with them; for you were formerly darkness, but now you are Light in the Lord; walk as children of Light (for the fruit of the Light *consists* in all goodness and righteousness and truth), trying to learn what is pleasing to the Lord. Do not participate in the unfruitful deeds of darkness, but instead even expose them; for it is disgraceful even to speak of the things which are done by them in secret. But all things become visible when they are exposed by the light, for everything that becomes visible is light. For this reason it says, "Awake, sleeper, And arise from the dead, And Christ will shine on you." Therefore be careful how you walk, not as unwise men but as wise, making the most of your time, because the days are evil. So then do not be foolish, but understand what the will of the Lord is. (Ephesians 5:1–17)

The warning for Sardis is so very timely for the affluent church of the West today. She had deceived herself and others; she was considered by them to be really living, though in fact she was dead. Their works were not perfect before God. They were okay before men but not before God. Their works were considered "dead." These works—their prayers, their alms, and their service—were as hypocrites, "to be seen of men." Before men, they had the appearance as spiritual, and they had their reward: people talked of them and gave them credit as having life. But before God, they were dead. It is only before God that everything is measured and truly evaluated.

The apostle Paul said, "It is a small thing to me to be judged of you or of any human judgment: he that judges me is the Lord; I labor to be accepted of him" (1 Corinthians 4:3). The one question for us all is, how will our work appear before God? Jesus' severe tone in this letter reveals His great displeasure with them. He is not pronouncing a judgment on their vice or their heresy. Rather, something more corrupt and deadly: a religious spirit of deception.

THE UNVEILING

Jesus' exhortation contains no encouragement, only correction. What was the problem? Jesus said that His disciples were "in the world but not of the world" and Sardis had become "of the world but not in it." Just an empty shell. Many churches today suffer from the same isolation. A dead church is isolated from the culture it is supposed to shine light into but so worldly that it is just as deceived as the world it believes it is above, stumbling in the darkness.

Jesus said that His disciples were "in the world but not of the world" and Sardis had become "of the world but not in it."

The church of Sardis had become deceived. The worst kind of deception is self-deception. The old saying is true: most people want to be delivered from temptation but would just like to stay in touch.

It has been reported that President Abraham Lincoln loved to employ a brainteaser to make a point to constituents. He would ask, "How many legs would a sheep have if you called his tail a leg?" Naturally, they would meekly respond, "Five." "Wrong! You are mistaken. The sheep would still have just four legs. Calling something a leg doesn't make it so."

We live in a time that is swimming in lies, and these lies are repeated again and again with the intention of deception. We are inundated with advertising, political self-promotion, and slanderous attacks. We must be awakened to the voluntary process of self-deception. The apostle Paul exposed this dangerous and deceptive downward spiral toward outer darkness.

> So this I say, and affirm together with the Lord, that you walk no longer just as the Gentiles also walk, in the futility of their mind, being darkened in their understanding, excluded from the life of God because of the ignorance that is in them, because of the hardness of their heart; and they, having become callous, have given themselves over to sensuality for the practice of

every kind of impurity with greediness. But you did not learn Christ in this way, if indeed you have heard Him and have been taught in Him, just as truth is in Jesus, that, in reference to your former manner of life, you lay aside the old self, which is being corrupted in accordance with the lusts of deceit, and that you be renewed in the spirit of your mind, and put on the new self, which in the likeness of God has been created in righteousness and holiness of the truth. (Ephesians 4:17–24)

We would do well to learn the lesson of the WWII pilot who was commissioned to gather intelligence behind enemy lines. He escaped the Nazi soldiers to a preplanned farm location in northern France. A small plane had been hidden under the hay in the barn for his flight to England. He cleared the plane and the way for takeoff. As he was taxiing toward the field, he heard a gnawing sound under the console. He rightly assumed it was a rat. He was very concerned at the critical nature of the wiring where the sound was heard. He had no choice but to take off to insure his safety. The gnawing continued, so he had to come up with a solution to survive. He placed his oxygen mask on and began to ascend steeply. The higher he rose, the thinner the oxygen level in the cockpit became. Eventually, the lack of oxygen killed the gnawing rat and it fell out on the floor.

Jesus' solution exhorts His church to take similar action to move further up and further in. We must take radical action to survive. The consequences of sin come silently, stealthily, secretly, invisibly, and even unexpectedly "as a thief." Who can mark the hour when God's Spirit leaves a man? Today is the day of repentance!

> **The deadliest sin is the consciousness of no sin.**
> —**Thomas Carlyle**

God has His remnant. He has always protected those few who would overcome in the face of deception. God's enabling grace is sufficient and available. The Lord remembered these "few" in Sardis and promised them victory. The remainder also would learn that victory was possible for them through Him who had the "Seven Spirits of God." The overcomer is the one who perseveres until the end in the grace of God by His Spirit!

The reward of these who overcome is God's righteousness, God's remembrance, and God's affirmation. His promises are to the living souls in a dead church. Jesus reminds them of the symbolic white robe representing victory, purity, and joy. He also reminds them that He will retain their names in the Book of Life and will confess their names before His Father and His angels.

This Book of Life or Book of Remembrance is referenced in the books Daniel and Malachi in the Old Testament.

> Then those who feared the LORD spoke to one another, and the LORD gave attention and heard it, and a *book of remembrance* was written before Him for those who fear the LORD and who esteem His name. "They will be Mine," says the LORD of hosts, "on the day that I prepare My own possession, and I will spare them as a man spares his own son who serves him." So you will again distinguish between the righteous and the wicked, between one who serves God and one who does not serve Him. (Malachi 3:16–18, emphasis added)

Jesus also references this truth in the Gospel of Luke.

> Nevertheless do not rejoice in this, that the spirits are subject to you, but rejoice that your names are *recorded in heaven*. (Luke 10:20, emphasis added)

The apostle Paul and the writer of Hebrews also remember this truth.

> Indeed, true companion, I ask you also to help these women who have shared my struggle in the cause of the gospel, together with Clement also and the rest of my fellow workers, whose names are in *the book of life*. (Philippians 4:3, emphasis added)

> To the general assembly and church of the firstborn who are *enrolled in heaven*, and to God, the Judge of all, and to the spirits of the righteous made perfect. (Hebrews 12:23, emphasis added)

The Scriptures remind us of God's faithfulness and His justice. He does not need a physical book to remember our deeds or us. He uses this expression as an exhortation to affirm us and encourage our hearts. We are also challenged to remember the only thing God chooses to forget: our sin. This He does by choice as we trust in His remedy, His redemption price paid for our cleansing.

Jesus also reminded the disciples further of His mutual confession as recorded in both Gospels of Matthew and Luke. He is a covenant God, and we are His covenant people. The covenant (cutting) revealed throughout Scripture is a threefold oath made in blood. Life is in the blood (Leviticus 17:11). Our covenant is an oath of loyalty, provision, and protection. Our loyalty to God is in our testimony as we live a life of faith. He reminds us of His loyalty.

> And I say to you, everyone who confesses Me before men, the Son of Man will confess him also before the angels of God; but he who denies Me before men will be denied before the angels of God. (Luke 12:8)

> Then the King will say to those on His right, "Come, you who are blessed of My Father, inherit the kingdom prepared for you from the foundation of the world. For I was hungry, and you gave Me something to eat; I was thirsty, and you gave Me something to drink; I was a stranger, and you invited Me in; naked, and you clothed Me; I was sick, and you visited Me; I was in prison, and you came to Me." Then the righteous will answer Him, "Lord, when did we see You hungry, and feed You, or thirsty, and give You something to drink? And when did we see You a stranger, and invite You in, or naked, and clothe You? When did we see You sick, or in prison, and come to You?" The King will answer and say to them, "Truly I say to you, to the

extent that you did it to one of these brothers of Mine, even the least of them, you did it to Me." (Matthew 25:34–40)

We live in a time of great compromise and intellectual hypocrisy. We would do well to heed Jesus' warning to the church of Sardis: "He who has an ear, let him hear what the Spirit says to the churches." Awake, oh sleeper!

> **Remember: "The deadliest sin is the consciousness of no sin."**

"And to the angel of the church in Philadelphia write:" (Revelation 3:7)

The focus of this oracle is the reality of the authority of God. Jesus introduces additional attributes in this letter to affirm the church and clarify His ultimate authority. They are wise to acknowledge His authority in their lives. "He Who is Holy!" He alone is holy—separate—set apart. These are the attributes of which this church needed to be reminded. The letter to the church of Philadelphia is addressed to the "faithful church." They were described as faithful to God and their calling, in their ministry and their troubles.

All authority is delegated authority. God is sovereign, God is the source, and Jesus is our access. The apostle Paul clearly stated and reaffirmed this attribute of God's sovereignty and His delegated authority for us in the letter to the Roman church.

> Every person is to be in subjection to the governing authorities. *For there is no authority except from God, and those which exist are established by God.* Therefore whoever resists authority has opposed the ordinance of God; and they who have opposed will receive condemnation upon themselves. (Romans 13:1–2, emphasis added)

The city of Aleshehir stands today at the ancient site of Philadelphia in western Turkey. It is one of the few remaining cities of that time, and the church remains in this Muslim country with its testimony of church bells and church buildings. It is reported to be the only remaining vibrant church of the original seven churches.

The church in Philadelphia is described as weak, "of little power." It has been tried many times, yet it has kept faith to God and His Word and has not denied Him. Jesus states that those who are against them will not continue; they will eventually fall. Those who claim to be of the true faith but are not will be shown the error of their ways. Those who deny Christ will, in the end, acknowledge those who were faithful to God. This church was promised the reward of not having to face the final trial and delivered from the threat of falling under the final temptations.

Christ reminds them of His imminent return. "I am coming quickly" (Revelation 3:11). He urges those who believe in Him to keep strong in their faith. Those who follow God will receive a reward that is unimaginable in the end. After the followers of God finish their trials through temptations, they will never have to suffer under them again. They will be with God in the end, and they will be known to God and to all who follow God. Those who seek truth and wisdom and life are to listen to the Holy Spirit so they may obtain it, remembering that in the end, the ones who suffered for Christ will be rewarded greatly and their oppressors will be rightly judged.

Jesus describes Himself as the One Who has the key of David. He is the fulfillment of the promised king. He has received this delegated authority—God's presence on sanctified shoulders. This is the key that King David received following the tragedy of Uzzah's death while transporting the Ark of the Covenant on a new oxcart rather than the sanctified shoulders of godly men (2 Samuel 6).

Philadelphia, "the open door," was designated a missionary city, a city for sending and expansion. It was about 150 years old and established on a trade route for economic gain and as a means to promote Hellenistic

THE UNVEILING

culture in the region with the protection of a military outpost. Jesus redefines their purpose as an "open door." He also restates His sovereignty in opening a door no one will shut. This is an encouragement to continue to evangelize in the face of difficulties. If God opens a door, who can shut it? Each local church exists for this purpose too: an open door for His Word and His people.

As a pastor of an urban church in an area resistant to the pursuit of growth and life, I am guilty of complaining to God of being called to serve in a difficult field of labor. So I have made a conscious decision to repent of my complaining about our inability to grow as an urban church. I believe that God is for us, so who can be against us? Faith is not believing that God *can*; faith is knowing that God *will*. We can do nothing outside of faith! I believe that the gates of hell shall not prevail! The location of our church plant was not of human design but Divinely orchestrated, an act of obedience to the Head of the church, so the outcome is in His hands. He opens doors that no man can shut.

The early church was continually harassed by the Judaizers and by pagan cults. The key cities of that era were competing for favor and finances from Rome. Many of these influential cities raised local money to honor Rome with commercial developments, cultural entertainments, and concentrated areas for pagan temples. These included the Jewish synagogues alongside the Imperial monolith. Since the Jewish community was so well established and served as key donors to such developments, the local synagogue was included in their monuments for political reasons.

Since they built the synagogue into the cultural expression of honor, and it was part of the temple of pagan worship and eventually Caesar worship, it was referred to as the synagogue of Satan. It was at this synagogue of Satan that their accusers would gather and pursue the persecution of the followers of Christ while claiming to be the people of God.

Many in this city would have personally remembered or been told the story of the calamity of the natural disaster that their city endured in AD 17. Philadelphia had endured total devastation of earthquakes and volcanic eruptions, so much so that they were referred to as the scorched earth of west Asia. They knew natural devastation. They were being warned of further testing in the midst of coming calamity. They were being exhorted to continue on in faithful ministry throughout their lives. Persevering in faith! Continuing until the end!

Jesus encouraged them by reminding them of His reward of a crown of perseverance. The New Testament lists five crowns of the faithful, crowns to throw at Jesus's feet. First is the incorruptible crown:

> And everyone who competes in the games exercises self-control in all things. They then do it to receive a perishable wreath, but we an imperishable. (1 Corinthians 9:25)

Not well known for her exhortations for Christ, Dolly Parton did make a relevant statement about perseverance. She came from a poor Appalachian family. When asked why she became successful when so many other poor mountain people did not, she replied, "I never stopped trying. And I never tried stopping." Faithfulness is highly regarded as a reflection of God's character.

The second crown is of rejoicing in the celebration of true fellowship:

> For who is our hope or joy or crown of exultation? Is it not even you, in the presence of our Lord Jesus at His coming? (1 Thessalonians 2:19)

The third crown is of righteousness:

> I have fought the good fight, I have finished the course, I have kept the faith; in the future there is laid up for me the crown of righteousness, which the Lord, the righteous Judge, will award to me on that day; and not only to me, but also to all who have loved His appearing. (2 Timothy 4:7–8)

THE UNVEILING

Someone once defined real failure as living without knowing what life is all about, feeding on things that do not satisfy, and thinking you have everything, only to find out in the end you have nothing that matters. The reality is that you haven't failed. You are just not finished yet.

Fourth, is the crown of life, the eternal reward and original intent of God's creation:

> Blessed is a man who perseveres under trial; for once he has been approved, he will receive the crown of life, which the Lord has promised to those who love Him. (James 1:12)

Fifth, is the crown of glory:

> And when the Chief Shepherd appears, you will receive the unfading crown of glory. (1 Peter 5:4)

It is in this faithful service that we overcome and He makes us a pillar in His house, the New Jerusalem. A pillar carries weight. The churches that are weak have few pillars and many caterpillars. A solid local church is built on strong pillars while the caterpillars crawl in and out. Many in today's churches lack the faithfulness and commitment required to become pillars capable of carrying weight. A majority of so-called church growth today is really a procession of caterpillars inching from church to church.

Solomon's temple had two key pillars named, Jachin and Boaz (1 Kings 7:21). Jachin stood on the left and is translated "founding" while Boaz stood on the right and is translated "in its strength." Jesus' promises to make those who overcome, those who persevere until the end, pillars in the temple of God, the place of His dwelling forever, *"established in strength."* He will write His name on your heart and your name in His book. He comes for us all—quickly! Therefore, persevere until the end in His authority.

"And to the angel of the church in Laodicea write:" (Revelation 3:14)

The church of Laodicea is known as the lukewarm church. They have been exposed as having a mistaken view of themselves. They are plagued with self-conceit and are self-deceived. Jesus commands them to focus on Him as their source and His Kingdom as their goal.

> For the kingdom of God is not eating and drinking, but righteousness and peace and joy in the Holy Spirit. (Romans 14:17)

If Jesus is worth anything, He is worth everything! He is the source! He references a commonly known local expression, of there being "neither hot nor cold." His statement is a strong correction, pointing out their mixed and corrupted carnal lives. He announces,

> I know your deeds, that you are neither cold nor hot; I wish that you were cold or hot. So because you are lukewarm, and neither hot nor cold, I will spit you out of My mouth. (Revelation 3:15–16)

This region is well known for its water supplies. Laodicea was geographically located between the two cities of Hierapolis and Colossae. Hot thermal springs vented from the continual volcanic activity of the area in what was referred to as the "Holy City," Hierapolis. This hot water was mixed with the cold, refreshing drinking water carried from Colossae. Hierapolis became a healing center where doctors used the thermal springs as a treatment for their patients. When these waters were mixed, both benefits of healing and refreshing were lost. If this water was consumed, the intense flavor of the mineral water would make a person nauseated and throw up.

This region was also known for the active volcanic eruptions. In AD 60, during the rule of Nero, a severe earthquake left the city completely in ruins. Another key component of this city is the relocation of two thousand Jewish families to Lydia and Phrygia from Babylon and Mesopotamia by Antiochus the Great. They were later joined by more families from Judea. The Jewish congregation grew in Hierapolis and has been estimated as high as fifty thousand in 62 BC.

This was a wealthy, self-supporting town known for its shiny black wool. Following the earthquake of AD 60, they did not ask Rome for imperial assistance to rebuild. They were very proud of their self-reliance. This was also manifested in spiritual pride. Spiritual pride and a lukewarm profession of faith are frequently produced by the accumulation of worldly prosperity.

Spiritual pride and a lukewarm profession of faith are frequently produced by the accumulation worldly prosperity.

The apostle Paul founded this church when he was in Ephesus. When Paul wrote the letter to Colossae, he made reference to Laodicea (Colossians 4:16–17). He warned the bishop, Archippus, to "take heed to fulfill the ministry."

Jesus advises them to buy from Him, "gold refined in the fire," to gain their wealth, true wealth, in Him. This was a reference to their smug self-sufficiency, economic independence, and their healing arts. God is not so concerned with our affluence and personal peace—our cash and our comfort—as with our relationship with Him, He is our source! God is able to comfort the afflicted, and for our good, He will afflict the comfortable.

But how are they to buy gold if they "are wretched and miserable and poor and blind and naked"? (Revelation 3:17)

> The sacrifices of God are a broken spirit; A broken and a contrite heart, O God, You will not despise. (Psalm 51:17)

> So that the proof of your faith, being more precious than gold which is perishable, even though tested by fire, may be found

> to result in praise and glory and honor at the revelation of Jesus Christ. (1 Peter 1:7)

Jesus concludes with an invitation to a lukewarm church. He promises to show His love with His discipline (verse 19). Jesus' plea is an intimate calling on His part for our return. The call for an open door is not an evangelistic closing line, but His expressed desire to spend quality time with His children.

> Behold, I stand at the door and knock; if anyone hears My voice and opens the door, I will come in to him and will dine with him, and he with Me. (Revelation 3:20)

> It is for discipline that you endure; God deals with you as with sons; for what son is there whom his father does not discipline? (Hebrews 12:7)

Conclusion

These first two keys open the door and set the stage for The Revelation. Jesus is the primary focus of The Revelation with His Church as His audience. All the epistles to the seven churches begin with "I know your works." He is omniscient and imminent. He knows all things and is in our midst. He walks among the seven candlesticks, and the seven stars are in His hand. Each epistle ends with the same plea: "He who has an ear, let him hear what the Spirit says to the churches."

Jesus' title in each epistle is taken from the introduction in Revelation 1:12–16 and reflects the nature of His address to the church. "His Name is a strong tower!" (Proverbs 18:10).

> For since the creation of the world His invisible attributes, His eternal power and divine nature, have been clearly seen, being understood through what has been made, so that they are without excuse. (Romans 1:19–20)

THE UNVEILING

Jesus reveals Himself to His Church with these appropriate attributes:

> To Ephesus: He holds the stars in His right hand and walks among the candlesticks.
>
> To Smyrna: He is the first and last, who was dead and is alive!
>
> To Pergamos: He is the sharp, two-edged sword.
>
> To Thyatira: He is the Son of God with eyes as fire and feet as bronze.
>
> To Sardis: He who has the seven Spirits of God and the seven stars.
>
> To Philadelphia: He that is holy and true and has the key of David.
>
> To Laodicea: He is the Amen, the faithful and true witness.

Jesus promises great blessings to the overcomers, the morally victorious, for those who do not compromise with the temptations that this temporary world offers.

> To Ephesus: They are granted to eat of the Tree of Life in the paradise of God.
>
> To Smyrna: They will not to be hurt by the second death.
>
> To Pergamos: They are to receive some hidden manna, a white stone, a new name.
>
> To Thyatira: They will receive authority over the nations and the morning star.
>
> To Sardis: They shall be clothed in white garments and their names written in the Book of Life and confessed before God and the angels.

To Philadelphia: God will make them a pillar in the temple of God and He will write God's name upon them.

To Laodicea: They will sit down with Jesus on His throne.

The prophet Isaiah records this promise of assurance:

> Remember this, and be assured; Recall it to mind, you transgressors. Remember the former things long past, for I am God, and there is no other; I am God, and there is no one like Me, declaring the end from the beginning, and from ancient times things which have not been done, saying, "My purpose will be established, and I will accomplish all My good pleasure;" Calling a bird of prey from the east, the man of My purpose from a far country. Truly I have spoken; truly I will bring it to pass. I have planned it, surely I will do it. (Isaiah 46:8–11)

Key #3

DISCLOSURE: THE INTENT OF THE REVELATION.

God is self-revealing!

The Revelation of Jesus Christ, which God gave Him to *show* to His bond-servants, the things which must soon take place; and He sent and *communicated it* by His angel to His bond-servant John, who *testified* to the word of God and to the testimony of Jesus Christ, even *to all that he saw*. Blessed is he who reads and those who hear the words of the prophecy, and heed the things which are written in it; for the time is near.
—Revelation 1:1–3, emphasis added

All God's revelations are sealed to us until they are opened to us by obedience. You will never get them open by philosophy or thinking. Immediately you obey, a flash of light comes. Let God's truth work in you by soaking in it, not by worrying into it. Obey God in the thing He is at present showing you, and instantly the next thing is opened up. We read tomes on the work of the Holy Spirit when ... five minutes of drastic obedience would make things clear as a sunbeam. We say, "I suppose I shall understand these things some day," You can understand them now: it is not study that does it, but obedience. The tiniest fragment of obedience, and heaven opens up and the profoundest truths of

God are yours straight away. God will never reveal more truth about Himself till you obey what you know already. Beware of being wise and prudent.

—Oswald Chambers

A Mystery to be Discovered

The God of creation—the Living God—is infinite and The Infinitely Creative Being. The scratches we have made in the surface of our understanding of His creation have revealed the order and elegance of His mind. From the smallest particle chased by our rudimentary and obtuse tools to the grandest imagination of the known universe, it is His marvelous mind that is being revealed.

God does not desire that we bump around in the dark, arrogantly pursuing knowledge without His revelation. Rather, it is just the opposite. His will is to reveal—to open—to invite us into His truth. All that we know, or think that we know, is but a reflection of His grace enabling us to see, to become aware, or even just to question. His leading is mercy itself and always points toward Him, and our questions are a manifestation of His grace.

> The secret [inner counsel] of the Lord is with those who fear Him, And He will show them His covenant. (Psalm 25:14)

The apostle Paul boldly pronounces his vocation—his calling and our prospect—to the Corinthian church:

> Let a man regard us in this manner, as servants of Christ and stewards of the mysteries of God. (1 Corinthians 4:1)

The simplicity of this calling is not unique to him but a calling for all who consider themselves "Jesus followers." We are His servants, living to accomplish His will, and He opens His truth to our hearts more and more. As the petals of a rose open in the heat of the sun, so the

THE UNVEILING

truth of God's mysteries are opened to His own for His purpose in the light of His Word by His Spirit. We then have the wonderful charge and responsibility to steward these mysteries as the Lord opens them to our hearts. The truths revealed are the mysteries of God, and as stated earlier, they are so simple that a child can grasp their meaning yet so deep we will spend eternity plumbing their depths. Mystery is a challenge for our minds, our deep channels of thought, to challenge us to the reality of discovery and knowledge. A mystery is something to be obtained, yet to be realized. Mysteries are always unsettling, as they are things revealed, not explained.

As the petals of a rose open in the heat of the sun, so the truth of God's mysteries are opened to His own for His purpose in the light of His Word by His Spirit.

We exist for His pleasure, and as a result, living to please Him is what fulfills us, this our fulfillment. It is only when we are fully alive—quickened and fully awake—that we can possibly find this fulfillment. God's revelations of His mysteries—His unpacking of the truth, the exposure of reality and facts—is the process of building a case that brings us to the point that we know something we didn't know. Or we are introduced to an ultimate truth.

Concerning Scripture, it is something that can be known but is not yet known. It is a mystery that is revealed to some and hidden from others, to be made known to all in the end. When we unpack known historical reality that relates to Scripture, it sheds light or gives us insight. When we unpack an etymological puzzle, pursuing the history of words, their origins, and how their form and meaning have changed over time, we gain clarity concerning the use of a word. This gives us some insight of its meaning in its context and history. When we remove the limits of what have been imposed—what has been established to express current word usage—a mystery can be revealed. We love to pursue and open mysteries as we gather information and insight to grow in knowledge. Unfortunately, the environment of elevated human reason can present a temptation of arrogance and we can consider our knowledge superior in the accumulation of information.

But The Unveiling, The Revelation of Jesus Christ, is something so much greater than the incremental progression of knowledge. It is overwhelming in the sense that it is not just a glimmer of truth, not just an insight. It is the revelation of God! For this very reason, many in our cynical postmodern mode of thinking have discounted it. God's intention is clear. The Apocalypse was given to show His people His plan, to reveal His heart, and to unravel the mystery of the ages.

Our challenge is to realize that He does so *from His perspective*. I suggest that this is the only coherent and encompassing perspective. In unraveling or opening the mystery, He is telling His story from His perspective, but He does so within our limited language and understanding. He works and reveals, within our comprehension, ideas that can be grasped in our minds. This is revealed in a number of mysteries that become clear following the resurrection of Jesus Christ.

> And He was saying to them, "To you has been given *the mystery of the kingdom of God*, but those who are outside get everything in parables, so that while seeing, they may see and not perceive, and while hearing, they may hear and not understand, otherwise they might return and be forgiven." (Mark 4:11–12, emphasis added)

> Now to Him who is able to establish you according to my gospel and the preaching of Jesus Christ, according to the *revelation of the mystery which has been kept secret* for long ages past, but now is manifested, and by the Scriptures of the prophets, according to the commandment of the eternal God, has been made known to all the nations, leading to obedience of faith; to the only wise God, through Jesus Christ, be the glory forever. Amen. (Romans 16:25–27, emphasis added)

> Yet we do speak wisdom among those who are mature; a wisdom, however, not of this age nor of the rulers of this age,

THE UNVEILING

who are passing away; but we speak God's wisdom in a *mystery, the hidden wisdom which God predestined before the ages to our glory*; the wisdom which none of the rulers of this age has understood; for if they had understood it they would not have crucified the Lord of glory. (1 Corinthians 2:6–8, emphasis added)

These mysteries revealed in and through Jesus Christ are realized in Him and continue to open through Him for His own. Paul opens the mystery of the appearing of Christ at the end of the age that results in the fact that not all sleep (1 Corinthians 15:51). His letter to the Ephesian church is filled with revelation of the mysteries of God. He writes of the mysteries of God's will, of Christ, the church, and the mystery of the gospel. In the letter to the Colossians, he adds the mystery of the Gentiles, the mystery of God, both of the Father and of Christ. His second letter to the Thessalonians reveals the mystery of lawlessness. His letters to Timothy reveal the mystery of the faith. Now John documents for us the mysteries of The Revelation of Jesus Christ.

It is the glory of God to conceal a matter, But the glory of kings is to search out a matter. (Proverbs 25:2)

This is the challenge of the Unveiling: the mind of God to the mind of man. The infinite being exposed and poured into the finite vessel, as a teacup attempting to receive the ocean. It is the Big Picture revealed to one with a small view. So we humbly look, listen, and receive the truth revealed. We are to be faithful witnesses and faithful stewards of the mysteries of God. We are to pursue them without fear as God reveals. This is how we are to receive The Revelation. This is the attitude of humility by which we approach this amazing book.

This is the challenge of the Unveiling:

the mind of God to the mind of man.

As an act of mercy and a token of our inclusion, the Creator God pulls back the curtain of His Story. He unveils the holy, revealing His plan and the process for His purpose in the explosive events and deep symbols used to tell His story. From the prophetic promise of salvation to Adam and Eve in the Garden of Eden and the symbolic shedding of blood to cover their nakedness, God has been revealing His plan and purpose of redemption and restoration. God was not reacting; He was revealing! Jesus *is* the Lamb of God slain from the foundation of the world! God was not surprised at the response of man and the liberties he would take with his free will. He knew what it would cost to create and love mankind, created beings that would choose to love Him—or not. He was willing to pay that price and provide that life and love for mankind. The Revelation is God's opening of this story to His own.

The Revelation of Jesus Christ is just that: His revealed truth. John's documentation of this "Apocalypse" is the final addition of the early church to the canon of Scriptures of the New Testament. Justin Martyr, a second-century Christian apologist, acknowledges him with "And with us a man named John, one of the Apostles of Christ, who in the Revelation made to him …" (Dialogue to Trypho the Jew, chapter 81).

This unveiled truth has comforted and confused many through the centuries. It comforted those who trusted in Him and His ultimate victory and restoration of all things. It confused those who attempted to divine the future with a temporal perspective and a pseudoscience. The Scriptures intentionally contain mysteries to be explored and discovered. We are instructed to keep on asking, keep on seeking, and keep on knocking.

God intentionally tells stories with imagery, symbols, poetry, songs, and history. When we lose sight of God's method of revealing Himself, His plans and His purpose, we look at the words as a literal tool or a mere human book to be compared with all other human documents and evaluated with the same literary assumptions. It is the Word of God! It is The Revelation of Jesus Christ! It was given for our edification and encouragement, not for division or divination.

Christianity is a revealed religion; God has spoken! As His bond servants, we begin with the assumption that "God is" a person with a will. That

"God is" personal. That God has spoken. He has communicated His will. Therefore, truth is knowable—through His revealed will, His Word.

Revelation is central to Christianity.

> He who has My commandments and keeps them is the one who loves Me; and he who loves Me will be loved by My Father, and *I will love him and will disclose Myself to him.* (John 14:21, emphasis added)

We are exhorted to receive His Word. To read His Word. To memorize His Word—and to hide it in our heart.

> For the word of God is living and active and sharper than any two-edged sword, and piercing as far as the division of soul and spirit, of both joints and marrow, and able to judge the thoughts and intentions of the heart. And there is no creature hidden from His sight, but all things are open and laid bare to the eyes of Him with whom we have to do. (Hebrews 4:12–13)

The Revelation is not a puzzle book for our entertainment. It is not a tool to promote our eschatological diminutions. God never intended His unveiling as a tool for man to use to divine the future or explain the past from a merely human perspective. Rather, He intends to reveal His heart, His plan of redemption, His restoration of all things. His revelation exposes His plan from the beginning in multiple stories with the intent of revealing His purpose to His people so they might endure until the end. This life is brief as a puff of smoke in the wind and should be placed in the proper light.

> God, after He spoke long ago to the fathers in the prophets in many portions and in many ways, in these last days has spoken to us in His Son, whom He appointed heir of all things, through whom also He made the world. And He is the radiance of His glory and the exact representation of His nature, and upholds all things by the word of His power. When He had

made purification of sins, He sat down at the right hand of the Majesty on high, having become as much better than the angels, as He has inherited a more excellent name than they. (Hebrews 1:1–4)

God is considered unreasonable to many people. The mystery of faith is not a natural approach but a spiritual reality for those who seek God Who is Spirit. Sometimes we just don't get it. We question God, His plan, His purpose, His intentions, and even His character. Our limited understanding inhibits our ability to grasp the infinite in faith, as we measure reality by our understanding. This is a relationship of trust, of humility, and of need.

The frustration experienced in our attempt to grasp what we do not understand is similar to Winston Churchill's quoted radio broadcast in October 1939. He was commenting on the actions of Russia and defined them as "a riddle, wrapped in a mystery, inside an enigma." As a Westerner who was blessed to serve the Lord in Kazan, Tatarstan, in central Russia in the 1990s, I also experienced the mystery of a culture that seemed just out of reach. They were the most Western of the Easterners and the most Eastern of the Westerners. They were a mystery to me. Through the years of service and a growing familiarity, the mystery of the culture began to unravel. This same disorientation is the initial reaction to The Revelation, as a riddle, wrapped in a mystery, inside an enigma.

Our limited understanding, preconceived ideas, and presuppositions, not to mention our individual limitations or capabilities, all provide a sense of frustration in an attempt to grasp the infinite. Our cultural worldview and other hereditary limitations need to be exposed and understood in light of God's revealed character in His Word. The humility required to receive revelation is a continual process of acquisition and the practice, or way, of a disciple.

Our personal arrogance resists such acknowledgements. Our limitations are illustrated in our assumptions. Just as the child who believes that her

THE UNVEILING

grandmother lives at the airport because when she wants her to visit her house they go there to get her and then they take her back to the airport after her visit, our perceptions are limited. Some people think God lives at church because we meet Him there on Sunday. A more mature understanding is of faith that comes from the entrance of His Word. His revealed Word introduces an infinite truth that reveals the attributes of God. He is omnipresent! There is no place hidden from His sight.

When our personal experiences line up with His revealed truth, it becomes our reality. A faith that is lived out. This is pleasing to God. This explains why glimmers of light in a moment of contemplation can produce a sacred place or a sacred act. The experience sanctifies the place or the action with memory and emotions to reignite the reality. This is the power of testimony. Our personal experiences are reinforced and sanctified by the testimony of the Holy Spirit and the Word of God. I recall a testimony by a Catholic nun who could not express her certainty of the presence and power of the Holy Spirit in her life with any other words than to say, "I know down in my knower!" And we get it. Mysteries are difficult for us to put into a simple package.

I have been blessed with numerous such experiences throughout my life that have become spiritual benchmarks of faith. Each one was used of God, if not initiated by Him, for my good. Each experience was reinforced by His Word and gave it credibility. The subjectivity of faith is a mystery itself. The litany of the faithful in the book of Hebrews testifies to this subjective instruction and followed obedience. It concludes clarity of motive but not an affirmation of comprehension.

> And all these, having gained approval through their faith, did not receive what was promised, because God had provided something better for us, so that apart from us they would not be made perfect. (Hebrews 11:39–40)

John documented the divinely intended experiences in The Revelation as an overwhelmed but obedient servant who needed repeated instruction to "write down what you see." The very event described in the introduction that he was "in the Spirit" as an explanation for what follows leaves us blinking like a toad in a hailstorm. This was a real experience orchestrated by God for the benefit of His bond servants. It is to be received in the Spirit of which it was given. It is a mystery to be opened. The author is the interpreter. His church is His instrument to keep, to communicate, and to forward The Revelation in this age. The writer of Hebrews reminds us:

> All these died in faith, without receiving the promises, but having seen them and having welcomed them from a distance, and having confessed that they were strangers and exiles on the earth. For those who say such things make it clear that they are seeking a country of their own. And indeed if they had been thinking of that country from which they went out, they would have had opportunity to return. But as it is, they desire a better country, that is, a heavenly one. Therefore God is not ashamed to be called their God; for He has prepared a city for them. By faith Abraham, when he was tested, offered up Isaac, and he who had received the promises was offering up his only begotten son; it was he to whom it was said, "In Isaac your descendants shall be called." He considered that God is able to raise people even from the dead, from which he also received him back as a type. (Hebrews 11:13–19)

Before the revelation of Jesus Christ in the earthly fulfillment of all the prophecies of Him from the beginning, the purpose of God was shrouded in mystery. The prophet Isaiah announced as much.

> I will give you the treasures of darkness and hidden riches of secret places, that you may know that I, the LORD, Who call you by your name, Am the God of Israel ... Truly, You are a God who hides Himself, O God of Israel, Savior! (Isaiah 45:3, 15)

God has disclosed Himself to us throughout our history. When Jesus announced the final word of His sacrificial ministry, "It is finished," God tore the curtain that concealed His glory and restricted our access to

Him—The Unveiling. He exposed the Holy of Holies and invited us into His presence. He intends to disclose Himself to all who will receive Him even now. A day will come when all of creation will acknowledge Him.

> Being found in appearance as a man, He humbled Himself by becoming obedient to the point of death, even death on a cross. For this reason also, God highly exalted Him, and bestowed on Him the name which is above every name, so that at the name of Jesus every knee will bow, of those who are in heaven and on earth and under the earth, and that every tongue will confess that Jesus Christ is Lord, to the glory of God the Father. (Philippians 2:8–11)

The reality and process of opening the mystery of the revelation of God rests in our relationship to Him. He discloses Himself to His own. Today's rational approach of an "answering theology," a sequential and logical rationalization with a relevant "takeaway" is the expectation, even a demand. The world asks a question, and theology is supposed to answer. There is a pressure to find a relevant response that meets the felt needs and demands of the crowd. But the world does not know the right questions. God must reveal the questions and the answers.

> **Throughout our lives we are either growing closer to God or further from Him.**
> —C. S. Lewis

The Christian Film and Television Commission reported in January 2007 that by the time the average American child reaches seventeen, that child will have spent more than sixty thousand hours with the mass media of entertainment, only eleven thousand hours at school, two thousand hours with their parents, and only nine hundred hours at church if they attend every week! Jesus responded to this demonically inspired formation of the mind with His exhortation to Satan in the wilderness.

> But He answered and said, "It is written, 'Man shall not live on bread alone, but on every word that proceeds out of the mouth of God.'" (Matthew 4:4)

We desire the light of revelation and the knowledge of the mysteries of God, but we can't hear over the noise of life filled with the bread of the world. To know God's mysteries is not the equivalent of mastering the facts. It is a matter of knowing God.

> This is eternal life, that they may know You, the only true God, and Jesus Christ whom You have sent. (John 17:3)

When Jesus was questioned by the Pharisees, He responded very clearly.

> So they were saying to Him, "Where is Your Father?" Jesus answered, "You know neither Me nor My Father; if you knew Me, you would know My Father also." (John 8:19)

Jesus is speaking of an indwelling reality of knowing, not as collected data or information. They have not acquired new ideas or experiences but a relationship with the living God.

> O righteous Father, although the world has not known You, yet I have known You; and these have known that You sent Me; and I have made Your name known to them, and will make it known, so that the love with which You loved Me may be in them, and I in them. (John 17:25–26)

Jesus is stating that the knowledge that dwells in us is in fact knowledge of Him. Christ Himself is the revealer, the revealing, and the revealed. Our faith is not mere creed or static content, but the dynamic reality of the living Christ. God's revelation is revealed to His own. Our faith is a revealed faith.

Christ Himself is the revealer, the revealing, and the revealed.

THE UNVEILING

The personal revelation we receive, the inspiration, or *rhema*, the God-breathed Word, radically changes and transforms us from the inside out. When we receive this clear instruction and exhortation, we also receive His grace to fulfill His Word. When this is incorporated into our lives, it becomes alive and life changing. This revelation by inspiration and conviction is called a pearl by Jesus. A pearl is a result of a source of irritation that is responded to by grace, like the bit of sand that becomes lodged in the soft tissue of a clam. It is not the bit of sand, the irritation, but the result of the response of the irritation. Layer by layer, response by response, the irritation can become something beautiful. When we have been blessed to receive this grace from God due to areas of sin and need, we can develop some beautiful Christian character: pearls.

While Jesus was responding to questions of sin and judgment, He gave a strong exhortation to those who would receive the revelation of God concerning sin and then impose this received grace and growth on others who have not received it. He called it "throw[ing] your pearls before swine."

> Do not give what is holy to dogs, and do not throw your pearls before swine, or they will trample them under their feet, and turn and tear you to pieces. (Matthew 7:6)

This is not a judgment of character on those we attempt to stand in judgment of; rather, it is an exhortation to those who apply their grace-received discipline on those who have not receive that grace. This is a rationalization of our revelation. We cannot correct that which needs to be converted. Only God can transform a person's heart.

Disclosure is God's intention. Our intention and our efforts to apply this revelation and make it easily accessible by simple instruction or rote memory is a waste of spirit. This can only be known in relationship and realized through mystery, paradox, and contradiction. We are His bond servants. We don't walk by sight; we live by faith. It has been well stated that sometimes what passes for theology can easily be little more than one swine discussing pearls with another.

Moses announced this in the beginning of the instruction of God's people.

> The secret things belong to the LORD our God, but the things revealed belong to us and to our sons forever, that we may observe all the words of this law ... For this commandment which I command you today is not too difficult for you, nor is it out of reach. It is not in heaven, that you should say, "Who will go up to heaven for us to get it for us and make us hear it, that we may observe it?" Nor is it beyond the sea, that you should say, "Who will cross the sea for us to get it for us and make us hear it, that we may observe it?" But the word is very near you, in your mouth and in your heart, that you may observe it. (Deuteronomy 29:29; 30:11–14)

God's mysteries are meant to be opened! They are given to reveal destinies, plans, strategies, and tactics. He does not hide them from us. He invites us to participate with Him.

> So I say to you, ask, and it will be given to you; seek, and you will find; knock, and it will be opened to you. For everyone who asks, receives; and he who seeks, finds; and to him who knocks, it will be opened. (Luke 11:9–10)

The Revelation of Jesus Christ is a series of seven visions seen, experienced, and documented by John for our benefit. They are brilliant reflections of God's unveiling as seven facets of a beautiful jewel, one truth from multiple perspectives. As we read and imagine the scenes displayed before us, without any assumptions or presuppositions outside of the revealed Word of God, we will be caught up with John in his experience. The same Holy Spirit who empowered him to accomplish this task will work in us to lead us into all truth. An overview of The Revelation follows to lay out the flow of the experiences that John wrote of for our benefit.

> Jesus answered them, "To you it has been granted to know the mysteries of the kingdom of heaven, but to them it has not been granted. For whoever has, to him more shall be given, and he will have an abundance; but whoever does not have, even what he has shall be taken away from him." (Matthew 13:11–12)

THE UNVEILING

The Seven Visions of The Revelation

An Outline of the Apocalypse

Chapter 1:1–8   Prologue and introduction

First Vision: Chapter 1:9–3:22

> The glorified Christ to His Church. The seven specific epistles to the historical churches of Asia Minor that represent the churches through all ages.

Second Vision: Chapter 4:1–11:19

> The throne room of God's presence with the heavenly hosts of eternity acknowledging the Lamb of God worthy of worship and of releasing the seals of judgment on humanity's sin. These seals are a graceful restraint of judgment due. Jesus is the only One worthy of releasing them as He is the One Who has paid the price and absorbed the judgment for those who trust in His salvation, the escape from ultimate judgment, the second death.
>
> The first seals broken reveal the judgments that fell on sinful man. They were released in the initial days of humanity and continue through to the consummation of the age. Their progression is described as four horsemen galloping through the history of man.
>
> 1)   The white horse and rider is representative of delegated human government with authority and strength.
>
> > Every person is to be in subjection to the governing authorities. For there is no authority except from God, and those which exist are established by God. (Romans 13:1)

2) The red horse and rider represent the response of chaos and anarchy that resists the authority of the white horse, resulting in conflict and death.

3) The black horse and rider are representative of the unjust economies and the manipulation of the wealthy over the poor in this fallen world.

4) The gray (ashen) horse and rider is representative of the march of death and sheol, the place of the dead. This seal represents the overwhelming reality of the means of death from the first three horsemen. This is an announcement of the gruesome reality that 25 percent of all human deaths will result from the wars, famine, pestilence, and accidents.

5) The fifth seal represents the limited but numerous martyrs throughout the history of man, beginning with Abel (Matthew 23:35; Psalm 72:14).

For this reason also the wisdom of God said, "I will send to them prophets and apostles, and *some* of them they will kill and *some* they will persecute, so that the blood of all the prophets, shed since the foundation of the world, may be charged against this generation, from the blood of Abel to the blood of Zechariah, who was killed between the altar and the house *of God;* yes, I tell you, it shall be charged against this generation." (Luke 11:49–50)

6) The sixth seal is the "beginning of the end" of ages, the beginning of the two tracks of consummation. This is represented in the concluding judgment on Israel in the first age and the final and cataclysmic end of our current age. In both worlds, it is global and catastrophic. "The great day of their wrath has come."

7) The seventh seal is the conclusion of the matter resulting in the consummation of the ages, the end of the intercession

of prayer before the throne, and the seven trumpets of announced judgment.

The voice of the seventh angel when he is about to sound, then the mystery of God is finished as He preached to the servants the prophets. (Revelation 10:7)

Chapter 7 reveals the heavenly description of the sealed bond servants of God. They are numbered first as a symbolic fulfillment of the government of God in His creation to rule and reign with Him. This is why only selected names are drawn from the tribes of Israel. Both Dan and Ephraim are excluded, as they represented the tribes that allowed the false worship of the golden calves to replace Jerusalem and the presence of God for worship in Jerusalem.

Then the bond servants are described as the great multitude from every nation and all tribes and people and tongues that have been clothed in the righteousness of God. They are God's covenant people. (See Key #2)

Chapter 10:8–11:14 is a parenthetical inclusion of the final judgment on the remaining and religious sacrificial system and the city of Jerusalem and her temple. This is the fulfillment of Jesus prophetic announcement made in Matthew 24 and Luke 21. This is the end of this age, and this method of access to God is now fulfilled in Jesus Christ. This is also the finality of Daniel's seventy-week prophecy of Israel.

Chapter 11:15–19 is the conclusion of the second vision. The last trumpet, the seventh trumpet of God. All is completed in the deluge of released concluding judgments.

Then the seventh angel sounded; and there were loud voices in heaven, saying, "The kingdom of the world **has become** *the kingdom* of our Lord and of His Christ; and He will reign forever and ever." (Revelation 11:15 emphasis added)

Third Vision: Chapter 12:1–14:20

God gives us these seven great signs to disclose His plan and process of God in bringing His promised remedy, the protoprophecy given in Genesis 3:15. These signs represent all the inclusive events in this grand narrative for our salvation in the war of the seeds. They are revealed as follows:

1. The first sign is the "woman clothed with the sun" representing the "Seed of the woman" from the first mentioned prophetic promise. God's people had waited from the beginning for this fulfillment. This is the source of the assumption of barrenness as a curse, as the barren woman was already excluded from bringing God's purposes into the world. She was realized in the nation of Israel and ultimately in Mary, the biological mother of Jesus, who was conceived by the Holy Spirit.

2. The second sign is the "great red dragon" representing the snake in the garden and the fullness of earthly authority that he offered to Jesus in the wilderness temptation. This is the enemy of God and God's plan of salvation through His promised remedy.

3. The third sign is the "male child" representing the fulfilled promise of Jesus Christ now seated at the right hand of the Father. This also includes the ongoing persecution of God's people, both of the nation of Israel, resulting in her destruction, and the predestined people of God.

4. The fourth sign is the angelic warfare that has ensued from the beginning. This is represented by Michael (meaning "Who is like God?") and his angels. These ministering spirits were sent out to render service for the sake of those who will inherit salvation (Hebrews 1:14).

Chapter 12:10–17 reveals a parenthetical view of the dual tracks of consummation in the ongoing battle and the immediate conclusion of the released judgment on Israel, Jerusalem, the temple, and the sacrificial system.

5. The fifth sign is the "beast from the sea," later revealed as the "great harlot" in the fifth vision. She represents the demonically inspired systems of the devil that fulfill his conspiracy to "steal, kill, and destroy" (John 10:10). These again include the consummation of judgment on Jerusalem and perseverance of the saints.

6. The sixth sign is the "beast from the earth" representing the historical characters that rise up in Earth's Babylonian systems both in the concluding judgment on Jerusalem and the ongoing persecution of the saints. These are referred to as the "antichrists" of the first and second epistles of John and the "man of sin" or "man of lawlessness" the apostle Paul refers to in the second epistle to the Thessalonians. These are the satanically inspired individuals who are empowered in counterfeit signs and wonders to bring destruction to humanity generally and to God's people specifically. *Encyclopaedia Romana* has documented a clear explanation of the impact of Caesar Nero during the era of the "Beast from the sea." This will be more clearly addressed in Key #6 Judgment: The Result of The Revelation. Again, the dual tracks of consummation are to be considered, especially in light of the meaning intended for the original hearers (Revelation 13:18; 17:9).

7. The seventh sign is the Lamb that was slain. This is the sign of the eternal and victorious Lamb with the co-ruling people of God. These people have seven descriptive attributes:

    1) The Lamb and the Father's Name are written on their foreheads.
    2) They sing a new song with the heavenly hosts.
    3) They have been redeemed, purchased from the earth.

4) These are physically and spiritually chaste (cleansed by the blood of the Lamb and faithful witnesses).
5) They follow the Lamb.
6) They are the first fruits of God to the Lamb.
7) There is no lie found in them. (They are blameless before God.)

This vision concludes with the remaining six angels who are introduced in the angelic warfare of the fourth sign. The seven angels of this vision are the ministering spirits that work with God in the consummation of the ages. They are described as from the heavenly temple sent by God as follows:

1) the warfare led by Michael in the fourth sign
2) the proclaiming angel of the Gospel of God to the nations of the earth
3) the angel of judgment on the "great harlot" of Babylon
4) the angel of judgment on those loyal to the beast
5) the first reaping angel
6) the second reaping angel
7) the third reaping angel

Fourth Vision: Chapter 15:1–16:21

The fourth vision is a narration of the effects of the release of the seven angels of the concluding seven plagues, or bowls of wrath. God Himself commands the angels to complete the judgment with the outpouring of His accumulated and restrained wrath in the earth until He announces in verse 17, "It is done." These judgments mirror the plagues poured out on a rebellious Egypt and her gods as a judgment for refusing to let God's people go.

1) The first angel poured out the wrath of God, resulting in the unabated suffering of those who rejected God's remedy.
2) The second angel's bowl of wrath represents the death of rebellious humanity as the "sea turns to blood as a dead man."

3) The third angel was God's wrath poured out on the remains of the earth and her life-giving waters.
4) The fourth angel poured out God's wrath reflected in the removal of God's protective covering in the atmospheric protection, resulting in the scorching of the sun.
5) The fifth angel is the wrath of God poured out on the throne of the beast, the seat of earthly and demonically inspired temporal power.
6) The sixth angel is the poured-out wrath of God on the removal of God's protective boundaries represented by the river Euphrates that Abraham crossed to enter into the promises of God.
7) The seventh and final bowl of wrath is poured by the angel into the second heavens in concluding judgment on the fallen humanity and the cursed earth.

Fifth Vision: Chapter 17–18

The sin-filled and demonically inspired systems of the earth are symbolically seen in the Babylon of old. The Genesis account of her initiation as an offense against God in human achievement is then referenced throughout man's history as a descriptive sign of man's rebellion. The desecrated city of Jerusalem is specifically acknowledged in her destruction in AD 70 and the city of Rome in the context of the writing along with all the cities of the earth that serve as an earthly capital of temporary dominion in the earth. She is called Babylon and is completely and quickly destroyed as a result of the pouring out of God's wrath.

Sixth Vision: Chapter 19–20

Chapter 19 begins with the fourfold hallelujahs of the heavenly hosts for the justice and salvation of God:

1) acknowledging His judgment of the harlot Babylon
2) the celebration of the eternal completion of this judgment
3) the beginning of worship before the throne for His salvation
4) the concluding expression of worship of His bond servants

The marriage of the Lamb and His bride, the blessing of those invited. This vision is the final and heavenly expression of the coming of Christ. This is the heavenly perspective of His first coming and His second coming, the beginning of His work and its conclusion. It is the Word of His mouth that brings the ultimate judgment to those opposed to God.

Chapter 20 describes the result of Christ's finished work. At His first coming, He victoriously exposed and defeated the works of the devil. The devil has been bound and has no authority unless delegated to him by man or that which emanates through his destructive, demonically inspired Babylonian systems.

> The Son of God appeared for this purpose, to destroy the works of the devil. (1 John 3:8b)

> When He had disarmed the rulers and authorities, He made a public display of them, having triumphed over them through Him. (Colossians 2:15)

At His return, following this symbolic element of one thousand years (representing the fullness of human time between Christ's first coming and His second coming), He will expose the righteous judgment on the deceiver and his minions. He again acknowledges the martyrs of the faith. These include both those who were violently put to death in this "Millennial" era as well as all those who chose to die to self and live in Christ in their earthly life. The symbol of death that is displayed in water baptism is the first resurrection of the dead.

> Therefore we have been buried with Him through baptism into death, so that as Christ was raised from the dead through the glory of the Father, so we too might walk in newness of life. (Romans 6:4)

> Having been buried with Him in baptism, in which you were also raised up with Him through faith in the working of God, who raised Him from the dead. (Colossians 2:12)

This vision reveals the ultimate judgment falling on the earth in the final days of the age when Satan will be release for a brief moment (relative to the one thousand years) to expose the hearts of men and the justice of God in His dealings with rebellion. It seems we are in such a day!

The judgment of God is complete and all-inclusive at His "Great White Throne." This resurrection and judgment includes all who are not included in the first resurrection.

Seventh Vision: Chapter 21–22:5

The final revelation is the fulfillment of God's plan of salvation. All creation is renewed and restored—a new heaven and new earth. Again, the symbols used previously in The Revelation describe the elimination of the chaos of humanity in the passing away of the sea. The New Jerusalem represents the dwelling of God with man and the new creation. The description of the size and elements of the new existence reveals the elegance, clarity, and value of God's intimacy with His people in His new creation. It also has a "bizarro world" reflection, a mirror-opposite image of the final earthly Roman Empire roughly covering the same length and width yet without a heavenly altitude. Here, there is no need for a temple, as God's people are His temple. A garden of Eden has been recreated and restored in this new creation with living water that flows continuously for those who will reign with Him forever and ever.

Chapter 22:6–21   Conclusion and final encouragement

Key #4

HEAVEN: THE PERSPECTIVE OF THE REVELATION

We can never know what might have been but what is to come is another matter entirely.
—C.S. Lewis

"I am the Alpha and the Omega, the Beginning and the End," says the Lord, "who is and who was and who is to come, the Almighty."
—Revelation 1:8

He said to them, "It is not for you to know times or epochs which the Father has fixed by His own authority."
—Acts 1:7

This fourth key might be considered the least obvious, yet it may produce the most dramatic redefinition of our perspective. The fresh vantage point of the seven visions as they are described by John clearly delineates their unique facets and their interrelated paradigms. When the language of The Revelation refers to the timelessness of the events disclosed, we are forced to stretch our understanding and incorporate our imagination to try to see what John is experiencing. The Revelation opens with the God of time and eternity introducing Himself and His intentions within the framework of our comprehension while introducing that which is beyond our full understanding. Again, the infinite being poured into the finite.

If we recognize and incorporate the first three keys: Jesus—the focus, the Church—the audience, and Disclosure—the intent of The Revelation, we are in a place of trust and expectation to use the fourth key that introduces "Heaven time." There is an awareness of this perspective disclosed in many of the prophecies of Scripture. The prophetic word is like a pebble thrown into a pond. The initial point of impact is an immediate reflection of that word to the original hearers, but the ripples of that word are ultimately realized in the first and/or second coming of the Messiah. The two cataclysmic conclusions prophesied in Scripture include the end of the sacrificial system, or age (Old Testament—BC) and the end days (the current age—AD). Heaven time reveals and treats both these eras in a conclusive manner. It is difficult for us to see such large brushstrokes as to conclude these ages in similar fashion.

Therefore, the redefinition of our perspective, a fresh view, is initiated by opening our sights to incorporate these possibilities, attempting to see God's great reveal from His perspective. I suggest that this view discloses the overlap of released judgments and reveals the similarities in their conclusions.

I have come to see that all apocalyptic literature is expressing God's truth from the heavenly perspective, an eternal or seemingly timeless view. God, in His apocalyptic, or unveiling Word is opening our view and expanding our paradigm that ultimately unveils reality to His creation. So our reading of apocalyptic Scriptures is especially challenging. In our attempt to experience and grasp what He has revealed, we are introduced to the unique dimensional comprehension of the heaven time, the spiritual dimension. This key is *required* to gain a fresh view of The Revelation of Jesus Christ. The Unveiling appears to be a timeless display of the Divine perspective of His interventions in the affairs of man in the fullness of time from seven different vantage points. Jesus is

THE UNVEILING

the Alpha and Omega, the beginning and the end. Not a timelessness but a timeliness and a completeness of time.

Armed with an awareness of this perspective, we can begin to open our minds and forge fresh and possibly new deep channels of thought that give the light we need. We can begin to perceive the bigger picture revealed through the seven visions of The Revelation. We can also see the overlapping conclusions of both ages, the age of the old covenant and the conclusion of the current age. This perspective of reality also opens a greater understanding for the perseverance required in the tribulations of man in our broken world awaiting the restoration of all things.

God has chosen to reveal His truth in broad brushstrokes. He answers the two greatest questions of humanity concerning our origination and our destiny in His Unveiling. They are precariously illustrated and detailed in His Scripture. It is our pleasure and our charge to search out the truth.

It is my hope the application of this key will begin to open a fresh perspective on The Revelation of Jesus Christ. All seven keys, if applied, serve to unlock The Revelation and simplify a perspective on the divinely orchestrated events. With them, we can then see that the seven visions interrelate and tell a complete story.

All humanity suffers from the same disease of sin, and as a result, we are all terminal. All the generations from Adam to this current generation have proved this out. We all quickly progress through this life and produce a history for the next generation. Our ability to see God's Unveiling from heaven's perspective reveals the timelessness of The Revelation and its application to all generations. In Christ, our eternal hope is realized, resulting in our first resurrection from the dead as we are born again in Him and "raised again to newness of life" (Romans 6:4). We have been "raised up with Him through faith in the working of God" (Colossians 2:12) and have received "the abundance of grace and of the gift of righteousness will reign in life through the One, Jesus Christ" (Romans 5:17).

With this heavenly perspective, we can begin to see the operation of the free will of man functioning *within* the sovereign will of God as He reveals and fulfills His ultimate will. This truth is revealed throughout the Scriptures.

> The heavens are telling of the glory of God; And their expanse is declaring the work of His hands. Day to day pours forth speech, And night to night reveals knowledge. There is no speech, nor are there words; Their voice is not heard. Their line has gone out through all the earth, And their utterances to the end of the world. In them He has placed a tent for the sun, Which is as a bridegroom coming out of his chamber; It rejoices as a strong man to run his course. Its rising is from one end of the heavens, And its circuit to the other end of them; And there is nothing hidden from its heat. (Psalm 19:1–6)

> And, "Forever, O LORD, Your word is settled in heaven" (Psalm 119:89).

> Jesus reaffirms this by proclaiming, "Heaven and earth will pass away, but My words will not pass away" (Matthew 24:35).

Charles Dickens captured the frustration of the human mind in his 1943 classic *A Christmas Carol*. This is a Victorian morality tale of an old and bitter miser, Ebenezer Scrooge, who undergoes a profound experience of redemption over the course of one Christmas Eve.

In the opening scene, Ebenezer is exhorted by the ghost of his old, now-deceased business partner, Jacob Marley. This conversation exposes Scrooge's frustration and unbelief as well as his limited temporal and pragmatic evaluation of the situation. During this brief encounter, Scrooge attempts to convince himself of a rational explanation for his experience. He deduces that he has but to swallow a toothpick and "be for the rest of my days persecuted by a legion of goblins, all of my own creation." Marley's reaction to Scrooge's stubbornness explodes with "Man of the worldly mind! Do you believe in me or not?"

THE UNVEILING

When we read The Revelation with a limited and linear perspective, our understanding is also limited. Our insistent empirical evaluations combine with a natural resistance to overcome the insecurity of our confusion, resulting in inconsistent conclusions. We have a similar reaction to the mystery of The Revelation given us in "Heaven time." Our view of apocalyptic truth while functioning in our chronological time frame can result in disorientation like the disciples experienced when they saw Jesus after the resurrection: a mystery.

Creatures of Time

The heavenly perspective is not timeless but inclusive of all time. It is an all-inclusive timeliness without the limitations we are bound to in our sequential chronological experience. I prefer to refer to it as "heaven time."

The timelessness of the view given in apocalyptic literature is an unnerving and disorienting aspect.

Our human perspective of time is always linear as "creatures of time," living in the now with the influence of the past and the anticipation of the future. Our perspectives can be limited to our experience and existence. The timelessness of the view given in apocalyptic literature is an unnerving and disorienting aspect. It is, though, a key to perceiving the insight of the different facets and overlapping visions of The Revelation. Their kaleidoscopic display can be dizzying as our finite minds receive, experience, and attempt to process that which is revealed from the infinite.

In a concluding chapter of considerations entitled "Lenses," I detail the dominant perspectives that influence current views of comprehension and application of Jesus' Revelation. I have found that the reactive approach to any of the current perspectives is limiting and directive. That is, the initial assumptions provide a lens or perspective that is intended to be limiting or directive. The intention is that the presupposition, or lens, initiates a system that must then be applied throughout the Scripture reading. I have attempted to remove those lenses and step back to attempt to see it from a fresh perspective. It is true that this is yet another lens, but I've found that this lens of a "Heaven time" view of seven separate visions serving and revealing one full story, seven facets of the same gem, maintain an intellectual continuity that includes all generations in all time.

The limitation of the preterist perspective is illustrated in James Stuart Russell's application of his perspective in his comments on *The Parousia In The Apocalypse*. His initial references to the immediacy of the application of John's words results in his presupposition and perspective applied to all seven visions. He writes,

> And does not this very obvious consideration suggest the true key to the Apocalypse? Must it not of necessity refer to matters of contemporary history? The only tenable, the only reasonable, hypothesis is that it was intended to be understood by its original readers; but this is as much as to say that it must be occupied with the events and transactions of their own day, and these comprised within a comparatively brief space of time."
>
> His deduction then is "To neglect the obvious and clear definition of the time so constantly thrust on the attention of the reader of the book itself is to stumble on the very threshold.[2]

This is the result of the assumptive preterist view. This can further result in a discounting inclusion of the heavenly perspective that accuses Scripture of hyperbole—an unacceptable literary exaggeration.

With this key of the heavenly perspective (Heaven Time), I hope to introduce a fresh perspective that opens the window for a heavenly view. The application of this all-encompassing timeliness is a comprehensive perspective that applies the seven visions to these last days, this period between Christ's first coming and His second coming. This timeless key of heaven time is the threshold to be crossed in reading and experiencing the visions and their application in The Revelation.

The apostle Peter refers to this sublime truth in his cryptic but simple statement concerning God and time and God's creation. Like fit-over sunglasses, Peter makes an assumptive blanket statement that effects our perspective.

> But, beloved, do not forget this one thing, that with the Lord one day is as a thousand years, and a thousand years as one day. (2 Peter 3:8)

I don't believe that Peter was stating a mathematical formula for defining history or for divining the future. He was revealing the reality of God interfacing in time with man. He was lifting the edge of the veil so we might get a clearer look. As mentioned, we exist in the now; our past is memory, and our future is imagination. Though the past and the future do not exist in the present, they definitely affect our "now."

We can never know what might have been but what is to come is another matter entirely.
—C. S. Lewis

The reality that God exists, in our comprehension, outside of time and yet is interfacing with man in time is an important idea in order to grasp the images of apocalyptic literature. When we catch a glimpse of this interaction in the Scripture, we have a natural tendency to apply the limited perspective of our sequential chronological experience. I suggest that we apply this lens of timelessness, or heaven time, in our reading of the apocalyptic literature of Scripture as an unlocking key to begin to enter into the revealed truths.

God's disclosure is His act of unveiling truth from His perspective. We are introduced to the reality that God dwells in the third heaven. This is a description of the Holy of holies of His existence. Only God has the wisdom to "stretch out" the heavens, and they have served Him as a veil.

> He has made the earth by His power; He has established the world by His wisdom, and stretched out the heaven by His understanding. (Jeremiah 51:15)

Heaven has become to us the curtain of God's tent, separating His dwelling place from that of humanity on earth, as the curtain on the Holy of Holies represented that partition between a holy God and sinful man.

> Who cover Yourself with light as with a garment, Who stretch out the heavens like a curtain. (Psalm 104:2)

> It is He who sits above the circle of the earth, and its inhabitants are like grasshoppers, Who stretches out the heavens like a curtain, and spreads them out like a tent to dwell in. (Isaiah 40:22)

As a creature of God's creation, it is difficult to comprehend the obvious declaration of the timelessness of God and the dimension of the third heaven. However, it is from this perspective that all things are Divinely orchestrated. One of the repeated revelations of the attributes of God is that "He is, He was, and He always will be." He is the "I AM" of ultimate reality. We receive this description of God in the mystery of His infinite Being. My intention with the unveiling of this key is to apply this reality as *the vantage point* of apocalyptic Scripture. We are being introduced to God's proceeding and intervening actions in His creation both in His timelessness and our timeliness.

> He said to them, "It is not for you to know times (*chronos*) or epochs (*kairos*) which the Father has fixed by His own authority." (Acts 1:7, emphasis added)

The New Testament uses two Greek words to describe time, *chronos* and *kairos*. Simply stated, we are *creatures of time* (*chronos*), and God intervenes in the affairs of man in the *fullness of time* (*kairos*), the right, supreme, or opportune moment. These measures are referenced in our understanding and throughout Scripture as "time and eternity" resulting in "the end of days." There are many Scriptural maxims expressed to be considered:

"Everything in its time"—There is an appointed time for everything. And there is a time for every event under heaven. (Ecclesiastes 3:1)

"The fullness of time"—But when the fullness of the time came, God sent forth His Son, born of a woman, born under the Law. (Galatians 4:4)

"The shortness of time"—Remember what my span of life is; For what vanity You have created all the sons of men! (Psalm 89:47)

"Making the most of time"—Therefore be careful how you walk, not as unwise men but as wise, making the most of your time, because the days are evil. (Ephesians 5:15–16)

"The uncertainty of time"—And He told them a parable, saying, "The land of a rich man was very productive. And he began reasoning to himself, saying, 'What shall I do, since I have no place to store my crops?' Then he said, 'This is what I will do: I will tear down my barns and build larger ones, and there I will store all my grain and my goods—And I will say to my soul, "Soul, you have many goods laid up for many years to come; take your ease, eat, drink and be merry."' But God said to him, "You fool! This very night your soul is required of you; and now who will own what you have prepared?" So is the man who stores up treasure for himself, and is not rich toward God. And He said to His disciples, "For this reason I say to you, do not worry about your life, as to what you will eat; nor for your body, as to what you will put on. For life is more than food, and the body more than clothing." (Luke 12:16–23)

"Accomplished in time"—For he was looking for the city which has foundations, whose architect and builder is God. (Hebrews 11:10)

"God works in time"—And saying, "Men, why are you doing these things? We are also men of the same nature as you, and preach the gospel to you that you should turn from these vain things to a living God, Who made the heaven and the earth and the sea and all that is in them. In the generations gone by He permitted all the nations to go their own ways; and yet He did not leave Himself without witness, in that He did good and gave you rains from heaven and fruitful seasons, satisfying your hearts with food and gladness." (Acts 14:15–17)

"The purpose of time"—The Lord is not slow about His promise, as some count slowness, but is patient toward you, not wishing for any to perish but for all to come to repentance. (2 Peter 3:9)

"God the everlasting God"—Lord, You have been our dwelling place in all generations. Before the mountains were born or You gave birth to the earth and the world, Even from everlasting to everlasting, You are God. You turn man back into dust And say, Return, O children of men. For a thousand years in Your sight Are like yesterday when it passes by, Or as a watch in the night. You have swept them away like a flood, they fall asleep; In the morning they are like grass which sprouts anew. In the morning it flourishes and sprouts anew; Toward evening it fades and withers away. For we have been consumed by Your anger And by Your wrath we have been dismayed. You have placed our iniquities before You, Our secret sins in the light of Your presence. For all our days have declined in Your fury; We have finished our years like a sigh. As for the days of our life, they contain seventy years, Or if due to strength, eighty years, Yet their pride is but labor and sorrow; For soon it is gone and we fly away. Who understands the power of Your anger And Your fury, according to the fear that is due You? So teach us to number our days, That we may present to You a heart of wisdom. Do return, O LORD; how long will it be? And be sorry for Your servants. O satisfy us in the morning with Your lovingkindness, That we may sing for joy and be glad all our

days. Make us glad according to the days You have afflicted us, And the years we have seen evil. Let Your work appear to Your servants And Your majesty to their children. Let the favor of the Lord our God be upon us; And confirm for us the work of our hands; Yes, confirm the work of our hands. (Psalm 90)

We comprehend existence as a sequential process, moment by moment. We discover history by uncovering and learning of the past sequence of events. God, however, knows all, the beginning and the end, and at the same time. He is omniscient, knowing all things. He is the Alpha and the Omega, the A and the Z. He is not bound by His creation, but He obviously relates to and interacts with it. He does so with the revealed purpose of becoming One with it in His incarnation.

The story of creation states in the poetically explosive and simplistically descriptive initial verses of Genesis that *time is a creation of God.*

> In the beginning God created the heavens and the earth. The earth was formless and void, and darkness was over the surface of the deep, and the Spirit of God was moving over the surface of the waters. Then God said, "Let there be light"; and there was light. God saw that the light was good; and God separated the light from the darkness. God called the light day, and the darkness He called night. And there was evening and there was morning, one day. (Genesis 1:1–5)

Both the described sequence of creation and the resulting sequence of events introduce a chronological series of actions: time. The following cause and effect of the creative words are instructive in the physical and functional process. The root Hebrew words used in the description of the Creator's actions are translated, "The heavens (*shamayim*) and the earth (*erets*)." The Biblical principle of *first mention* focuses our attention on these words as foundational to our comprehension of physical existence. There was nothing, and then there was something! God said, God saw, and it was good!

First, the heavens—what we clumsily describe as space and generally describe as the atmospheric layers of our universe—we conclude with an ultimate description of the spiritual dimension. We need not limit the intention of the words used to our finite experience. The words God used to describe His creation are not limited, and we do ourselves a disservice when we assign diminishing meanings to His words.

In this "space," or "the heavens," God spoke again and there was "earth." Again, this is the first mention of a root word that infers the very basic element of matter itself, the element in the universe that undergoes formation and alteration. With this understanding, underscored by the recent gift of Einstein's theory of relativity, we can begin to comprehend the next phases of God's creative process that resulted in the creation of time (*chronos*).

"Matter," translated "earth," was not yet placed in order, or organized, and therefore described in Hebrew as *tohu wa bohu*, that is, formless (*tohu*) and void (*bohu*). As a result of this initial inert presence of created matter within created space, "darkness was over the surface of the deep." Until God spoke and initiated the motion of matter within space, there was no light. Light is a description of radiant energy. When God spoke those creative words, "Let there be light," there was light! The matter began its motion in space, producing the radiant energy we describe as light. This deduction also answers the question for those who ask how there could be light before the sun was formed. The organization and formation of the created matter followed this initial command. The creation of time was a result of the command. Now a sequence began, a cause-and-effect process that we can relate to and has proceeded until now. This is God's functional order of occurrence, our chronology.

All the following descriptions proceeded from this foundation in sequence. Again, we are creatures of time. We have a past, described now as our memory and recorded as history. We anticipate our future, described as our hope or imagination. But as creatures in time, we only live and exist in the present, our "now." This is also why the heavenly perspective is so important in our walk with God. Our hope for the future tremendously affects our now. "Now faith is ..."

I believe that this perspective will assist our ability to receive what God intended; this key is not just to make a point but to make a difference. We limit our comprehension of God's revealed Word when we force a stunted application and our narrow comprehension into a linear sequential series of events rather than attempting to grasp what is revealed in the light that it is given.

> **If you read history you will find that the Christians who did most for the present world were just those who thought most of the next... It is since Christians have largely ceased to think of the other world that they have become so ineffective in this. Aim at Heaven and you will get earth "thrown in": aim at earth and you will get neither.**
> —C. S. Lewis, *Mere Christianity*

Marking Time

It is interesting that the Lord initiated an *experiential* daily and lunar calendar for the people of Israel rather than an *empirical* solar calendar. This method is difficult to accept and correlate within our historical understanding and the current Western, or Gregorian, calendar. The Hebrew calendar is a lunar calendar initiated by the visual acknowledgement of the first sight of the crescent of the new moon. The Hebrew word for month is *chodesh*, meaning "the new moon." This sighting by the high priest began the month (Exodus 19:1). The lunar cycle intentionally played a significant role in the cultural and religious life of the people. The new moon was a festival day, observed by burnt offerings and sacrifices as well as banquets (Numbers 29:6; 1 Samuel 20:5; 1 Chronicle 23:31). The New Moon Festival, along with the weekly Sabbath, was an important religious observance (2 Kings 4:23; Ezekiel 45:17). Likewise, the middle of the month, or the observance of the full moon, was an important marker of the passing of time. Both the spring feast of Passover and the fall Feast of Tabernacles were to be celebrated on the full moon in the middle of the month.

> Blow the trumpet at the new moon, at the full moon, on our feast day. (Psalm 81:3)

The Hebrew calendar contained twelve months and added the thirteenth month, or *second adar*, to keep the lunar calendar coordinated with the seasons of the year. This additional month occurred seven out of every nineteen years. Again, the leaders of God's people determined this by observation and experience. So the Hebrew day had no fixed length but was modeled on the Genesis 1 creation account that announced that "there was evening and there was morning."

> God called the light day, and the darkness He called night. And there was evening and there was morning, one day. (Genesis 1:5)

The Hebrew day began at sunset, the start of the evening, to the next sunset. There is no clock to determine the hour in this system but the observation of God's creation and a natural division of the time between the observed key points of sunrise, full day (noon), and sunset. This is restated for the fall feast of the Day of Atonement.

> You shall do no work at all. It is to be a perpetual statute throughout your generations in all your dwelling places. It is to be a sabbath of complete rest to you, and you shall humble your souls; on the ninth of the month at evening, from evening until evening you shall keep your sabbath. (Leviticus 23:31–32)

In general, the hour is defined as one half of the time from sunrise to sunset, the morning hour and the afternoon hour. However, the day was still divided by functional hours, and its equivalent was recorded by the prophet Daniel. Jesus also referenced the hour in His words and the measurement of His suffering.

THE UNVEILING

Jesus answered, "Are there not twelve hours in the day? If anyone walks in the day, he does not stumble, because he sees the light of this world." (John 11:9)

The measuring of the day, our chronological process, or the hours of the day, are experienced in creation rather than imposed on a day. Throughout the Scriptures, the term *hour* refers to a period of time measured as one-twelfth of the daylight part of the day. While daylight is longer in summer than in winter, and therefore summer "hours" were longer than winter "hours," as a general rule, the first hour was equivalent to six to seven a.m. on a modern-day clock, and so on:

The first hour	= 6 to 7 a.m.
The second hour	= 7 to 8 a.m.
The third hour	= 8 to 9 a.m.
The fourth hour	= 9 to 10 a.m.
The fifth hour	= 10 to 11 a.m.
The sixth hour	= 11 a.m. to 12 p.m.
The seventh hour	= 12 to 1 p.m.
The eighth hour	= 1 to 2 p.m.
The ninth hour	= 2 to 3 p.m.
The tenth hour	= 3 to 4 p.m.
The eleventh hour	= 4 to 5 p.m.
The twelfth hour	= 5 to 6 p.m.

The weekday starts with *Yom Rishon*, the first day, and proceeds to the seventh, *Yom Shabbat*. The week, or *shavua*, is a cycle of sevens. This also mirrors the seven days of creation in Genesis 1. The names for the days of the week, like those in the creation account, are the listed day number within the week. So the days of the week run from sunrise to sunset and are determined locally.

Also the days of the week were enumerated and named by sevens. The seventh, or Sabbath, concluded the week, and the end of the day was marked by sundown. A new day began at sunset. The reference to "the hour" referred to the half time from sunup to sundown.

The Hebrew days of the week are a numerical value and are listed Day 1 through Day 7:

1. Yom Rishon, meaning first day, corresponding to Sunday.
2. Yom Sheni, meaning second day, corresponding to Monday.
3. Yom Shlishi, meaning third day, corresponding to Tuesday.
4. Yom Revi'I, meaning fourth day, corresponding to Wednesday.
5. Yom Chamishi, meaning fifth day, corresponding to Thursday.
6. Yom Shishi, meaning sixth day, corresponding to Friday.
7. Yom Shabbat, meaning seventh day, corresponding to Saturday.

The reality of our existence is measured in a sequential chronology of events. Our relationship with God in His creation is detailed also as a chronology of events marked in His creative cycle and our experiential relationship with it. However, these events are *Kairos* moments that are ordained by God in our sequential *chronos* existence. In the same way, The Revelation of Jesus Christ is a series of seven visions unveiling God's "in the fullness of time" events from seven different vantage points.

The Challenges of Heaven Time—Chapter and Verse

One of the most basic structural forms included in modern Bibles is the application of chapter and verse. This is very helpful—most of the time. The Bible is a compilation of sixty-six books written by at least forty authors in three languages over a fifteen hundred-year period and assembled by God's people into the canon (or rule) of Scripture. Most of these books have been divided into chapters since the thirteenth century. Since the mid-sixteenth century, they have been further divided into verses. These applied divisions assist the location of particular stories and verses. They have historically applied the understood order of books and divisions. However, these applied divisions also introduce difficulty by assigning starting and stopping points throughout Scripture that were not originally intended but are now inferred.

Language is dynamic. The interpretation of language is a challenge. The grammatical structures do not simply follow in the process. So

THE UNVEILING

the interpretive application of paragraphs, sentence structure, and punctuation can be helpful, or not.

When reading apocalyptic Scripture, the chapters and verses impose a sequence that was not necessarily intended. When chapter one precedes chapter two, it is natural to assume a chronological sequence to the events described. However, rather than the imposed chapters and verses, we should follow the transitions, conjunctions, and instructions given within the text, as they are revealing and instructive. The Revelation is described as Jesus' disclosure that John saw and heard. He was then instructed to document these visions. I introduced the seven visions in Key #3 Disclosure: The Intent of The Revelation. I will consider the literature of The Revelation in the next chapter, Key #5 Scripture: The Library of The Revelation.

The transitions introduced in John's writing are very helpful in disclosing John's current experience, but the assumption of sequence is just that—an assumption. The language clearly states experiential transitions. The first is his Patmos vision that began with his experience of "hearing a loud voice" (Revelation 1:10) behind him. This is described as a historical moment in his life while he was isolated for his faith. He proceeds to describe what he saw and heard in his familiar language. He was shown things he could comprehend that would describe what God wanted to reveal to John and to us. Each sight was described as an experience; each phrase was documented as heard. Occasionally there is an interpretation, but this is not the regular flow. So apocalyptic Scripture differs from other Scripture in that it is an observation and a report, whether by experience or prophetic insight (vision) that is obediently and accurately recorded from the human perspective.

Revelation's mysteries are God's unveiling literature that incorporates descriptive and mystical images that open His story to us. The Biblical exposition of these mysteries, both the critical explanation and the interpretations of the text, unfold the revealed events in "Heaven time." Biblical mysteries are God's truths revealed to be received. All mysteries are not immediately explained. Mysteries are always unsettling.

> **Any chronological sequence applied by the reader is assumed. John clearly expresses the complete changes that occur within his visions without trying to tie them together.**

The Church is the audience of The Revelation. God has revealed Himself and His story to ordinary people. He intends that we receive His unveiling and live by His Word. The apostle Paul emphasizes this simple truth to the church at Corinth.

> For consider your calling, brethren, that there were not many wise according to the flesh, not many mighty, not many noble; but God has chosen the foolish things of the world to shame the wise, and God has chosen the weak things of the world to shame the things which are strong, and the base things of the world and the despised God has chosen, the things that are not, so that He may nullify the things that are, so that no man may boast before God. But by His doing you are in Christ Jesus, who became to us wisdom from God, and righteousness and sanctification, and redemption, so that, just as it is written, "Let him who boasts, boast in the Lord." (1 Corinthians 1:26–31)

And Mark reports in his gospel that the common people heard Him. "And the large crowd enjoyed listening to Him" (Mark 12:37b).

John repeatedly notes the transitions from one event or vision to another. Any chronological sequence applied by the reader is assumed. John clearly expresses the complete changes that occur within his visions without trying to tie them together. The first transition is so astounding in that there is a complete change of location. He first heard and saw the glorified Christ among His church and relayed His message to the churches. When this vision concluded, he was taken with the next.

> **Revelation's mysteries are God's unveiling literature that incorporates descriptive and mystical images that open His story to us.**

THE UNVEILING

There is a sequence to the seven visions, and there is a sequence within each vision, but the chapter delineations do not clarify their chronology. This is why all seven of the visions are relevant to the Christians of the first century and also to the church today. The glorified Christ is the same yesterday, today, and forever (Hebrews 13:8). The messages to the seven churches are relevant to the church today as are all the epistles of the New Testament.

Each of the seven visions is complete and could stand alone as a full unveiling of God's heavenly scene in time and eternity. We see the eternal Lamb of God, His worthiness to release the judgment on the sin of man resulting in death, the unfolding description of the result of this judgment, and its ultimate and cataclysmic conclusions, both of the initial and typical justification in the sacrificial system as well as the consummation of the age. The concluding statements are enclosed in this vision.

> But in the days of the voice of the seventh angel, when he is about to sound, then the_mystery of God is finished, as He preached to His servants the prophets... Then the seventh angel sounded; and there were loud voices in heaven, saying, "The kingdom of the world *has become* the kingdom of our Lord and of His Christ; and He will reign forever and ever." (Revelation 10:7; 11:15, emphasis added)

The third vision is a complete disclosure of the spiritual battle waged in the heavens and the earth. It could stand alone as a description of the "War of the Seeds" introduced in the Genesis 3:15 remedy promised by God describing the unfolding of events in the personification of the key characters and events that result in the conclusion of judgment and the restoration promised.

Almost as a parenthetical expansion of the judgment we see the "Behold" moments of the reapers and the final outpouring of judgment. This is reflective of the creation story detailed in Genesis 1–2:3 followed by a parenthetical expansion of the details of the formation of Adam and Eve in Genesis 2.

The fifth vision is a clear pronouncement of judgment on the Babylonian systems that were demonically inspired to bring death, injustice, and ungodly control of the earth. This pronouncement and following vision detail her complete destruction.

> Then one of the seven angels who had the seven bowls came and spoke with me, saying, "Come here, I will show you the judgment of the great harlot who sits on many waters, with whom the kings of the earth committed acts of immorality, and those who dwell on the earth were made drunk with the wine of her immorality." (Revelation 17:1-2)

The final two visions detail the victory of God and the reward of His holy ones. The declaration and brief description of the defeat of the enemies of the Kingdom of God are included with their ultimate judgment and the celebration of the saints of the first resurrection. Both of these visions, though complete and all-inclusive, add to the full unveiling of God's plans and purposes. Each facet, each vision, is a beautiful revelation of the plan and purpose of God. Each could be a separate book, detailed as the plan of God. However, like a beautiful stone cut with each facet highlighting and enhancing the other, these seven visions, or facets, unveil the full plan of God.

In conclusion, the chapter and verse divisions are helpful in navigating the book but are not to be imposed upon the book to define its chronology.

The Challenges of Heaven Time—Imminent and Transcendent

Time is of the essence. This essence includes more than the writer's (or reader's) contemporary timeline. So the application of this perspective of the unveiling of the documented events is described as given from an eternal or timeless perspective, "Heaven time." Again, God's perspective is both Alpha and Omega—beginning and end—revealing all aspects of time in what is expressed as a series of visions.

Since the reader of apocalyptic literature is naturally attempting to find meaning (or assign meaning) to the text with a limited chronological perspective, a willful attempt must be made to receive it with the view in which it is given. Contemporary realities, historical data, and imaginative explanations from past and present understanding, along with the overriding scenarios that have developed, I believe are based on the misunderstanding of the element of "Heaven time."

This is further exacerbated by the fact the church also continues to suffer from the problems of false prophets, false teaching and poor Biblical exegesis. The eschatological views that have developed through the past two millennia are based in a unique—and sometimes limiting—paradigm. Again, these eschatological systems are detailed in the chapter entitled "Lenses" in the consideration of Part 3 for an explanation of these perspectives.

The transitions throughout The Revelation are instructional and directive as to the separation between experiences and focus of the current vision. The Revelation is observed and experienced in scenes. The application is for all of God's people in "these last days." Since it was given in the middle of the first century, it must apply both to the fulfillment of Jesus' prophetic announcement of the end of days for the Hebrew sacrificial system and the temple as well as the end of days for the current age in "these last days" between the first and the Second Coming of Christ.

There are many dozens of Bible verses documenting "these last days" in both the Old Testament and the New. They all indicate an immediate and ultimate realization of the concluding events. Due to the inclusion of God's Divine perspective, the descriptions of their imminent realization and ultimate consummation are understandable. Both at the beginning and the end of The Revelation the immediacy of fulfillment is indicated while at the same time pronouncing that there is clear direction for comprehending the end of the age. The phrases, "the time is near," (Revelation1:3) "shortly," "quickly," and "shall take place" are expressed along with concluding statements of completion at the end of the age.

> Therefore write the things which you have seen, and the things which are, and the things which will take place after these things ... But in the days of the voice of the seventh angel, when he is about to sound, then the mystery of God is finished, as He preached to His servants the prophets. (Revelation 1:19; 10:7)

Since God's Word is always relevant for application, it is the work of the student to pursue what it meant to the original hearers for greater insight. The application of His eternal Word is not malleable, but it is contemporary. When the prophet Daniel was given the vision of the four beasts, the interpretation was given that represented the four remaining earthly kingdoms that would dominate in the history of Israel. This time covered from Daniel's day until the coming of Messiah and His "cutting off" (Daniel 9:26). He understood the shocking reality of the judgment of God on a disobedient people. He also realized that God's eternal Kingdom would be established in the process and this settled his immediate concern with an eternal hope.

> In the days of those kings the God of heaven will set up a kingdom which will never be destroyed, and that kingdom will not be left for another people; it will crush and put an end to all these kingdoms, but it will itself endure forever. (Daniel 2:44)

> I kept looking in the night visions, and behold, with the clouds of heaven One like a Son of Man was coming, and He came up to the Ancient of Days and was presented before Him. And to Him was given dominion, Glory and a kingdom, that all the peoples, nations and men of every language Might serve Him. His dominion is an everlasting dominion which will not pass away; and His kingdom is one which will not be destroyed. (Daniel 7:13–14)

But the saints of the Highest One will receive the kingdom and possess the kingdom forever, for all ages to come. (Daniel 7:18)

Then the sovereignty, the dominion and the greatness of all the kingdoms under the whole heaven will be given to the people of the saints of the Highest One; His kingdom will be an everlasting kingdom, and all the dominions will serve and obey Him. (Daniel 7:27)

Now at that time Michael, the great prince who stands guard over the sons of your people, will arise. And there will be a time of distress such as never occurred since there was a nation until that time; and at that time your people, everyone who is found written in the book, will be rescued. Many of those who sleep in the dust of the ground will awake, these to everlasting life, but the others to disgrace and everlasting contempt. Those who have insight will shine brightly like the brightness of the expanse of heaven, and those who lead the many to righteousness, like the stars forever and ever. (Daniel 12:1–3)

The Revelation weaves together the visions of Daniel in the conclusion of the judgment on Israel with the "end of days" and the final and complete consummation of the ages. The seven visions of The Revelation give us a contemporary understanding of the imminent expectation of judgment while revealing the ultimate and transcendent fulfillment of the promise of God to make all things new, a new heaven and a new earth.

The Challenges of Heaven Time—John's Experience

The initial reading of The Revelation clearly displays that it was written differently from other New Testament books. The canon of Scripture contains categories of defined types of literature: allegory, poetry, metaphor, and symbolic "types" that are related in history, poetry, songs, and narrations. The New Testament includes the Gospels, the Acts, the Epistles, and The Revelation. The Gospels are reports inspired by the Holy Spirit to display the moral nature of God in four aspects of Jesus Christ—Matthew (the lion as King of the Jews), Mark (the ox as the Servant of all), Luke (a man as the Son of Man), and John (the eagle as the Son of God)—all in the fulfillment of God's prophetic Word. These are also reflected in the apocalyptic references of Isaiah 6, Ezekiel 1, and Revelation 4 with the reflective glory of the "burning ones" (*seraphim*) before the throne of God. The book of Acts, like the Gospels, were composed as Luke reports,

> The first account I composed, Theophilus, about all that Jesus began to do and teach, until the day when He was taken up to heaven, after He had by the Holy Spirit given orders to the apostles whom He had chosen. (Acts 1:1-2)

The letters (epistles) to the churches are apostolic correspondence that reveal the application of the grace of salvation in the life and context of the believer. The Revelation is John's documented experience of the visions, captured for our benefit at the exhortation of the angel.

The Hebrew Old Testament, the *Tanakh*, is also an accumulation of God's revealed truth and the documented histories of Israel and the nations and the poetic and prophetic words revealing God to us. The *Tanakh* is the canonical collection of Jewish texts. This is an acronym from the first Hebrew letter of each of the three traditional subdivisions. TaNaKh: (Ta)—Torah (teachings or the five books of Moses), (Na)—Nevi'im (prophets), and (Kh)—Ketuvim (writings). These documents also include apocalyptic portions as documented events that occurred in the lives of the Old Testament saints. They are the writings of the patriarchs, the prophets, and the poets preparing the way for Messiah.

John was obviously a historical person. He lived and died in our past. His faith was lived out in time. In fact, the chronology of his life and ministry are recorded in the first verses as he identifies with the church.

> I, John, your brother and fellow partaker in the tribulation and kingdom and perseverance which are in Jesus, was on the island called Patmos because of the word of God and the testimony of Jesus. (Revelation 1:9)

John testifies to the reality of walking out his faith in time. As a "fellow partaker," he is one joined in the suffering of the church. He is one who believes and has paid a price for his faith. He acknowledges his part in the tribulation, living in a broken world in a body destined to die, in a spiritual environment opposed to the Kingdom of God.

He also identifies the reality of the Kingdom that now exists and has since Jesus preached, "The Kingdom of God is among us." This was John's faithfulness, his long obedience as a steward of the gospel. This was not just a moment in time but a process of time, his perseverance in the Spirit. However, his recorded experience of the visions he received is a timeless report for our benefit of the revelation he received on that day.

Again, John's experience was an obedient documenting of what he saw and heard. So it was in that order he heard or saw and responded emotionally but obediently to the vision he was experiencing. He was repeatedly reminded by the angel to write it down, with one exception. This exclusion is not explained but obviously another act of God's mercy in judgment.

> Now when the seven thunders uttered their voices, I was about to write; but I heard a voice from heaven saying to me, "Seal up the things which the seven thunders uttered, and do not write them." (Revelation 10:4)

The Revelation is complete as the Holy Spirit Himself is the author. As with His work in the church, He chooses to work through His vessels. John was overwhelmed with the experiences of the visions.

> And when I saw Him, I fell at His feet as dead ... Now I, John, saw and heard these things. And when I heard and saw, I fell down to worship before the feet of the angel who showed me these things. (Revelation 1:17a; 22:8)

The conclusion of The Revelation confirms that John's coherent writings were not lacking due to his distraction or his overwhelming experience but were Divinely inspired!

I, Jesus, have sent My angel to testify to you these things in the churches. I am the Root and the Offspring of David, the Bright and Morning Star. And the Spirit and the bride say, "Come!" And let him who hears say, "Come!" And let him who thirsts come. Whoever desires, let him take the water of life freely. For I testify to everyone who hears the words of the prophecy of this book: If anyone adds to these things, God will add to him the plagues that are written in this book; and if anyone takes away from the words of the book of this prophecy, God shall take away his part from the Book of Life, from the holy city, and from the things which are written in this book. He who testifies to these things says, "Surely I am coming quickly." Amen. Even so, come, Lord Jesus! The grace of our Lord Jesus Christ be with you all. Amen. (Revelation 22:16–21)

The Challenges of Heaven Time—Past-Present-Future

The introduction of the Unveiling gives us an immediate awareness of the all-encompassing timeliness of the coming Revelation. He begins with an announcement of God's intention and His authority.

> Behold, *He is coming* with the clouds, and every eye *will see* Him, even those *who pierced* Him; and all the tribes of the earth *will mourn* over Him. So *it is to be*. Amen. "I am the Alpha and the Omega," says the Lord God, "who is and who was and who is to come, the Almighty." (Revelation 1:7–8, emphasis added)

Notice the language of the tenses used to describe God's intention and His audience. First, this is about Jesus coming! The two descriptions of His coming refer to judgment and the fulfillment to the disciples on the Mount of Olives. He is coming—present and future. In the immediate expected present, He comes to conclude the final judgment on Israel and her failed covenant of sacrifice. This will fulfill Jesus' prophecy concerning the temple and Jerusalem. Then, He is coming—future, in the consummation of the ages. Both of these are in the clouds, the

THE UNVEILING

clouds of judgment as described throughout the Old Testament of a vast marching army, first in the Roman armies of Vespasian and Titus on the city of Jerusalem, and every eye will see them, and then the ultimate return in the clouds at the conclusion of the age as promised the disciples on the Mount of Olives, and again, every eye will see Him.

This initial verse looks at the *present* and then to the *future*: "Behold He is coming." The focus then shifts to the *past* and identifies "even those that pierced Him." Finally, it looks to the *future*: "All the tribes of the earth will mourn over Him."

He introduces Himself in the same way. "I am" now and always, "Alpha and Omega," the first and the last, encompassing all of time. He clarifies and amplifies with "who is and who was and who is to come" and places the exclamation point on "the Almighty."

As with all Scripture, it is originated in the heart of God. He has revealed Himself to man in many composite ways throughout history. From the burning bush and the still, small voice to the *Shekinah* presence seen in the pillar of cloud by day and the pillar of fire by night. But in these last days, He is seen in Jesus.

> God, after He spoke long ago to the fathers in the prophets in many portions and in many ways, in these last days has spoken to us in His Son. (Hebrews 1:1–2)

Throughout the seven visions, we are opened to the vast spectrum of events of this age from seven different vantage points to the finished work of God. This work has been accomplished from the foundation of the world.

> All who dwell on the earth will worship him, whose names have not been written in the Book of Life of the Lamb slain from the foundation of the world. (Revelation 13:8)

> For the Son of Man is going to come in the glory of His Father with His angels, and will then repay every man according to

his deeds. Truly I say to you, there are some of those who are standing here who will not taste death until they see the Son of Man coming in His kingdom. (Matthew 16:27–28)

The seven visions of The Revelation are each a stand-alone unveiling of God's truth as well as a blended addition to each of the other visions. They each have their own timely perspective.

The first vision of the glorified Christ addressing the Church is occurring in the past, from our perspective, with a heavenly resurrected Christ who is the same yesterday, today, and forever.

The second vision of the heavens and the throne room of God with His attending audience is a picture of completion and is timeless. The scene reveals a past, present, and future disclosure of the restraint of judgment by the Lamb of God. Breaking the seven seals is the release of judgment that has been realized since the sin of Adam and is visualized by the scroll and the Lamb's worthy response from the beginning of judgment until its conclusion.

The third vision of the seven signs depicting the "War of the Seeds" gives us a timeless and heavenly perspective of the spiritual battle from the fall of Lucifer referenced in Isaiah 14:12–15 and Ezekiel 28:12–19. This vision covers a period of chronological time that would include all of the creation in this age and then some! The heavenly perspective is described with earthly symbols disclosing the ongoing battle initiated by Lucifer and carried on through the history of man while God reveals His revealed remedy that He promised in the garden of Eden to the end of the age.

The fourth vision of the outpoured bowls of wrath is a promised future conclusion, an all-consuming release of the promised judgment of sin as a quick, concluding, and merciful outpouring of the deserved judgment on sin and rebellion.

The fifth vision of the doom of Babylon is a parenthetical description of the judgment on the affairs of men over the span of human history.

THE UNVEILING

These demonically revealed deadly systems are doomed at the end of the age. Both the fourth and fifth visions are expansive descriptions of the judgment released at the end of the second and third visions.

The sixth vision is a victorious revelation of the commencement celebration of the Marriage Supper of the Lamb and recognition of the concluding judgments on Satan and sin.

The seventh and final vision details the fulfilled promise of future restoration of the relationship of God and man and the new heaven and the new earth.

All seven visions are overlapping, sometimes kaleidoscopic, but thoroughly complete in the conclusion of all things in this age from God's perspective, heaven time.

Key # 5

SCRIPTURE: THE LIBRARY OF THE REVELATION

This is the challenge of The Unveiling: the mind of God to the mind of man, the infinite poured into the finite. The Big Picture to the one with the small view. Now we are to be stewards of the mysteries of God and pursue them and not fear when they are revealed. This is how we should receive revelation.

> All Scripture is inspired by God and profitable for teaching, for reproof, for correction, for training in righteousness.
> —2 Timothy 3:16

The fifth key is foundational in that all Scripture is to be read in light of Scripture. Due to the source and intention of the canon of Scripture, its authenticity is a testimony of the Spirit. Those who do not have this testimony would argue against the self-authentication of this circular logic. All truth is rational, but Scriptural truth is received relationally through revelation. Since the acceptance of Scripture is a matter of faith reinforced by reason, archaeology, and history, Judeo-Christian Scripture is a genre all its own.

One of the church fathers, Tertullian (c.150–212), is quoted in relation to his conviction that God's Word was the only safe source of truth on earth. Those who desire to walk with God are people of faith first. We are citizens not of earth but of "the city above … [who] have nothing to do with the joys of the world, nay [who] are called to the very opposite ... And I think the Lord affirms, that those who mourn are happy, not those who are crowned."[3]

> But as it is, they desire a better country, that is, a heavenly one. Therefore God is not ashamed to be called their God; for He has prepared a city for them. (Hebrews 11:16)

Scripture is the body of God's work written by Him through His creation for humanity and recognized by His church. It is His nature, culture, and language revealed in this age. The ancient adage is true that all truth is God's truth wherever it may be found. The crescendo of His revealed Word is realized in the Incarnation, and The Revelation is His all-inclusive conclusion and consummation. The results of His intentions are unveiled in His apocalyptic announcements throughout His Word and disclosed in full in The Revelation of Jesus Christ. Apocalyptic Scriptures are those given from a heavenly perspective and usually reveal the spiritual dimension in a unique disclosure to accomplish God's intention for His people.

Scripture is the body of God's work written by Him through His creation for humanity and recognized by His church.

Restoring this spiritual dimension to man is God's intention and the topic of the seventh key, Restoration: The Promise of The Revelation. We can see from the beginning that Genesis reveals God's motive of love and His intention for relationship in His creation. This is realized in the formation of Adam with the addition of His breath in Adam's nostrils. All creation was spoken into being, but Adam was formed from the stuff of earth, and God breathed into him the breath of life. Adam became a living soul, the first human being, made for heaven and earth. Man is God's priestly connection in His creation. The original dimensional existence of man was not limited to our current earthly realm. These include the four dimensions of our limited existence—height, width, depth, and time. However, we were also made for the fifth dimension—the spiritual dimension—with full access to the presence and speaking voice of God and our cooperation with Him in His creation. We were formed of the stuff of heaven and of earth. We were made for heaven and earth!

The wisdom of God is manifested in His creation and is expressed and personified throughout the book of Proverbs, especially in chapter eight. This wisdom—the eternal speaking voice of God—is an all-encompassing and eternal expression that resonates within His creation. This is the speaking voice that is responsible for everything that is and is also responsible for holding all things together by the Word of His power.

> For by Him all things were created, both in the heavens and on earth, visible and invisible, whether thrones or dominions or rulers or authorities—all things have been created through Him and for Him. He is before all things, and in Him all things hold together. (Colossians 1:16–17)

When we listen to and receive the speaking voice of God, our hearts resonate with Him, and we can live and move and have our being in Him. His written Word is the accumulation, documentation, and revelation of this interaction throughout history. It is then described in history, law, wisdom, poetry, prophecy, gospel, epistles, and apocalyptic writings. We can see and appreciate the history of man and the intervention of God. He has given His revelation in many literary forms, including parable, allegory, cultural poetry, and prose, as well as many types, and the narration of His work and man's response. He also uses the literation of numbers and numeration of letters (*gematria*) as seen throughout apocalyptic writings. The Revelation begins with such a literation referring to Jesus as the first and last, Alpha and Omega.

Of all the books of the Bible, none is introduced like The Revelation of Jesus Christ. Though there are other portions of Scripture that contain apocalyptic literature, there is none like it. It discloses an ever-increasing light of the compounding revelation of God. We know this is true of all Scripture, but The Revelation is unique.

> All Scripture is inspired by God and profitable for teaching, for reproof, for correction, for training in righteousness. (2 Timothy 3:16)

The specific revelation of Scripture is so much more than its immediate literal value. From the simplicity and yet infinite introduction of God in Genesis to His realized fulfillment in the consummation of the ages of The Revelation of Jesus Christ, God's Word is just that—His Word. He has infused the finite of our reality with the infinite of His "I Am"! The Scriptures are layered in types and allegories, in similitudes and symbols. The Scriptural infrastructure of these revealing truths is the foundation of God's disclosure to humanity. The personified wisdom of Proverbs proclaims the spoken Word of God as that which forms all of His intentions in His creation.

The apostle Paul was a student of the Scripture. He writes to the Corinthian church to encourage them to invest in the study of Scripture so they might gain revealed wisdom. The stories and histories were written down for God's people as a warning. God's revelation and interaction with His people through the ages is for our good and our understanding. This is expressed in the biblical truth of Augustine's axiom that "The Old Testament is the New Testament concealed, the New Testament is the Old Testament revealed."

> Now these things happened to them as an example, and they were written for our instruction, upon whom the ends of the ages have come. Therefore let him who thinks he stands take heed that he does not fall. No temptation has overtaken you but such as is common to man; and God is faithful, who will not allow you to be tempted beyond what you are able, but with the temptation will provide the way of escape also, so that you will be able to endure it. (1 Corinthians 10:11–13)

The typology of the Scriptures from Genesis through the prophets reveals God's truth in impressions, patterns, images, and figures that are all ultimately fulfilled in Jesus Christ. Adam is a type of Christ, and the flood is an expression of the mercy of God in the ultimate fulfillment of His plan realized in the incarnation.

> Nevertheless death reigned from Adam until Moses, even over those who had not sinned in the likeness of the offense of Adam, who is a type of Him who was to come. (Romans 5:14)

> For Christ also died for sins once for all, the just for the unjust, so that He might bring us to God, having been put to death in the flesh, but made alive in the spirit; in which also He went and made proclamation to the spirits now in prison, who once were disobedient, when the patience of God kept waiting in the days of Noah, during the construction of the ark, in which a few, that is, eight persons, were brought safely through the water. Corresponding to that, baptism now saves you—not the removal of dirt from the flesh, but an appeal to God for a good conscience—through the resurrection of Jesus Christ, who is at the right hand of God, having gone into heaven, after angels and authorities and powers had been subjected to Him. (1 Peter 3:18–22)

We begin to see in the book of Genesis the revelation of God's moral nature and man's need. We can see God's planned cooperation from the foundations of the earth and His promised restoration. His patience is revealed in His interaction with His chosen seed and ultimately the nation of Israel, as His mercy is new every morning. The strong types of the composite expressions of God are revealed in the relationship of Abraham and Isaac, the patriarchal leadership with His people, and the prophetic pronouncements. When Christ came, everything changed. All the promises of God throughout the past age found their fulfillment in Him. Now the mysteries of the past are revealed in the light of God's mercy and God's provision through Jesus Christ.

Each of the seven visions of The Revelation is filled with descriptions, allegories, symbols, and dramatic scenes introduced throughout the Old Testament. God's allegories are a sacramental turn of mind. He begins with a revealed and immaterial fact of the conflict of good and evil, of the demonically inspired attempt to discredit God or devalue His creation, and depicts these realities in a visible and experiential facet of the whole revelation. We then attempt to read and perceive that turn of mind, that something else, through the types and symbols. The Biblical literary structures God uses to communicate truth are redundant facets, or perspectives, that reveals and teaches His moral reality. The sequence of the seven visions is God's literary device depicting a spiritual experience for John and an unveiled mystery to the church.

The sequence of the seven visions is God's literary device depicting a spiritual experience for John and an unveiled mystery to the church.

As mentioned before, Christianity is a revealed religion—God has spoken! By faith, we accept that God is—God is personal—God is a person with a will! We believe that truth is knowable through His Scriptures. The Revelation is central to unveil the big picture, the grand narrative. It is not a book of religion but a unique interpretation of universal history, the history of the whole creation, and the history of the human race.

> To you it has been granted to know the mysteries of the kingdom of heaven. (Matthew 13:11)

So the mystery of the Bible is simple enough that a child is able to grasp a foundational meaning, and yet it is deep enough that we will spend eternity observing God's truth bloom to full disclosure, an eternal opening. Mystery is a challenge for our mind, a way of thinking that there is something to be obtained and yet to be realized. God is unpacking His truth in the mysteries of the seven visions. He is revealing facts, building a case, and disclosing His intention. He intends to disclose something to His people that was not previously known. He intends to reveal the ultimate truth to our hearts. Scripture is intentionally revealing, yet it is progressively opening in greater layers and relationship. This is why a mystery can be known and experienced by some yet hidden from others to be made known in the end.

THE UNVEILING

Our goal is to search out the historical reality that is known so we might shed light on a given subject and produce a greater insight. We unpack an etymological clarity concerning the words used, how they are used, and what the words mean in context and history. We remove the veil of what has been imposed, what it has been made to mean in its current usage, and a mystery is revealed, a layer pulled back. It is glorious to lift the corner of revelation and glimpse at the blinding light of truth.

Now, we love and pursue these kinds of mysteries as we gather information and garner apparent insight, so we might grow in knowledge and, as a result, feel superior in the accumulation of that knowledge. But The Revelation of Jesus Christ is something much greater and overwhelming in the sense that it is not just a glimmer, not just an insight; it is the revelation of God. As a result of its basis in faith, it is discounted in our postmodern cynical thinking. God intended to show His plan, to unravel the mystery of the ages in His written Word. But He does so from His perspective, the only correct and encompassing perspective. In unraveling the mystery, He is telling His story from His perspective, but in our limited language, understanding, ideas, and minds.

This is the challenge of The Unveiling: the mind of God to the mind of man, the infinite poured into the finite. The Big Picture to the one with the small view. Now we are to be stewards of the mysteries of God and pursue them and not fear when they are revealed. This is how we should receive revelation.

We are to receive The Unveiling in a literal manner. "Literal" does not mean historical or bound to a contemporary understanding. It means, "according to the letter"; that is, "What does the text actually say?" When Jesus introduces Himself as the Alpha and the Omega, we understand the inference to be a simile that He is the first and the last. He is not a Hebrew letter. Rather, He is timeless, and the source of the beginning and the end. I intend to pursue and detail each symbol in its context as I continue to study and teach this book. This is the unique reality of The Unveiling. It is from heaven's perspective and requires parabolic symbols and similes to communicate the heavenly truth. God is very artistic in His communication. He is an artist, a poet, a creator, and Jesus is the apex of His communication. So His Word needs to be read poetically and valued artistically and yet received personally and practically, as John concluded in His gospel so this is true in all of God's Word "that we might believe."

> Therefore many other signs Jesus also performed in the presence of the disciples, which are not written in this book; but these have been written so that you may believe that Jesus is the Christ, the Son of God; and that believing you may have life in His name. (John 20:30–31)

Reading Scripture introduces us to God's truth and types that open His Revelation. These pictures begin to unfold in Genesis, and the characters, types, and symbols are repeated and amplified throughout the Old Testament stories. The prophetic and poetic pictures introduce God's language of symbolic description envisioned and realized in His Revelation. The conclusion of the seventh vision is the fulfillment of God's accumulated pictures. He began in the Garden of Eden and concludes in the Garden of God's New Creation. A lamb was sacrificed in the first garden to cover the sin of Adam and Eve. The Lamb has risen from the dead and now sits on the throne in the Kingdom of God and the New Jerusalem, the City of the Lamb. Throughout the Scriptures, this Edenic existence is the plan of God for man. The Psalms are filled with such images and promises. The prophets Isaiah, Ezekiel, Daniel, and Zechariah are clearly reflected and fulfilled in this conclusive vision. All the patriarchal, prophetic, and poetic pictures are realized in Jesus Christ, for the spirit of prophecy is the testimony of Jesus. The Scripture is our reference library to comprehend The Revelation.

Signs and Wonders

As stated, each of the seven visions of The Revelation is unveiled with many symbols of shocking facts, stark clarity, ominous expectations, amazing promises, and fearful judgments.

The first vision is of the glorified Christ and gives us descriptions that reflect and fulfill the One introduced to Israel at the Jabbok (Genesis 32:30), to Joshua at the entrance to the Promised Land (Joshua 5:14), and to three men thrown in the furnace and to Nebuchadnezzar: "One like the Son of God" (Daniel 3:25).

The second vision is of the heavens and the throne room of God with His attending audience and is a full description of the experience described by the prophet (Isaiah 6:1-5) and experienced by the apostle Paul (2 Corinthians 12:2). The Lamb slain from the foundation of the world is a description of Jesus and a fulfillment of the inferred animal that God sacrificed in the garden of Eden to shed its blood and cover the nakedness of Adam and Eve (Genesis 3:21). This is the realization of the typified Passover lamb whose blood was shed to cover the doorposts and lintel of the people of God for the death angel to pass over (Exodus 12:1-13). The scroll with seven seals is a familiar and commonly understood concept, and it is sealed for limited access. However, this scroll is God's living Word released into His creation, and as the seals are broken, the Word is released. This is the topic of the sixth key of Revelation, Judgment: The Result of The Revelation, which will be covered in the next chapter.

The third vision includes all of the key characters of our Biblical history. We see the woman fulfilling the protoprophecy (Genesis 3:15) in the War of the Seeds and the Holy Offspring of that promise, the male child. We see the primordial spiritual battle in the heavens (Isaiah 14:12-15; Ezekiel 28:12-19) typified by a snake in the garden and a dragon in the battles. We also see God's messengers, His angels, who do His bidding. This vision extends the spiritual battle for our understanding into the pre-creation era. He reveals the Satanic attempt to undermine the will of God and destroy His ultimate remedy of redemption and restoration. The expansion of this battle is revealed as the overarching influence on humanity and her idolatrous interaction with the dragon.

The fourth vision is a promised future conclusion of judgment on the earth. It is an all-consuming release of the promised judgment of sin as a quick, concluding, and merciful outpouring of the deserved judgment on this sin and rebellion. Many of these symbols were used to describe God's intervention with Israel (Zechariah 9:14–17). The bowl is symbolic of a limited container, complete, and, because of its limited capacity, merciful in its conclusion.

The fifth vision is a parenthetical description of judgment on the affairs of men over the span of human history. These demonically inspired deadly systems are doomed at the end of the age. Both the fourth and fifth visions are expansive descriptions of the conclusive judgment released at the end of the second and third visions. The great symbol of this fifth vision is defined and described, even personified as Babylon. Throughout Scripture, this name has been referenced spiritually and symbolically and even maintained geographically throughout history. The beasts of the prophet Daniel's visions are remembered as the expression of evil that arises in the Babylonian systems of corruption, injustice, and violence in the earth.

The sixth vision is a victorious revelation of consummation and the beginning of an eternal celebration with recognition of the concluding judgments on Satan and sin. The Church is known as the Bride of Christ and is given in marriage to the Bridegroom, concluding in the marriage supper of the Lamb. Now the concluding horse of The Revelation is revealed as beginning His march. He is victorious, clothed in His own blood, and signed as the King of kings and Lord of lords. The enemies of God and His people are destroyed by His own Words as a sword that proceeds from His mouth. The conclusion of all judgment is revealed in these few words with its final closing of the books.

THE UNVEILING

The seventh and final vision details the fulfilled promise of future restoration of the relationship of God and man and the new heaven and the new earth. This vision will be detailed in the seventh and conclusive key, Restoration: The Promise of The Revelation.

Key # 6
JUDGMENT: THE RESULT OF THE REVELATION

The release of His wrath is measured by grace for our benefit, and we will yet realize it as His mercy!

Behold He is coming with the clouds, and every eye will see Him, even those who pierced Him; and all the tribes of the earth will mourn over Him.
—Revelation 1:7

The sixth key is the dominant and overwhelming focus for most students of The Revelation. Though the explosive disclosures of the heavenly visions are overwhelming in all their aspects, the conclusive judgments become the focal point. This is especially true for those who are actively looking for "signs" and attempting to divine the future. All of us are curious; however, some are actively preparing for a coming catastrophe while others for an escape. As a result, the anticipation of judgment has become the most culturally influencing aspect of Scripture and is being pursued with a liberal artistic license. Many would consider God's judgment the only theme of the Apocalypse, if not the only purpose of the book. As we have seen from the previous keys that open The Revelation, the focus is Jesus and His eternal purpose. It is also clear from the introduction that the initial purpose of Jesus' Revelation is to prepare and exhort His bond servants, the saints, for both persecution and perseverance in their brief time in this life. The consequences of sin are deadly but the good news has been promised and realized in Jesus.

The apostle Paul clarified that the wages of sin is death (Romans 6:23), and this death has ruled in creation and us since man's rejection of life. The fact that death exists is not a reactive punishment sent to us from God but a result of turning from God Who is the source of life. Man chose to break fellowship with God and, as a result, death remained. God is life, light, love, and humanity's only Source. Man was created by God for His pleasure and does not have life in himself. Therefore, man's choice to separate from God resulted in separating from life itself. Life is a gift of God. Genesis relates the story of Adam and Eve, God's warning to them, and man's fall. The resulting reality of turning from God was death. This was not God's reaction but man's choice.

As we consider the unveiled and conclusive judgment of God, we must not lose sight of man's choice and God's revealed nature. God is love. God is holy. Man's disobedience did not produce a vengeful act from God, but it did produce a deadly consequence.

> The Lord God commanded the man, saying, "From any tree of the garden you may eat freely; but from the tree of the knowledge of good and evil you shall not eat, for in the day that you eat from it you will surely die." (Genesis 2:16–17)

Many early commentators on Scripture were careful to note that God did not say, "In the day you eat of it I will kill you," but "In the day you eat of it you shall die." This truth is repeated throughout Scripture.

> Now as for you, son of man, say to the house of Israel, "Thus you have spoken, saying, 'Surely our transgressions and our sins are upon us, and we are rotting away in them; how then can we survive?'" Say to them, "'As I live!' declares the Lord GOD, 'I take no pleasure in the death of the wicked, but rather that the wicked turn from his way and live. Turn back, turn back from your evil ways! Why then will you die, O house of Israel?'" (Ezekiel 33:10–11)

> I call heaven and earth to witness against you today, that I have set before you life and death, the blessing and the curse. So

choose life in order that you may live, you and your descendants, by loving the LORD your God, by obeying His voice, and by holding fast to Him; for this is your life and the length of your days, that you may live in the land which the LORD swore to your fathers, to Abraham, Isaac, and Jacob, to give them. (Deuteronomy 30:19–20)

God did not take life from man. Life was a gift, but we separated ourselves from it. Death is the result that is not limited to the physical conclusion of this life, but it includes the corruptive process of death that is at work in us. Our daily lives bring to light the reality that this entire "age," from the fall of man to the restoration of all things, is an age of tribulation. Since the "fall," mankind has lived in a broken world. We daily manage and endure life in bodies destined to die. We enter the Kingdom through tribulation. This is not a cynical and defeated position of perpetual existence, but a reality check for the passing world in which we live and an explanation for the chaos, suffering, and death that exists in this world.

Those who are unaware of this truth and are distant from the God of creation ask the accusing questions that naturally stem from the result of this sin and death: "Why do the innocent suffer?" "Why do the wicked prosper?" Where is God in all this?" A lack of understanding of the free will of man operating under the sovereign will of God results in accusations that question the motives of God. In this ignorance, man angrily accuses God, questioning His character and purpose. From this lack of knowing come comments like "If God is all good but not all-powerful or knowing, perhaps He doesn't have the ability to intervene in the affairs of man." Others accuse God of a mean or vindictive nature, or that He is just not interested or involved in His creation. The result is that man's responsibility for the consequences of sin are reflected back on God, and in a fatalistic accusation, God is accused of creating evil.

The defined study of the defense of the justice of God is called theodicy. This is a term derived from two Greek words, *theos* (God) and *dike* (justice). This is an attempt to justify or defend God in the face of evil, that is, why a perfectly good, almighty, and all-knowing God permits evil. This "problem of the existence of evil" is a distraction from the consequence of sin. The full unveiling of Jesus Christ gives us the complete picture of the source of evil and the provision of a merciful God. Evil is not a created entity; rather, it is a result of free will, a choice for death and rejecting life. God knew what it would cost Him, and us, for our free will to exist. He was willing to pay the price for our deliverance and salvation from our own poor choices and, with free will, offer us the gift of eternal life with Him. Jesus is the Lamb of God slain from the foundation of the world.

The reality of our free will operating within God's sovereign will is a mystery we live with but cannot completely comprehend. It is only the revealed knowledge of His holiness and goodness that graces the believer to walk with peace in this brief life as a volitional being.

> And we know that God causes all things to work together for good to those who love God, to those who are called according to His purpose. (Romans 8:28)

Some have chosen to turn away from any hope of comprehension or revelation. In their agnostic conclusions, the cynicism of the heart results in a greater sorrow as the weight of reality crushes their souls. No one intentionally invites trouble or enjoys tribulation, but our world is filled with both. The mystic Bernard of Clairvaux (1090–1153) has so poignantly stated, "It is a misery to be born, a pain to live, a trouble to die." Yes, we enter the Kingdom through tribulation.

Tribulation

The word *tribulation* carries a heavy anticipation and realization of life, as well as our own mortality. It also carries the meaning of affliction, sorrow, and anguish. Tribulation is derived from the Latin *tribulum*, which was an ancient farming tool for threshing the grain. This word is drawn from the Latin *terere,* meaning "to rub or to grind." This was the process of separating the grain from the husks. In the practical use of this ancient method of threshing grain, one man would stir up the sheaves while another would ride over them in a cart equipped with rollers with attached bits of iron and sharp stones. There were no wheels, so the weight of the cylinders and attached tools helped separate the husks from the grain.

Translators of both the Hebrew and the Greek have appropriated this word to describe the trouble and anguish of the soul and difficulties of life. When the great afflictions of this life come to us, we feel as if our lives are being torn to pieces under the cruel pressures of adverse circumstances. No farmer ever harvested his grain or a thresher yoke his *tribulum* for the mere purpose of destroying the crop. This threshing was intended not for destruction but for revealing the precious grain. Jesus has also made this clear. He never puts us under the pressure of sorrow and disappointment needlessly. Adversity can either destroy or build up, depending on our chosen response. The poet Oliver Goldsmith (1730–1774) wrote,

> Aromatic plants bestow
> No spicy fragrance while they grow;
> But crushed or trodden to the ground
> Diffuse their sweetness all around.

The sorrow and trials of this life are a result of a world under judgment. The apostle Paul describes the ongoing reality of this judgment in the earth. God's grace and mercy keep us in this age while at the same time multiplying the souls gifted with life and the free will to choose Him for a life of eternal reward and relationship. The wrath of God is experienced in this cursed world that has separated itself from the source of life and hope. The release of His wrath is measured for our benefit, and we will yet realize it as His mercy. As introduced in the first two keys that open The Revelation, the apostle Paul states the reality and the result of man's choices in his letter to the church in Rome.

> For the wrath of God is revealed from heaven against all ungodliness and unrighteousness of men who suppress the

truth in unrighteousness, because that which is known about God is evident within them; for God made it evident to them. For since the creation of the world His invisible attributes, His eternal power and divine nature, have been clearly seen, being understood through what has been made, so that they are without excuse. For even though they knew God, they did not honor Him as God or give thanks, but they became futile in their speculations, and their foolish heart was darkened. Professing to be wise, they became fools, and exchanged the glory of the incorruptible God for an image in the form of corruptible man and of birds and four-footed animals and crawling creatures. Therefore God gave them over in the lusts of their hearts to impurity, so that their bodies would be dishonored among them. For they exchanged the truth of God for a lie, and worshiped and served the creature rather than the Creator, who is blessed forever. Amen. For this reason God gave them over to degrading passions; for their women exchanged the natural function for that which is unnatural, and in the same way also the men abandoned the natural function of the woman and burned in their desire toward one another, men with men committing indecent acts and receiving in their own persons the due penalty of their error. And just as they did not see fit to acknowledge God any longer, God gave them over to a depraved mind, to do those things which are not proper, being filled with all unrighteousness, wickedness, greed, evil; full of envy, murder, strife, deceit, malice; they are gossips, slanderers, haters of God, insolent, arrogant, boastful, inventors of evil, disobedient to parents, without understanding, untrustworthy, unloving, unmerciful; and although they know the ordinance of God, that those who practice such things are worthy of death, they not only do the same, but also give hearty approval to those who practice them. (Romans 1:18–32)

Those blinded by arrogance and unbelief, who suppress the truth in unrighteousness, are pawns in this world overshadowed with demonically inspired Babylonian systems for their destruction. The enemy comes to steal, kill, and destroy (John 10:10), and his Babylonian systems accomplish this goal throughout the whole world in this era. The result *is* the wrath of God in our broken world, and this sets the stage for despair and an attitude of resignation for those who have no hope in Him.

When God's grace is rejected, the only thing that remains are our own devices, our own strength, and our manufactured purposes and the anticipation of failure. This results in our helpless and hopeless pursuits. These false altruisms pursue the salvation of the humanity of the future while discarding the humanity of the day. Carl Sagan was one of the most influential humanistic voices of the last generation that proposed this very purpose. He served as a consultant to NASA and as the David Duncan Professor of Astronomy and Space Sciences and director of the Laboratory for Planetary Studies at Cornell University. He concluded,

> Our planet is a lonely speck in the great enveloping cosmic dark. In our obscurity, in all this vastness, there is no hint that help will come from elsewhere to save us from ourselves. (*Pale Blue Dot: A Vision of the Human Future in Space*)

The reality is opposite from this hopelessness. The heavens do not proclaim the insignificance of man, but they do declare the glory of God (Psalm 19:1). Mr. Sagan's philosophical influence is rampant today in the thinking of those who live in a broken world with the fear that we, humanity, must DO SOMETHING to save ourselves. From the recent fearful projections of a new Ice Age prophesied in the 1970s as settled science, followed by the threats of global warming of the 1980s and 1990s, we now live with daily prophecies of doom from the changing weather. These fears have led to increasing attempts to control global wealth and the human population by diminishing the number of people on Earth and by managing the prosperity of the masses in a spirit of lack.

The Scriptures reveal that humanity has been given a mandate to steward God's creation for His glory. The bond servants of God are comforted with the revelation of His provident hand. Fulfilling His cultural mandate results in our great benefit.

> God created man in His own image, in the image of God He created him; male and female He created them. God blessed them; and God said to them, "Be fruitful and multiply, and fill the earth, and subdue it; and rule over the fish of the sea and over the birds of the sky and over every living thing that moves on the earth." (Genesis 1:27–28)

Those who trust in God are blessed with the revelation of this anthropic principle introduced in Genesis. God's creation is for His glory and man's *(anthropic)* benefit. We trust that He has blessed us with life and has gifted us with His creation. The minuscule physical parameters required for our survival on this planet and within this environment reveal the hand of God, His provision and keeping power. This wisdom is exhorted in Proverbs for our confidence in this place of dependence on God for survival.

> Incline your ear and hear the words of the wise, and apply your mind to my knowledge; For it will be pleasant if you keep them within you, That they may be ready on your lips. *So that your trust may be in the* LORD, I have taught you today, even you. Have I not written to you excellent things of counsels and knowledge, *To make you know the certainty of the words of truth* That you may correctly answer him who sent you? (Proverbs 22:17–21, emphasis added)

The apostle Peter also addressed this lack of wisdom in the first century with a reminder for the issue that has come to the surface in every century since. The grace and mercy of God are inherent in His judgment. They keep us in this interim age while at the same time increase the opportunity for many more to come into the Kingdom.

> Know this first of all, that in the last days mockers will come with their mocking, following after their own lusts, and saying, "Where is the promise of His coming? For ever since the fathers

fell asleep, all continues just as it was from the beginning of creation." For when they maintain this, it escapes their notice that by the word of God the heavens existed long ago and the earth was formed out of water and by water, through which the world at that time was destroyed, being flooded with water. But by His word the present heavens and earth are being reserved for fire, kept for the day of judgment and destruction of ungodly men. But do not let this one fact escape your notice, beloved, that with the Lord one day is like a thousand years, and a thousand years like one day. The Lord is not slow about His promise, as some count slowness, but is patient toward you, not wishing for any to perish but for all to come to repentance. But the day of the Lord will come like a thief, in which the heavens will pass away with a roar and the elements will be destroyed with intense heat, and the earth and its works will be burned up. Since all these things are to be destroyed in this way, what sort of people ought you to be in holy conduct and godliness, looking for and hastening the coming of the day of God, because of which the heavens will be destroyed by burning, and the elements will melt with intense heat! But according to His promise we are looking for new heavens and a new earth, in which righteousness dwells. Therefore, beloved, since you look for these things, be diligent to be found by Him in peace, spotless and blameless, and regard the patience of our Lord as salvation. (2 Peter 3:3–15a)

The mockers question, accuse, forget, and cherry-pick what they want to remember. They are blinded by their agnosticism. They misunderstand God's grace and mercy and do not fear the Lord. But it is clear that in His time, a measured time, the fullness of time, He will bring the consummation of His judgment on the elements again. These who mock also refuse to acknowledge the cataclysmic judgment of the past flood and will not turn their hearts to Him Who will protect them from the prepared and yet-to be-released conclusion of judgment on sin and death in the near future.

The questions and doubts have proliferated in fallen humanity. They are everywhere. God's judgment is in the earth. I have been privileged to travel to many nations and experience many different cultures. Before I was drafted to serve in the military, I had only known the world from my young and blessed American vantage point. Now that I have experienced dozens of languages and cultures with their own histories, I more clearly recognize demonically influenced lifestyles and their consequences. I have come to realize that we in the United States live in a Disneyland of entertainment and comforts. We are truly a blessed nation. The gratitude and awareness of this blessing has been lost by too many in their childish expectations and demands of the current entitlement culture. It appears that our culture has come to believe that peace, prosperity, and opportunity are demanded rights to be grasped rather than bestowed blessings to be received and appreciated. The greater our departure from the gracious foundations that have afforded us these blessings, the faster our decline into the darkness of the Babylonian systems that have dominated world history from the beginning. Demanded entitlements produce deadly entanglements. These deceptions open humanity to accept the unacceptable and result in even greater tribulation.

Fellow Companion

As stated before, John includes his own participation in this world's tribulation in the ninth verse of the opening chapter. He identifies himself as a fellow brother and companion in three distinct things.

> I, John, your brother and fellow partaker in the tribulation and kingdom and perseverance which are in Jesus, was on the island called Patmos because of the word of God and the testimony of Jesus. I was in the Spirit on the Lord's day, and I heard behind me a loud voice like the sound of a trumpet ... (Revelation 1:9–10)

First, he acknowledges the ongoing result of God's judgment on sin with his phrase "in the tribulation." He lives his life, not in anticipation of a coming tribulation, but in the ongoing tribulation of life.

Second, he proclaims the gospel and the reality of this age by including "and kingdom." The tension of this age, an inaugurated eschatology, acknowledges that the Kingdom of God is in our midst (Luke 17:21), but its ultimate expression is yet to be consummated.

John's final phrase exposes the difficulty of our brief lives in the time between Jesus first coming and His second coming with the conclusion "and patience of Jesus Christ." Again, He was not fearfully looking to the future for a tribulation to come but acknowledges the tribulation of this life with a challenge to be faithful to the end.

This is an important foundation for reading and applying The Revelation to our lives and for the lives of all Christians in "these last days" between Christ's first coming and His second coming. These words were applicable to the saints in the first century and to all the saints in every century since. Jesus included us in His encouraging words spoken to the disciples in His earthly ministry:

> These things I have spoken to you, that in Me you may have peace. In the world you will have tribulation; but be of good cheer, I have overcome the world. (John 16:33)

The Gospel of Jesus Christ is the proclamation of His victory. The Unveiling of Jesus Christ has detailed His full story with the consummation of that victory in overcoming the corruption of this world system. We, then, in our brief time on Earth are to take up our cross and follow Him. James refers to this breath of a life like a vapor, a mere puff of smoke (James 4:13–14).

> And He was saying to them all, "If anyone wishes to come after Me, he must deny himself, and take up his cross daily and follow Me." (Luke 9:23)

The Lord's Day

John describes his environment as a place of persecution and isolation, his current cross to bear. This speaks to all Christians that they are to minister in the place where they find themselves. John introduces and includes himself as one being persecuted. He is in fellowship with the church in this tribulation. He is a faithful witness that is persevering in this faith for the Kingdom of God. He gives us some background for our understanding. He reports that he was being detained on the Isle of Patmos, an isolated Roman outpost, for his faith. He boldly announces that he was "in the Spirit" on "the Lord's Day." I suggest that this phrase introduces another possible factor of his persecution.

As early as the fourth century, the phrase "The Lord's Day" had been assigned a meaning that referred to the first day of the week. At that time, Eusebius referenced this phrase in a noncanonical book, *The Teaching of the Twelve Apostles*, known as the *Didache*, where the "Lord's Supper" and the "Lord's Day" are observed together. This early Christian manual for worship and instruction became an influential document and the dominating reference for the current definition of Sunday as the "Lord's Day."

Due to the three centuries between the life of John and the assigned meaning of the Lord's Day as Sunday I would like to suggest another possible indication for John's reference to this day. Keeping in mind the politics of the first century and the use of this phrase in context of that era could open a different meaning of the phrase "The Lord's Day." The primary influence of the first century church as a Jewish sect was its Hebrew roots. As a result, the Sabbath was still the commanded and cultural day of prayer, rest, and celebration. The New Testament documents that the early church began its week in celebration "on the first day of the week" (Acts 20:7; 1 Corinthians 16:2). It would gather for an early morning celebration on Sunday to remember the resurrection of its Lord prior to the week's activities. The church did not dictate a change in worship from Saturday to Sunday until the fourth and fifth centuries. So "The Lord's Day" that John is referring to is probably referring to something other than Sunday.

The history of Caesar Nero in the first century indicates that during his reign a day had been designated each year by the Imperial Cult requiring his subjects to acknowledge him as "Lord and Savior" and proclaim that "Caesar is lord." This imposed sign of yielding to Rome was locally imposed throughout the Empire and was increasingly promoted in the city-states that were vying for Roman favor and wealth. This demand had been developing in the Imperial Cult of the Caesars throughout the Empire and was encouraged by Nero himself. The defined and imposed day of yielding was called the "Day of the Lord." Roman subjects were to bow before a symbol of Rome's Caesar, the flag or crest or a bust of Caesar. They were to burn incense and bow and hail him as lord and the savior of the world.

It is possible that this is the very day that John received the vision of the glorified Christ. This is God's proclamation from heaven to His people contrasting the deception and the imposition of the Babylonian world systems with the Kingdom of God.

> He who sits in the heavens laughs, The Lord scoffs at them. Then He will speak to them in His anger And terrify them in His fury, saying, "But as for Me, I have installed My King Upon Zion, My holy mountain." (Psalm 2:4–6)

The "Revelation in a sentence" (Revelation 1:7) that proceeds this announcement places all things in the proper light.

This phrase could be translated "the Lord's Day" or "the Day of the Lord." Again, the context infers the pronouncement of the victorious Messiah in the midst of a broken world coming to her consummation. Throughout Scripture, "the Day of the Lord" describes any day that the Lord brings judgment and this concludes with "the Great Day of the Lord." This "Great Day" refers to the final conclusion of these judgments on all nations and, in this case, includes the old covenant sacrificial system and the nation of Israel itself, which is fully consummated at the end of the age. Both of these are included in the preceding "Revelation In A Sentence."

The Seven Judgment Announcements of The Revelation

I. Revelation in a Sentence: The First Announcement of Judgment

The introductory verse of revealed judgment serves as "The Revelation in a sentence." It is included in the opening remarks of the introduction, laying the foundation for the results revealed throughout the seven visions recorded by John.

> Behold He is coming with the clouds, and every eye will see Him, even those who pierced Him; and all the tribes of the earth will mourn over Him. So it is to be. Amen. "I am the Alpha and the Omega," says the Lord God, "who is and who was and who is to come, the Almighty." (Revelation 1:7–8)

This announcement in the introduction of The Revelation of Jesus Christ is the intended focal point of the Unveiling, reflecting His moral nature, attributes, and ministry and its completion. Jesus intends that we see this first—that we realize His intention—that we anticipate His return. This verse serves as the eyepiece for a telescopic view of all the prophetic judgments that will follow. I suggest that it serves as a comprehensive, though condensed, disclosure of the ministry of Jesus Christ, His fulfilled purpose, the consummation of the ages, and the judgment He releases and concludes throughout the seven visions and the announced judgment scenarios. This announcement was intended for the first century and every century that would follow until His coming is realized. It exposes the fulfillment of the warnings and prophesies of God for judgment, on the nation of Israel specifically and on all the nations generally. The parallel and fulfilling visions bring a conclusion to the Word of God concerning His covenants and His people as well as a conclusion for those who reject Him.

THE UNVEILING

This verse serves as the eyepiece for a telescopic view of all the prophetic judgments that will follow.

Throughout the Old Testament, God's people were warned of the consequences of their sin of disobedience and unbelief. Their idolatry was revealed as a foolish pursuit and would result in their demise, they chose poorly. God continually reminded them that He would retain a remnant of faithful ones and added that He would graft in the believing Gentiles to His holy nation, a chosen race, a royal priesthood, a people for His own possession (1 Peter 2:9).

Daniel the prophet was given the apocalyptic visions he recorded in response to his prayer for the restoration of his nation following the chastisement of God in judgment. He was soon overwhelmed with the received answer, a revelation of the next few centuries and the introduction of the end of the age (Daniel 9:20-27). He saw that the seventy years prophesied by Jeremiah was coming to an end and sought the Lord on the completion of this era of judgment. He was clearly informed of the conclusion of the current era of judgment under Babylon, but then he was shown the continued disobedience of his people resulting in the ongoing subjection to a series of Gentile nations. This is the reason for his sickened response (Daniel 10:8). The current Babylonian domination would be followed by the Medo-Persian Empire. This blessed but dominating era would be followed by yet another kingdom. The third ruling Greek empire would include a precursor to the ultimate judgment on Jerusalem with the rise of Antiochus Epiphanes and his demonically inspired desire for Jerusalem. Jesus referred to this event in His prophecy of the final destruction of the temple and Jerusalem. Finally, the most violent and dominating force, the Roman Empire, would rise and be in power at the coming of Messiah. These visions were given to Daniel and interpreted for him and for us. His seventy weeks prophecy, yet another message in sevens, details a precise series of events leading to this momentous provision. They detail and lead up to the introduction and death of the Messiah and conclude in the destruction of the temple and of the City of Jerusalem. The detail of these centuries is testimony to the sovereign source of these words.

> So you are to know and discern that from the issuing of a decree to restore and rebuild Jerusalem until Messiah the Prince there will be seven weeks and sixty-two weeks; it will be built again, with plaza and moat, even in times of distress. Then after the sixty-two weeks the Messiah will be cut off and have nothing, and the people of the prince who is to come will destroy the city and the sanctuary. And its end will come with a flood; even to the end there will be war; desolations are determined. (Daniel 9:25-26)

The vision of Daniel's "seventy weeks" is a key to understand the judgment of God on the nation of Israel and the old sacrificial system of weak men and weak blood. The context of the vision is the conclusion of judgment on Israel and the introduction of Messiah in humanity and His earthly ministry and sacrifice. God's final word is not one of failure but of fulfillment.

The precursor of focused judgment on Jerusalem is realized by the abomination of desolation foreshadowed by the actions of Antiochus Epiphanes of Syria and referenced by Jesus prophetic announcement on Jerusalem and the temple. The reference to and application of this event is where the fit-over glasses of our interpretive systems begin to impose an explanation and define an expectation. I will again refer to a concluding chapter of considerations, entitled "Lenses," to detail these interpretive systems. I suggest that Daniel's vision introduces the timeless and conclusive judgments on both the old sacrificial system and, in parallel, the consummation of the ages.

Seven Points of Focus

Following the prologue of the first six verses in The Revelation the seventh verse is "The Revelation in a sentence" and has seven points:

First, He commands our attention with this imperative statement, "Behold." He says to pay close attention, to be sure to see this. Don't miss this! This is the focus! These facts are clear and follow the command to start with this!

The second point is that "He is coming with the clouds." This introductory phrase is multifaceted and references the two primary judgments. The first judgment is on the failed covenant of the sacrificial system that Jesus had previously announced at the kangaroo court of His prosecution on the night of His passion.

> Now the chief priests and the whole Council kept trying to obtain false testimony against Jesus, so that they might put Him to death. They did not find any, even though many false witnesses came forward. But later on two came forward, and said, "This man stated, 'I am able to destroy the temple of God and to rebuild it in three days.'" The high priest stood up and said to Him, "Do You not answer? What is it that these men are testifying against You?" But Jesus kept silent. And the high priest said to Him, "I adjure You by the living God, that You tell us whether You are the Christ, the Son of God." Jesus said to him, "You have said it yourself; nevertheless I tell you, hereafter you will see THE SON OF MAN SITTING AT THE RIGHT HAND OF POWER, and COMING ON THE CLOUDS OF HEAVEN." (Matthew 26:59–66b)

When Jesus was questioned by the high priest, who was pressing Him for clarity about His claim to be the Son of God, Jesus answered with this truly awesome proclamation in Matthew 26. He identified Himself with the prophecy of Daniel 7:13–14 and Psalm 110:1. It is clear that the high priest fully understood what the Lord Jesus was saying and responded to it by condemning Him to death for blasphemy.

> I kept looking in the night visions, And behold, with the clouds of heaven One like a Son of Man was coming, And He came up to the Ancient of Days And was presented before Him. And to

> Him was given dominion, Glory and a kingdom, That all the peoples, nations and men of every language Might serve Him. His dominion is an everlasting dominion Which will not pass away; And His kingdom is one Which will not be destroyed. (Daniel 7:13–14)

> The LORD says to my Lord: "Sit at My right hand Until I make Your enemies a footstool for Your feet." (Psalm 110:1)

The second judgment is referenced by the angels when announcing His return at the ascension.

> And after He had said these things, He was lifted up while they were looking on, and a cloud received Him out of their sight. And as they were gazing intently into the sky while He was going, behold, two men in white clothing stood beside them. They also said, "Men of Galilee, why do you stand looking into the sky? This Jesus, who has been taken up from you into heaven, will come in just the same way as you have watched Him go into heaven." (Acts 1:9–11)

These two facets, judgment on Jerusalem and the temple and the consummation of the age, are inferred in this announcement of His coming. The image of "the clouds" is referenced throughout Scripture. Historically, "the clouds" have referred to the multitudes that surround the throne and minister to God, or the "hosts" of heaven. They have also referred to the "great cloud of witnesses" that surrounds us. In the original language and context of the Old Testament warfare, this image describes the effects of the galloping horses and marching armies on the fields of battle. Finally, angels on the Mount of Olives exhort the disciples when a cloud receives Jesus out of their sight at His ascension into heaven to expect His return in the same way.

Since there are over 150 references to clouds in the Bible, and while a few refer to clouds in the natural sense, such as pouring forth rain, most of these references have to do with God's presence, His nature, His revelation, His judgment, war, and the nations. Clouds are depicted as the place where God's majesty and presence are recognized in His creation. God has used this statement throughout Scripture as a means to express a lofty residence. The clouds are the chariot of God, as He rides on the "highest heavens" (Psalm 68:33). Finally, there is a very natural expression of the presence of clouds that refers to any disturbance in the atmospheric levels, whether the natural or spiritual dimensions. A disturbance in these areas produces an effect, or clouds. This was also experienced as a result of God's presence in the temple in the seventh month when the ark of the covenant was brought in at Solomon's dedication.

> It happened that when the priests came from the holy place, the cloud filled the house of the LORD, so that the priests could not stand to minister because of the cloud, for the glory of the LORD filled the house of the LORD. (1 Kings 8:10–11)

In summary, the prophetic announcement of His "coming on the clouds" is a multifaceted phrase that acknowledges God's power and glory and His ultimate judgment. This phrase describes the troubling disturbance in God's creation when He breaks into our limited dimensions with His fulfilled and concluding will. The inclusion of these two ages that come to their conclusion in God's judgment are revealed as "in that day," and further exposes the reflective and parallel reality of God's revealed judgment on these ages.

I suggest that the narrowing of these events to either a completely past and fulfilled event (preterist) or something yet to be realized (futurist) results in a diminishing of the words used and the heavenly perspective unveiled. This is reinforced by the language the Holy Spirit included in these apocalyptic announcements suggesting the inclusion of both events. God does not need nor does He employ hyperbole to make Himself clear. Apocalyptic literature cannot be devalued to a form of exaggeration in order to make a point without devaluing all of Scripture to a literary common denominator. It is God's unveiling of truth that challenges our comprehension and should be pursued in this light.

Apocalyptic literature cannot be devalued to a form of exaggeration in order to make a point without devaluing all of Scripture to a literary common denominator.

The third point in this sentence is the descriptive and timeless inclusion that "Every eye will see him." This is the prophetic announcement of the testimony of these events. The inclusion of the past, present, and future again reflects the heavenly perspective. This is referenced as a single description of an event that occurs in both eras. Both ages come to a close with catastrophic judgment as they are expanded and opened throughout the remaining visions of The Revelation. None will be excluded from the reality and conclusion of both final judgments.

The fourth point is the inclusion of the past, the guilty, and the ransomed: "even those who pierced Him." Since we are all included in the responsibility for His death, we are also included in this statement of the past. Those who witnessed the first conclusive judgment on Jerusalem and the temple are mentioned both in the experience of Titus's invasion as all in Jerusalem either escaped or were killed in this siege. This is a historical reality that fulfilled a prophetic expectation: "Truly I say to you, this generation will not pass away until all these things take place" (Matthew 24:34).

Every eye in and around Jerusalem saw the end of the sacrificial system with the total destruction of the city and the temple, and now we look back on that historic reality. And then, every eye will see Jesus in His second coming at the end of the age. This event will occur in the undivided spiritual and natural dimensions. It will be experienced by all, as prophesied here, "every eye," including those in the past, "even those who pierced Him."

The fifth point of this statement includes "all the tribes of the earth will mourn over Him." This infers a spiritual dimension to the event that includes a reality not yet realized and all souls of all families at the end of the age. The judgment seen then includes first the nation of Israel and second the judgment that will fall on this world and her Babylonian systems. The first refers to God's announced judgment on the nation of Israel by the prophets and then by Jesus announcement in Matthew 23:37–24:51 and restated in Luke 21:3–24. Both of these accounts prophesy the destruction of Jerusalem and the temple. The second reveals the prophesied final judgment at the end of this age.

The sixth point is a concluding "Amen." This is God's strong affirmation, the authoritative "so be it"—a finality to God's conclusive end of the judgment of death that was forewarned in the garden and has been realized throughout man's history.

The seventh point, the "I Am," is a reiteration of the timeless source that establishes this as a done deal!

> "I am the Alpha and the Omega," says the Lord God, "who is and who was and who is to come, the Almighty." (Revelation 1:8)

Jesus includes the infinity of His being and the reality that all time fits in the span of His hand. All the volition of men and angels exists under the overall rule of His sovereignty. He is not bound by time but rules over it and operates within it. Our past, present, and future are tied up in Him and His pronouncement. Those in the past, those in the present (the initial audience), and those in the future are all included in a miraculous spiritually dimensional aspect that includes all of creation.

> Who has measured the waters in the hollow of His hand, And marked off the heavens by the span, And calculated the dust of the earth by the measure, And weighed the mountains in a balance And the hills in a pair of scales? (Isaiah 40:12)

Since these words were heard and written, centuries have passed. There has been the initial fulfillment in the destruction of Jerusalem and the temple. Jesus prophesied this specific event and its timing in His prophecy of woes in Jerusalem prior to His crucifixion.

> Truly I say to you, all these things will come upon this generation. Jerusalem, Jerusalem, who kills the prophets and stones those who are sent to her! How often I wanted to gather your children together, the way a hen gathers her chicks under her wings, and you were unwilling. Behold, your house is being left to you desolate! For I say to you, from now on you will not see Me until you say, "Blessed is He Who comes in the Name of the Lord!" (Matthew 23:36-39)

The ongoing judgment in the earth includes this prophesied judgment and all the wrath of God revealed from heaven against ungodliness and unrighteousness of men who suppress the truth in unrighteousness (Romans 1:18). The "Revelation in a sentence" at the beginning of the unveiling of Jesus Christ is the focal point of The Revelation and serves the following prophecies as the eyepiece is to a telescopic view, even to the end. It is a comprehensive, though condensed, disclosure of the ministry of Jesus Christ, His fulfilled purpose, the consummation of the age, and the judgment He brings.

II. Warning to the Seven Churches: The Second Announcement of Judgment

The second announced judgment was expressed in Jesus' warning to the churches as detailed in Key #2 The Church: The Audience of The Revelation. These seven existing churches with their ongoing problems faced a real threat. Jesus' exhortations and resulting judgments are specific to them and applicable to all churches throughout this age. These warnings have already been realized in the churches of Asia Minor and are being realized in His church today.

> To Ephesus: If they would not repent from turning from their first love, His judgment would result in the removal of the lampstand of His presence.

> To Smyrna: In their ongoing tribulation, they would need to be faithful unto death.

To Pergamos: If they would not repent from the teachings of Balaam and the Nicolaitans, their judgment would be self-induced as they reject Him and He would make war with them with the sword of His mouth.

To Thyatira: If they continued to tolerate the woman Jezebel, who calls herself a prophetess, He warned them:

Behold, I will throw her on a bed of sickness, and those who commit adultery with her into great tribulation, unless they repent of her deeds. And I will kill her children with pestilence, and all the churches will know that I am He who searches the minds and hearts; and I will give to each one of you according to your deeds. (Revelation 2:22–23)

To Sardis: If they would not wake up and strengthen the things that remain and repent, He warned them, "I will come like a thief, and you will not know at what hour I will come to you" (Revelation 3:3b).

To Philadelphia: He does not warn of a judgment on them but exhorts them to persevere in the faith in the judgment that surrounds them.

To Laodicea: The church is accused of being lukewarm and, therefore, nauseating to Jesus Himself. He exposes them and counsels them,

So because you are lukewarm, and neither hot nor cold, I will spit you out of My mouth. Because you say, "I am rich, and have become wealthy, and have need of nothing," and you do not know that you are wretched and miserable and poor and blind and naked, I advise you to buy from Me gold refined by fire so that you may become rich, and white garments so that you may clothe yourself, and that the shame of your nakedness will not be revealed; and eye salve to anoint your eyes so that you may see. Those whom I love, I reprove and discipline; therefore be zealous and repent. (Revelation 3:16-19)

The Church has already come through judgment in Christ in that all our judgment has been absorbed in Him. However, whenever we choose to reject the propitiation (favor) of His provision, we then step out from under His umbrella of protection from the wrath of God that has been released in the earth. Jesus' words to the seven churches should awaken our hearts today to live in His holiness.

Therefore do not be partakers with them; for you were formerly darkness, but now you are Light in the Lord; walk as children of Light (for the fruit of the Light consists in all goodness and righteousness and truth), trying to learn what is pleasing to the Lord. Do not participate in the unfruitful deeds of darkness, but instead even expose them; for it is disgraceful even to speak of the things which are done by them in secret. But all things become visible when they are exposed by the light, for everything that becomes visible is light. For this reason it says, "Awake, sleeper, And arise from the dead, And Christ will shine on you." Therefore be careful how you walk, not as unwise men but as wise, making the most of your time, because the days are evil. (Ephesians 5:7-16)

III. The Seven Seals and Seven Trumpets: The Third Announcement of Judgment

The third announced judgment is all-inclusive. The heavenly perspective of God's released judgment is revealed as the fulfilled and realized consequence of God's warning. This heavenly vision is documented for us in chapters four through eleven. It begins in the throne room of God and reveals the Lamb of God slain from the foundation of the world. Since He is the only One capable of paying the redemption price, He is the only One worthy to release the judgment on mankind. Again, the promise of this released judgment was spoken in Genesis as a consequence of Adam's disobedience.

> The LORD God commanded the man, saying, "From any tree of the garden you may eat freely; but from the tree of the knowledge of good and evil you shall not eat, for in the day that you eat from it you will surely die." (Genesis 2:16–17)

The unveiling of this judgment is seen here as a sequence of increasing intensity as the seals are broken and the restrained judgment is released. The grace and mercy of God are evident in His patience with us over the span of time. God's mercy is revealed in His seeming delay in order that the number of souls included would increase, not wishing for any to perish.

> The Lord is not slow about His promise, as some count slowness, but is patient toward you, not wishing for any to perish but for all to come to repentance. (2 Peter 3:9)

The first four seals are described as horsemen, a symbol that signifies forward movement. They are released in sequence and continue to march through history until the end of this age.

The First Seal

The judgment of human government is seen as a horseman on a white horse: "I looked, and behold, a white horse, and he who sat on it had a bow; and a crown was given to him, and he went out conquering and to conquer" (Revelation 6:2).

The first result of rejecting the government of God released the delegated but perverse government of man, a false Christ. All authority is delegated authority (Romans13:1). The rider was given a bow representing power and a crown representing authority. This vision reveals the corruption of human governments that ultimately rule with violence and strength. The kingdoms of this world produce an authoritarian injustice. The motivations of human authorities, as seen in today's politicians, are to gain and maintain power. Their primary tool to accomplish this is manipulation of authority—political intrigue and military aggression.

There are some who begin to govern with good motives, but very few can function in this temporal and delegated power structure and maintain the unselfish motive of a statesman. The desire to continue in power is deceptive and selfish, resulting in politicians who become more concerned about the next election rather than the next generation. The values of this human system of government are based on money, sex, and power. This is opposite of the Kingdom of God in which faith, hope, and love abide. This white horse, the very appearance of the good intentions of order and justice, has produced many violent leaders, resulting in wars of expanding and protecting kingdoms, "conquering and to conquer."

The Second Seal

The reaction to the first horseman and its resulting human oppression is the second horseman of anarchy and chaos, rebellion and civil wars. This has produced an unending series of wars "taking peace from the earth."

> And another, a red horse, went out; and to him who sat on it, it was granted to take peace from the earth, and that men would slay one another; and a great sword was given to him. (Revelation 6:4)

The so-called peace of the first century, the *Pax Romana* (Latin for the "Roman Peace"), forced the Empire's authoritarian will on all the nations under its grasp. This is the peace the world offers: a temporary submission to the will of the empire at the end of a sword. This vision is the horseman on a red horse marching through human history. The reaction to injustice and the rebellion of those who vie for power continually take peace from the earth and produce untold number of deaths. This deadly horse has stomped through human history from the days of Cain and Lamech and continuing through the initiation of first Babylonian kingdom of Nimrod, even to the end of days. These imposing human authorities continue to produce a rebellious reaction resulting in anarchy and in more death. This is described in this ongoing vision of judgment.

The Third Seal

The next horseman revealed and released is the black horse of economic injustice represented by the rider with scales in his hand and his proclamation. The hypocrisy of the appearance of a just measure is revealed in the proclamation of market manipulations of those in power.

> When He broke the third seal, I heard the third living creature saying, "Come." I looked, and behold, a black horse; and he who sat on it had a pair of scales in his hand. And I heard something like a voice in the center of the four living creatures saying, "A quart of wheat for a denarius, and three quarts of barley for a denarius; and do not damage the oil and the wine." (Revelation 6:5–6)

The fruit of the first two horsemen galloping across human history has produced an economy of the powerful filled with greed and injustice based on the tension of that power. The currency of human government is the accumulation of power that controls the outcome of human efforts. The result of this accumulation is the control of land and its wealth. The selfish manipulations of that wealth, in a broken world dominated by a spirit of lack due to its rebellion to God, produces more violence and increased injustice, resulting in famine and pestilence. Those who can accumulate wealth want to keep it. They want to control it and believe they deserve it. This produces injustice, poverty, and corruption at every level of the world's economic systems. The inequity is displayed in the valuation for daily bread and the protection of luxuries. The rich get richer, and the poor get poorer.

The Fourth Seal

The last horseman is revealed as the gray, or ashen, horse of death. The result of the violence and injustice of a broken world has produced a human history filled with death and the place of the dead. The accumulation of dead souls is described in Scripture as temporary. There is a separation between the righteous and the unrighteous with a great gulf between them. Jesus has given us some insight of the place of the dead prior to His resurrection in His story of Lazarus and the rich man and His promise to the penitent thief. All those from Adam to Christ had looked forward in faith to God's promised remedy even as all can look back in faith to the cross now.

> I looked, and behold, an ashen horse; and he who sat on it had the name Death; and Hades was following with him. Authority was given to them over a fourth of the earth, to kill with sword and with famine and with pestilence and by the wild beasts of the earth. (Revelation 6:8)

This forth horseman of the apocalypse marches through history and reveals the result of death from violent sources. All humanity lives in the continuing dread of violence, disease, famine, epidemics, and pandemics as all men will die as a consequence of sin. This broken seal reveals that as many as one fourth of the human population dies as a result of violence and hunger and disease.

> And inasmuch as it is appointed for men to die once and after this *comes* judgment, (Hebrews 9:27)

Many die violently as a direct result of the consequences of the release of the first three horsemen. They were loosed on the earth as a consequence to sin. This is the judgment of God on the sinfulness of man. For the wrath of God is revealed from heaven (Romans 1:18)!

The Fifth Seal

When this seal is broken, we then see the consequence of the adversary's enmity: martyrdom.

> When the Lamb broke the fifth seal, I saw underneath the altar the souls of those who had been slain because of the word of God, and because of the testimony which they had maintained; and they cried out with a loud voice, saying, "How long, O Lord, holy and true, will You refrain from judging and avenging our blood on those who dwell on the earth?" And there was given to each of them a white robe; and they were told that they should rest for a little while longer, until the number of their fellow servants and their brethren who were to be killed even as they had been, would be completed also. (Revelation 6:9–11)

This accumulation of the martyrs is a casualty of the war of the seeds that began immediately following God's prophetic announcement to the serpent in the garden and His selection of Abel as the next in line from the seed of the woman as a "son of God."

> And I will put enmity between you and the woman, And between your seed and her seed; He shall bruise you on the head, And you shall bruise him on the heel. (Genesis 3:15)

The sovereignly separated (holy) lineage of the seed of the woman was God's promise and provision, His human portal into the human race and the target of the serpent's wrath. The mystery of God's remedy continued to unfold through the generations until it was revealed in Christ. The violent results of this enmity have been obvious throughout human history. The spiritual battle is evident, as the adversary has attempted to destroy this seed and ultimately all humanity in order to attack God and oppose His purpose.

This is also the context of the sovereign choices of God revealed throughout Scripture. The holy seed continues through the antediluvian patriarchs listed as the lineage of Noah. This lineage is clearly defined and marked with God's covenant relationship with Abraham, Isaac, and Jacob. The apostle Paul emphasizes this "God defined" lineage in his letter to the Romans concerning the Israelites and their heritage. God's selection is realized in Jacob over Esau, Isaac, and Rebecca's twin sons. He references the prophet Malachi as he describes the mystery in its result.

> The oracle of the word of the LORD to Israel through Malachi. "I have loved you," says the LORD. "But you say, 'How have You loved us?' Was not Esau Jacob's brother?" declares the LORD. "Yet I have loved Jacob; but I have hated Esau, and I have made his mountains a desolation and appointed his inheritance for the jackals of the wilderness." (Malachi 1:1–3)

> That is, it is not the children of the flesh who are children of God, but the children of the promise are regarded as descendants. For this is the word of promise: "At this time I will come, and Sarah shall have a son." And not only this, but there was Rebekah also, when she had conceived *twins* by one man, our father Isaac; for though *the twins* were not yet born and had not done anything good or bad, so that God's purpose according to *His* choice would stand, not because of works but because of Him who calls, it was said to her, "The older will serve the younger." Just as it is written, "Jacob I loved, but Esau I hated." (Romans 9:8–13, emphasis added)

Jacob, later renamed Israel, was chosen by God to father the nation that would serve as His vessel and the type of God's "called people," the church. This is obviously the language of sovereign selection, not of human emotions of love and hate. This does not exclude the remainder of the human race. Rather, it reveals God's mercy and provision in His sovereignty.

Man is made in God's image—*Imago Dei*—and is a spiritual being as a result of the breath of God. There have been no atheists from the beginning, and I contend that there are none today. The varied spiritual expressions of man have produced many religions. These are a direct response of his existence in God's creation. The witnesses of creation and conscience are revealed by the apostle Paul (Romans 1:18–20) and are the loudest voices that a fallen humanity hears, and they demand a response. Separation from the Divine source results in many religious expressions, both of worship (awe) of creation and of guilt (ought) from a troubled conscience. The arrogant heart demands control that deceptively defines and explains away creation as well as callousing the conscience against the sense of guilt toward any god that might impose such a response. Most people have either tried to appease the gods of this world for their favor or they shake their fists and rail at a god they say does not exist. This is seen in the first religious attempts to acknowledge and appease God, whether in faith or in works.

When Cain was demonically inspired to kill Abel, he produced the first martyr, a witness who was slain for the Word of God. Cain attempted to acquire righteousness by his own works rather than the sacrifice of blood. He insisted that the cursed ground that he worked to produce his sacrifice was worthy of its place before God as an acceptable offering. Man-made religion is always a result of self-righteousness and works. On the other hand, Abel offered the innocent blood of a lamb, and this was accepted. In the rejection of his offering, Cain responded in anger and envy, killing Abel. This process of human religion and self-righteousness has produced many martyrs and has continued through the ages, whether this terror is a result of the rage of envy or the deception of demonically inspired religions that promise a paradise to the obedient who would cut the throats of the infidels, "until the number of their fellow servants and their brethren who were to be killed even as they had been, would be completed also" (Revelation 6:11).

The mercy of this judgment is found in the eternal honor and recognition given to these witnesses as well as the realization that there is a limit to their numbers. This will come to an end. But for now, this judgment continues throughout human history until their number is completed.

The Sixth Seal

When Jesus breaks this seal, the end of all judgment has begun. This boulder of prophetic impact plunges into the pool of this world's events. The judgment introduced in this Word is two-fold. As the conclusions of The Revelation are unveiled in "Heaven time" and bring completion to God's judgments on earth's two ages, this seal's broken results express the beginning of the end for them both. It is realized first in the fulfillment of Jesus great prophecy of the destruction of the temple in Jerusalem and finally in the consummation of the age.

The previous five seals have been realized throughout human history. This final seal is introduced as a conclusive catastrophic sequence of events resulting in the consummation of both ages. The "heaven time" perspective complicates and challenges our perception of these events. Since God does not exist "in time" and sees "all time," His unveiling of this conclusive judgment covers both events and appears simultaneously, as revealed in John's disclosure following this seal.

Many of these signs were experienced in the Roman Empire in the first century and were recorded by historians of the day that reported a number of catastrophes. However, the unveiling of these concluding judgments in full produces the end of the natural world. The descriptive events detail the results of global upheaval from an initiating earthquake and the following sequence of events it produces.

> I looked when He broke the sixth seal, and there was a great earthquake; and the sun became black as sackcloth made of hair, and the whole moon became like blood; and the stars of the sky fell to the earth, as a fig tree casts its unripe figs when shaken by a great wind. The sky was split apart like a scroll when it is rolled up, and every mountain and island were moved out of their places. Then the kings of the earth and the great men and the commanders and the rich and the strong and every slave and free man hid themselves in the caves and among the rocks of the mountains; and they said to the mountains and to

the rocks, "Fall on us and hide us from the presence of Him who sits on the throne, and from the wrath of the Lamb; for the great day of their wrath has come, and who is able to stand?" (Revelation 6:12–17)

As the cataclysmic events unfold at the breaking of the sixth seal, a number of other things are unveiled from heaven. Revelation 7 reveals, again in "Heaven Time," the angelic restraint on this unfolding concluding judgment. First is the picture of the four angels stationed at four corners (north-south-east-west) of the earth as they wait for their instructions. It is announced that ultimate judgment will not fall until the full number of bond servants is accounted for and sealed, for God is not slow about His promise (2 Peter 3:9).

This scene is followed by an announcement (Revelation 7:40). John "heard" the number of those who were sealed. The "Heaven time" aspect of this predetermined and complete number acknowledges these bond servants as the complete family of God. The tribal definitions are listed first, excluding the tribal names of Dan and Ephraim. These tribes are symbolic of the complete and governmental number of the family of God, a holy nation that will rule with Him in His creation. The two tribes that are excluded represent the tribal names of those that housed the golden calves of Jeroboam (1 Kings 12:25–29) and therefore symbolize the rejection of God's rule and presence in Jerusalem.

The symbolic number *twelve* is the Biblical number of government. This vision represents God's delegated authority in His creation, His Divine election. The significance of this number as a symbol is reflected in the *twelve* months of the calendar year, the *twelve* patriarchs of the Holy Seed from Adam to Shem and then established in the *twelve* tribes of Israel. This is reinforced through the history of Israel with the *twelve* jewels on the priest's vestments and the inferred measurements and symbols of *twelve* in the construction of the temple. As the tribes began to acquire the Promised Land, there were *twelve* pillars, the *twelve* spies, and the *twelve* stones of dedication. This carries over into the New

Testament when Jesus chose *twelve* apostles. This symbol is concluded in the description of God's people in the New Jerusalem.

This symbol is used, therefore, to represent the complete multitude of *twelve thousand*. The number, *thousand*, is the Biblical round number for a large group, such as, myriad, or ten *thousand*, or a multitude. Numbers greater than this seem to lose relevance as an abstract amount. It is important to realize the symbolic references throughout The Revelation in the use of numbers. They speak volumes and open our understanding to God's greater intent. Numbers are symbols and these pictures are worth a *thousand* words.

In this case, I suggest that the "one hundred and forty-four *thousand*" and the "great multitude" are unique but redundant descriptions of God's people. These are all recognized as God's mixed multitude of faith and those who have come faithfully through the tribulation of this judged world. They are defined as those who are cleansed by the blood of the Lamb, all who had looked forward in faith—from Adam to the cross—for God's promised remedy, and all who now look back on that same event. These are they who "washed their robes and made them white in the blood of the Lamb" (Revelation 7:14b).

> They will hunger no longer, nor thirst anymore; nor will the sun beat down on them, nor any heat; for the Lamb in the center of the throne will be their shepherd, and will guide them to springs of the water of life; and God will wipe every tear from their eyes. (Revelation 7:16-17)

This reveals the fulfilled promise and the eternal paradise of God in His presence and under His care. It is in this dual description of God's holy nation, listed in the tribal names and the great mixed multitude, which no one could count, that the knowledge of the people of faith brings clarity and completion. As detailed in Key #2 The Church: The Audience of The Revelation, some commentators attempt to separate God's people into two distinct groups, ethnic Israel and the church. But the Scriptures are clear that God has separated "a people for His own possession" not by ethnic commonality but by covenant community.

The Seventh Seal

When Jesus breaks this seal, He releases the final blow of judgment that initiates the end. *Seven* is the number of fullness, completion and rest, and this releases the fullness of judgment that will ultimately bring rest. John states that silence falls on heaven for a brief period, as all prayer is concluded and now will be answered in completion. The saints have experienced one of three options in prayer up to this time. God has answered prayer with a yes, no, or not yet. The "yes" prayers are celebrated in their immediate satisfaction or forgotten in the lack of further concern. The "no" prayers are worked through. The "not yet" prayers have accumulated before His throne and will now be answered. Christians have been praying as the Lord instructed for many centuries, specifically, "Thy Kingdom come, Thy will be done on earth as it is in heaven" (Matthew 6:10). Now the Kingdom of God will come on earth as it is in heaven as the Lord instructs the angel to act. The prayers that have touched heaven will now change the earth.

> Then the angel took the censer and filled it with the fire of the altar, and threw it to the earth; and there followed peals of thunder and sounds and flashes of lightning and an earthquake. (Revelation 8:5)

Following this silence, the angels prepare themselves to sound the trumpets to release the final consequence of judgment. As each angel is instructed and released to blow the trumpet, the cascading catastrophic conclusion of judgment falls on creation as detailed in Revelation 8 and 9. This is now the sounding of the *seven* trumpets that signal each release.

The first trumpet: when sounded, it releases devastation on a third of the earth.

The second trumpet: when sounded, it releases devastation on a third of the seas.

The third trumpet: when sounded, it releases devastation on a third of the flowing fresh waters.

> The earth is poisoned from an asteroid named Wormwood. This name is associated with decay and bitterness in the Scriptures. (Proverbs 5:3–5; Lamentations 3:19)
>
> Wormwood is mentioned seven times in the Bible, always with the implication of bitterness. When this breaks through the earth's atmosphere and onto the earth, it produces the result of decay and bitterness.

The fourth trumpet: when sounded, it releases the fruit of an accumulation of such debris in the atmosphere as to filter a third of the light from the sun and moon, casting the earth into darkness.

The fifth trumpet: the dual fulfillment is exposed here first in the fall of Jerusalem and second as the end of days. This is a symbolic description of the Roman assault on Israel during the Jewish wars with Rome. They historically tormented the Jews for five months (May–September AD 66) in their initial attempt at taking Jerusalem. However, the global and cataclysmic insinuation of these words portend a much greater demonically inspired outpouring of judgment, and a nightmarish consequence is released on rebellious humanity.

The sixth trumpet: when this angel sounds, John hears yet another sound coming from the altar of judgment that is before God. The final blows are described that will result in human devastation. In the first century, the Roman armies stationed at the Euphrates River in Syria were commanded to march on to Judea, straight to Jerusalem (late AD 66) where they killed numerous Jews. The historian Josephus records about one million deaths in this siege. This incomprehensible number of warriors is described by first-century historians Josephus and Tacitus. Josephus writes, "Before the sun setting, chariots and troops of soldiers in their armor were seen running about among the clouds, and surrounding of cities."[4] And Tacitus writes, "In the sky appeared a vision of armies in conflict, of glittering armor."[5]

However, the fulfillment of this verse indicates that there will be a war involving more warriors in one place than anything the world has ever seen. The geographic location indicated also focuses on an area that has never seen such a battle. The current rise of powers in that portion of the earth reveal the very possibility. The Euphrates River begins in the mountains of northern Turkey and runs down through Syria, then Iraq, and into the Persian Gulf. This area was the focal point of the violent Islamic caliphate that conquered most of the known world beginning in the seventh century. This is now repeating the process again in the twenty-first century and in the same area. The two hundred million mentioned in this account reference a gathering of all those in this region who have opposed God and describe the oblivion of war that will conclude in their final judgment. This past century has been the deadliest with approximately two hundred million deaths by wars and genocide. The comparison is not lost as we race to the conclusion of this age.

The seventh trumpet: when this angel sounds, the angelic proclamation announces the accomplishment of the Kingdom of God and of His Christ. The forward look "and is to come" is not included in this pronouncement as in past proclamations, indicating the conclusion has come.

> We give You thanks, O Lord God, the Almighty, who are and who were, because You have taken Your great power and have begun to reign. (Revelation 11:17)

The Two Tracks of Consummation

These released judgments, seen in The Unveiling, had been realized in a limited and localized experience in the first century and will be realized in a global and catastrophic experience at the end of the age. Josephus has recorded a number of devastating events in the Roman Empire from natural causes leading up to Mount Vesuvius in AD 79. These "woes" are associated with Titus's destruction of Jerusalem and the temple. History has recorded the volcanic eruptions of the first century and the signs in the heavens. It is this very point of the "Heavenly Perspective" that is disorienting to our natural chronological perspective. However, if considered, it opens the understanding to parallel tracks of fulfillment in both eras. It also helps to comprehend the attempts of commentators to press all the events into a chronological and sequential series of events, either preterist or futurist. The transitional verses of this vision clearly bring one event to a close while opening yet another.

> But in the days of the voice of the seventh angel, when he is about to sound, *then the mystery of God is finished,* as He preached to His servants the prophets. Then the voice which I heard from heaven, I heard again speaking with me, and saying, "Go, take the book which is open in the hand of the angel who stands on the sea and on the land." So I went to the angel, telling him to give me the little book. And he said to me, "Take it and eat it; it will make your stomach bitter, but in your mouth it will be sweet as honey." (Revelation 10:7–9, emphasis added)

The passage that follows this instructive change in focus turns from the overview to the specific. The specific view is of the temple. This is not the conclusive heavenly temple but the last mention of the still-remaining earthly temple under earthly influences. This portion of Scripture details the conclusion of the sacrificial age, Jerusalem and her temple. John is instructed to prophecy again to the bond slaves of God concerning the ultimate judgment on Israel and the failed system of weak men and weak blood. The details of this prophecy mirror the final days of the siege of Jerusalem and the time of the Gentiles. Jerusalem is called Sodom, Egypt, and the place where Jesus was crucified (Revelation 11:8). The Roman invasion began in late AD 66 and ended in August of AD 70, relating to the forty-two months minus the eight months of withdrawal to Rome in November of AD 66 to address the political turmoil.

THE UNVEILING

The Old Covenant has come to a close in the fulfillment and the initiation of the New Covenant. The old sacrificial system is being removed even as Jesus' prophecy of Jerusalem to His disciples on the Mount of Olives is realized. The separation becomes clearer as we note John's words in the explanations and transitions he records. He directs the reader's attention to the focus of his received revelation. The detailed preterist explanations of these events help shine a clear light on the timing, intention, and fulfillment of Jesus' words and their prophetic fulfillment of the consummation of the Old Testament era. However, these preterist explanations come up short on the realization of the consummation of the age and the global impact these judgments rendered. So the dual tracks of consummation are exposed to acknowledge the consummation of both eras.

The mystery of the symbols used here relate to the prophecy of Zechariah but infer a conclusive reference to God's original covenant of blood that served as a portal for the ultimate and new covenant. The Old Covenant and the New Covenant come into fulfillment here as a full and complete testimony on the final judgments on Jerusalem and the temple with the conclusive judgment at the "end of days." The two witnesses are the two olive trees and the two lampstands that stand before the Lord. They fulfill the two-testimony principle of Scripture and the reflection of the Word of God and the testimony of Jesus. The olive trees (representing the people of God before and after the cross) and the anointing from the oil that brings light represent God's witnesses in the earth. The mystical beast of verse seven is detailed more clearly in the next vision and is the demonically inspired attempt to destroy the purpose and people of God.

Author George Peter Holford wrote a detailed report about the fall of Jerusalem in 1805. This document details the realized localized fulfillment of the catastrophes of these trumpets of Revelation in reference to the end of the temple and the sacrificial system of the Old Covenant.

He reports the earthquakes in Rome during Claudius's reign from AD 41 to 54 recorded by Tacitus. And another earthquake recorded during this same reign in Crete, along with recorded earthquakes at Smyrna, Miletus, Chios, and Samos. In Nero's reign, from AD 54 to 68, there was another earthquake at Laodicea, which also devastated Hierapolis and Colossae. Other earthquakes leading up to the destruction of Jerusalem occurred in Rome during the reign of Galba in AD 68–69. The first century was indeed tumultuous with many catastrophic events. Mr. Holford writes,

> *And great earthquakes shall be in divers places."*—Of these significant emblems of political commotions, there occurred several within the scene of this prophecy, and, as our SAVIOUR predicted, in divers places. In the reign of Claudius there was one at Rome, and another at Apamea in Syria, where many of the Jews resided. The earthquake at the latter place was so destructive, that the emperor, in order to relieve the distresses of the inhabitants, remitted its tribute for five years. Both these earthquakes are recorded by Tacitus. There was one also, in the same reign in Crete. This is mentioned by Philostratus, in his Life of Apollonius, who says, that 'there were others at Smyrna, Miletus, Chios, and Samos; in all which places Jews had settled." In the reign of Nero there was an earthquake at Laodicea. Tacitus records this also. It is likewise mentioned by Eusebius and Orosius, who add that Hieropolis and Colose, as well as Laodicea, were overthrown by an earthquake. There was also one in Campania in this reign (of this both Tacitus and Seneca speak ;) and another at Rome in the reign of Galba, recorded by Suetonius; to all which may be added those which happened on that dreadful night When the Idumeans were excluded from Jerusalem, a short time before the siege commenced. "A heavy storm (says Josephus) burst on them during the night violent winds arose, accompanied with the most excessive rains, with constant lightnings, most tremendous thunderings, and with dreadful roarings of earthquakes. It seemed (continues he) as if the system of the world had been confounded for the destruction of mankind; and one might well conjecture that these were signs of no common events.

Our LORD predicted *"famines"* also. Of these the principal was that which Agabus foretold would happen in the days of Claudius, as related in the Acts of the Apostles. It begun in the fourth year of his reign, and was of long continuance. It extended through Greece, and even into Italy, but was felt most severely in Judea, and especially at Jerusalem, where many perished for want of bread. This famine is recorded by Josephus also, who relates that "an assaron of corn was sold for five drachmae" (i.e. about 3 1/2 pints for 3s. 3d.) It is likewise noticed by Eusebius and Orosius. To alleviate this terrible calamity, Helena, queen of Adiabena, who was at that time in Jerusalem, ordered large supplies of grain to be sent from Alexandria; and Izates, her son, consigned vast sums to the governors of Jerusalem, to be applied to the relief of the more indigent sufferers. The Gentile Christian converts residing in foreign countries, also sent, at the instance of St. Paul, liberal contributions, to relieve the distresses of their Jewish brethren. (I Corin. xvi. 3.) Dion Cassius relates that there was likewise a famine in the first year of Claudius which prevailed at Rome, and in other parts of Italy; and, in the eleventh year of the same emperor, there was another, mentioned by Eusebius. To these may be added those that afflicted the inhabitants of several of the cities of Galilee and Judea, which were besieged and taken, previously to the investment of Jerusalem, where the climax of national misery, arising from this and every other cause, was so awfully completed.

Our Lord adds *"pestilences"* likewise. Pestilence treads upon the heels of famine, it may therefore reasonably be presumed, that this terrible scourge accompanied the famines which have just been enumerated. History, however, particularly distinguishes two instances of this calamity, which occurred before the commencement of the Jewish war. The first took place at Babylon about A.D. 40, and raged so alarmingly, that great multitudes of Jews fled from that city to Seleucia for safety, as hath been hinted already. The other happened at Rome

A.D. 65, and carried off prodigious multitudes. Both Tacitus and Suetonius also record, that similar calamities prevailed, during this period, in various parts of the Roman empire. After Jerusalem was surrounded by the army of Titus, pestilential diseases soon made their appearance there to aggravate the miseries, and deepen the horrors of the siege. They were partly occasioned by the immense multitudes which were crowded together in the city, partly by the putrid effluvia which arose from the unburied dead, and partly from spread of famine.

Our Lord proceeded, *"And fearful sights and great signs shall there be from heaven."* Josephus has collected the chief of these portents together, and introduces his account by a reflection on the strangeness of that infatuation, which could induce his countrymen to give credit to impostors, and unfounded reports, whilst they disregarded the divine admonitions, confirmed, as he asserts they were, by the following extraordinary *signs*:

1. "A meteor, resembling a sword, hung over Jerusalem during one whole year." This could not be a comet, for it was stationary, and was visible for twelve successive months. A sword too, though a fit emblem for destruction, but ill represents a comet.
2. "On the eighth of the month Zanthicus, (before the feast of unleavened bread) at the ninth hour of the night, there shone round about the altar, and the circumjacent buildings of the temple, a light equal to the brightness of the day, which continued for the space of half an hour." This could not be the effect of lightning, nor of a vivid aurora borealis, for it was confined to a particular spoil and the light shone unintermittedly thirty minutes.
3. "As the High Priest were leading a heifer to the altar to be sacrificed, she brought forth a lamb, in the midst of the temple." Such is the strange account given by the historian. Some may regard it as a "Grecian fable," while others may think that they discern in this prodigy

THE UNVEILING

a miraculous rebuke of Jewish infidelity and impiety, for rejecting the ANTITYPICAL Lamb, who had offered Up Himself as an atonement, "once for all," and who, by thus completely fulfilling their design, had virtually abrogated the Levitical sacrifices. However this may be, the circumstances of the prodigy are remarkable. It did not occur in an obscure part of the city, but in the temple; not at an ordinary time, but at the Passover, the season of our LORD'S crucifixion in the presence, not of the vulgar merely, but of the High Priests and their attendants, and when they were leading the sacrifice *to the altar.*

4. "About the sixth hour of the night, the eastern gate of the temple was seen to open without human assistance." When the guards informed the Curator of this event, he sent men to assist them in shutting it, who with great difficulty succeeded.—This gate, as hath been observed already, 'Was of solid brass, and required twenty men to close it every evening. It could not have been opened by a "strong gust of wind," or a slight earthquake;" for Josephus says, it was secured by iron bolts And bars, which were let down into a large threshold; consisting of one entire stone."

5. "Soon after the feast of the Passover, in various parts of the country, before the Setting of the sun, chariots and armed men were seen in the air, passing round about Jerusalem." Neither could this portentous spectacle be occasioned by the aurora borealis, for it occurred before the setting of the sun ; or merely the fancy of a few villagers, gazing at the heavens, for it was seen in various parts of the country.

6. "At the subsequent feast of Pentecost, while the priests were going, by night, into the inner, temple to perform their customary ministrations, they first felt, as they said, a shaking, accompanied by an indistinct murmuring, and afterwards voices as of a multitude, saying, in a

distinct and earnest manner, "LET US DEPART HENCE." This gradation will remind the reader of that awful transaction, which the feast of Pentecost as principally instituted to commemorate. First, a shaking was heard; this would naturally induce the priests to listen: an unintelligible murmur succeeds; this would more powerfully arrest their attention, and while it was thus awakened arid fixed, they heard, says Josephus, the voices as of a multitude, distinctly pronouncing the words "LET US DEPART HENCE."—And accordingly, before the period for celebrating this feast returned, the Jewish war had commenced, and in the space of three years afterwards, Jerusalem was surrounded by the Roman army, the temple converted into a citadel, and its sacred courts streaming with the blood of human victims.

7. As the last and most fearful omen, Josephus relates that one Jesus, the son of Ananus, a rustic of the lower class, during the Feast of Tabernacles, suddenly exclaimed in the temple, "A voice from the east a voice from the west—a voice from the four winds—a voice against Jerusalem and the temple—a voice against bridegrooms and brides—a voice against the whole people!" These words he incessantly proclaimed aloud both day and night, through all the streets of Jerusalem, for seven years and five months together, commencing at a time (A.D. 62) when the city was in a state of peace, and overflowing with prosperity, and terminating amidst the horrors of the siege. This disturber, having excited the attention of the magistracy, was brought before Albinus the Roman governor, who commanded that he should be scourged. But the severest stripes drew from him neither tears nor supplications. As he never thanked those who relieved, so neither did he complain of the injustice of those who struck him. And no other answer could the governor obtain to his interrogatories,

but his usual denunciation of "Woe, woe to Jerusalem!" which he still continued to proclaim through the city, but especially during the festivals, when his manner became more earnest, and the tone of his voice louder. At length, on the commencement of the siege, he ascended the walls, and, in a more powerful voice than ever, exclaimed, "Woe, woe to this city, this temple, and this people!" And then, with a presentment of his own death, added," Woe, woe to myself '" he had scarcely uttered these words when a stone from one of the Roman engines killed him on the spot.

Such are the prodigies related by Josephus, and which, excepting the first, he places in the Year immediately preceding the Jewish war. Several of them are recorded also by Tacitus. Nevertheless, it ought to be observed, that they are received by Christian writers cautiously, and with various degrees of credit. Those, however, who are most skeptical, and who resolve them into natural causes, allow the "superintendence of GOD to awaken his people by some of these means." Whatever the fact, in this respect, may be, it is clear that they correspond to our LORD'S prediction of "fearful sights, and great signs from heaven;" and ought to be deemed a sufficient answer to the objector, who demands whether any such appearances are respectably recorded.[6]

IV. The Seven Signs of the War of the Seeds: The Fourth Announcement of Judgment

The third vision describes the judgment of the war of the seeds. This enmity began with God's announcement in the Garden of Eden and is concluded at the end of days. This unveiled judgment begins with the vessel for God's remedy, the woman, who gives birth to the promised Messiah. Each of the seven signs revealed in this vision serves as a key component of the war throughout the history of man and specifically of God's bond servants in the earth. This vision is detailed in the seven facets, the seven visions in The Book of Sevens.

The *first* sign is of the woman who is at enmity with the *second* sign, the dragon of old. When the promised child is born, the *third* sign, there is a threat of annihilation that fails and the judgment continues. The consequence of this released judgment is described as spiritual warfare in the heavenly dimension that affects the earth, the *fourth* sign. The *fifth* sign is a result of this judgment and turmoil, as the demonically inspired human influence arises from the sea of human chaos and anarchy to deceive and destroy many, the beast of the sea. These judgments include, again, the consummation of judgment on Jerusalem and perseverance of the saints.

These judgments also incorporate the historical characters who are represented as the *sixth* sign, the beast that rises from the earth's corrupted systems, concluding the judgment on Jerusalem and the ongoing persecution of the saints. These characters are satanically inspired and empowered in counterfeit signs and wonders to bring destruction to humanity generally and to God's people specifically.

The *Encyclopaedia Romana* has documented a clear and preterist explanation of the impact of Caesar Nero during the era of the "Beast from the sea." This history is very descriptive of the events of the Jewish Wars that immediately preceded the destruction of the temple and the city of Jerusalem.

> During his reign many abuses were severely punished and put down, and no fewer new laws were made ... Punishment was inflicted on the Christians, a class of men given to a new and mischievous superstition. (Suetonius, Nero XVI.2)

The warning given to the original hearers is also reflected in this beast from the earth. The original hearers would understand the literation as a warning of a beast from the earth without specifically naming him. The letters of the Latin, Greek, and Hebrew languages are also represented as numerals. By adding the values of the letters as numbers, that number would represent a meaning. As previously acknowledged, numbers are used throughout The Revelation to convey meaning. The *Encyclopaedia Romana* documents that when the Greek letters of Nero Caesar (*Neron Kaisar*) are transliterated into seven Hebrew letters of (*nrwn qsr*), the numerical of these Hebrew letters equals 666 (50+200+6+50+100+60+200). Since the Greek and Hebrew did not have discreet numbers, the numerical values of the three letters would be expressed as 600, 60, and 6. So the name Nero encoded in the Hebrew for the first century Jewish cult was understood by the Christians receiving The Revelation in Greek.

> Here is wisdom. Let him who has understanding calculate the number of the beast, for the number is that of a man; and his number is six hundred and sixty-six. (Revelation 13:18)

The final judgment, the Lamb with the hosts of heaven, the *seventh* sign, brings a conclusion to the judgment in the earth. The Lamb is revealed as the "Lord of the Harvest."

> Then I looked, and behold, a white cloud, and sitting on the cloud was one like a son of man, having a golden crown on His head and a sharp sickle in His hand. (Revelation 14:14)

This judgment concludes in the final harvest of God's great ingathering represented in the fall Feasts of the Lord.

The reference to sixteen hundred stadia is a strong symbol of God's judgment. This measurement, foreign to us, was a common and comprehensible measurement of distance to the original hearers. The inferred meaning of *forty* times *forty*, or *forty* squared, reflects the consummation of tribulation. Throughout Scripture, the number *forty* refers to a time of testing or trouble. There are nine *forty*-day periods noted in Scripture. There are nine *forty*-day periods in the Hebrew lunar/solar year of 360 days.

Forty, as the number of tribulation, is first noted as the days of rainfall at the flood (Genesis 7:12, 17). Moses was separated from the people of the exodus for *forty* days on two occasions in the giving of the Law (Exodus 24:18; 34:28; Deuteronomy 9:9–18). There were *forty* days of testing for the fearful spies (Numbers 13:25; 14:34). Goliath defied Israel for *forty* days (2 Samuel 17:16). Elijah journeyed to Horeb for *forty* days (1 Kings 19:8). Jonah preached to Nineveh for *forty* days (Jonah 3:4). Christ was tempted in the wilderness for *forty* days following His baptism for righteousness sake (Matthew 4:2; Mark 1:13; Luke 4:2). Finally, the concluding *forty* day period was a glorious testing of convincing proof of Christ's physical resurrection.

> To these He also presented Himself alive after His suffering, by many convincing proofs, appearing to them over a period of forty days and speaking of the things concerning the kingdom of God. (Acts 1:3)

The Scriptural examples of these *forty* day periods were of intense times of testing and the final reference is a multiplication of the number *forty*, *forty* squared, or sixteen hundred.

> For I consider that the sufferings of this present time are not worthy to be compared with the glory that is to be revealed to us. (Romans 8:18)

V. The Seven Bowls: The Fifth Announcement of Judgment

Revelation 15 begins with the sight of another heavenly sign. This one is a conclusive unveiling of the *seven* last plagues.

> Then I saw another sign in heaven, great and marvelous, seven angels who had seven plagues, which are the *last*, because in them the wrath of God is *finished*. (Revelation 15:1, emphasis added)

These *seven* messengers of God disclose yet another facet of the concluding judgment that was released with the *seventh* seal. The all-inclusive and conclusive full display is described as *seven* angels with *seven* bowls pouring out the *seven* plagues to finish the wrath of God, both in Jerusalem and throughout the whole world.

These plagues reflect the plagues that were released on a hardened and rebellious Egypt that opposed God's will with His people at the beginning of their national experience. Now the resistance to God's ultimate will with His people will face the full and concluding wrath of God. Both the enemies of God's will and those that line up with that opposition will face the ultimate judgment and defeat. It concludes with an understatement of the final plague as extremely severe.

The first angel pours out his bowl of wrath on the earth—physical disease as a result of the idolatry revealed as the mark of the beast, those whose loyalty is not with God. This is an unabated suffering of those who reject God's remedy. As initially seen in Ezekiel's prophecy of the Babylonian destruction of Jerusalem, the Lord commanded an angel to place a mark on their foreheads.

> Then the glory of the God of Israel went up from the cherub on which it had been, to the threshold of the temple. And He called to the man clothed in linen at whose loins was the writing case. The LORD said to him, "Go through the midst of the city, *even* through the midst of Jerusalem, and put a mark on the foreheads of the men who sigh and groan over all the abominations which are being committed in its midst." But to the others He said in my hearing, "Go through the city after him and strike; do not let your eye have pity and do not spare. "Utterly slay old men, young men, maidens, little children, and women, but do not touch any man on whom is the mark; and you shall start from My sanctuary." So they started with the elders who *were* before the temple. (Ezekiel 9:3–6)

This mark was God's acknowledgment of the heart of the individual set apart in a symbolic way in a doomed city. This was His emblem of ownership, marked for preservation. This was not a literal mark or tattoo or a technological addition, but the omniscience of God of the heart of man.

The second angel pours out his bowl of wrath into the sea—a putrid judgment representing the death of rebellious humanity as the "sea turns to blood as a dead man."

The third angel pours his bowl of wrath into the rivers—this is the end of the flow of life as the life-giving waters are putrefied.

The fourth angel pours out his bowl of wrath onto the sun—that which has served as life-giving will now be a curse, as God's wrath is reflected in the removal of His protective atmospheric covering, resulting on the scorching of the sun.

The fifth angel pours out his bowl of wrath upon the throne of the beast—the seat of earthly and demonically inspired temporal power is unrestrained in the earth.

The sixth angel pours out his bowl of wrath on the river Euphrates—This symbolic natural boundary is breached as a judgment that represents the separation from the promises of God. This is the river that Abraham crossed from Paddan Aram to the land of Canaan and those who crossed were called "Hebrews", meaning "those who cross."

The seventh angel pours out his wrath upon the air—this is the judgment upon the second heavens in concluding judgment on the fallen humanity and the cursed earth. The final description of this judgment is very clear.

> And huge hailstones, about one hundred pounds each, came down from heaven upon men; and men blasphemed God because of the plague of the hail, because its plague was extremely severe. (Revelation 16:21)

VI. The Doom of Babylon: The Sixth Announcement of Judgment

The sixth judgment is unveiled in the fifth vision as the final blow on the city of Babylon. The angel reveals to John that this is a parenthetical explanation of the ongoing judgment. Babylon is the Biblical name that represents the failed efforts of man and the consequences of these efforts since Nimrod arose as the leader following the flood. Mankind attempted to build an edifice to reach God and protect himself from another flood with a waterproof ziggurat built of fired bricks and asphalt mortar. This building and the accumulation of fearful and religious people represent the social structures of man and the religions of the world.

There are only two religious realities in the earth. The first has a multitude of expressions. Babylon represents this first reality of man's attempt to reach up to God. Man's religious self-righteousness has resulted in numerous works attempting to tilt the scales of good and bad in man's favor to excuse the witness of the guilty conscience. This expression has morphed into more nuanced and sophisticated religions through the centuries that lead to an even greater deception, the acquisition of becoming a god or becoming part of the divine being as the deceiver initially implied (Genesis 3:5).

However, the only acceptable alternative is the faith reality: God reaching down to man. This is the Good News! God did what we could never do. He bridged the unsurpassable gap between the holiness of God and the sinfulness of man. He not only bridged the gap, He paid the ultimate ransom price for our deliverance and in Christ provided access to God restoring the broken relationship caused by man's sin.

The destruction of Babylon represents God's judgment on the attempts of man to use God's creation for his own benefit at the expense of all else. The schemes of the demonically inspired worldly leaders (the rider of the white horse of the first seal) have produced human, social, governmental, educational, medical, financial, and many other so-called civil systems in the earth. These systems provide a means to continue in a fallen world with the appearance of succeeding. These systems have also allowed the finite demonic influences to be multiplied in the nations and generations of the earth.

> And he carried me away in the Spirit into a wilderness; and I saw a woman sitting on a scarlet beast, full of blasphemous names, having seven heads and ten horns. The woman was clothed in purple and scarlet, and adorned with gold and precious stones and pearls, having in her hand a gold cup full of abominations and of the unclean things of her immorality, and on her forehead a name was written, a mystery, "BABYLON THE GREAT, THE MOTHER OF HARLOTS AND OF THE ABOMINATIONS OF THE EARTH." (Revelation 17:3–5,)

This Babylonian system is personified in a way that represents the prostitution of humanity to the ways of demonically inspired corruption. She opposed the will and people of God. She takes all she can from the world and gives nothing in return. She is clothed in the garments of wealth and royalty. The scarlet beast represents the full measure of human empires in the image of the seven heads symbolizing the full measure of human kings and authorities in the image of the ten horns.

The Old Testament warning and the accusation of the nation of Israel that had turned away from God in her idolatry is revealed as an adulterous prostitute. This judgment is, again, a parallel picture on the ultimate judgment on Jerusalem as well as on all the systems of the world. The blood of the martyrs is on the hands of those who have opposed God from the beginning, even the religious systems of the Jews. She also represents the historical Roman Empire to the original hearers. This was the final earthly kingdom that dominated Israel in Daniel's prophecy. She prostituted the position and place of the high priest and the temple. She is represented as riding the beast, her dependence on Rome in the initial fulfillment, and then the systems of the global economy and geopolitical nations of the earth in the conclusion of judgment in the end of days. Her end will come in one day!

VII. The Great White Throne: The Seventh Announcement of Judgment

The final announcement of judgment follows the four "Hallelujahs" of the heavenly hosts as they rejoice at the marriage of the Lamb. The focus of the prostitute of the previous judgment is replaced by the "Bride of Christ." This final scene of judgment is revealed in "Heaven Time" for the saints of God.

John documents the heavenly perspective of both the first and second comings of Christ in this sixth vision. Christ is seen as the victor on the white horse who wages war. He is the only one worthy to break the seals and the wrath that is released is from His mouth. He is clothed in a robe dipped in blood, His blood! This is the garment of His righteousness and our salvation. As with other scenes from the heavenly perspective, the past, the present, and the future are melded together in the vision as God has revealed His plan from the beginning. The great judgment on the earth that results in such devastation and death is described as a feast for the birds. The demonic beings that represent the deception of humanity are seized, bound, and thrown into the lake of fire. Jesus' judgment falls on all who oppose Him.

This final scene of judgment is expressed in conclusive actions covering the same period of time as all previously revealed judgment. Following the enemy's defeat at the cross, he is bound for the duration of "these last days." He has been exposed and defeated. The Holy Spirit has been poured out in the earth, and the church of Jesus Christ has been spreading throughout the earth in authority and victory. The kingdoms of this earth have become the kingdoms of our Lord.

> And Jesus came up and spoke to them, saying, *"All authority has been given to Me in heaven and on earth. Go therefore and make disciples of all the nations, baptizing them in the name of the*

Father and the Son and the Holy Spirit, teaching them to observe all that I commanded you; and lo, I am with you always, even to the end of the age." (Matthew 28:18–20, emphasis added)

This vision reveals that God has not finished with the testing He will accomplish on the earth as Satan is temporarily released for a short time at the end of days. This brief satanic appearance will reveal the hearts of men and prepare them for the final blow of the wrath of God as the sixth and seventh seals are broken and final judgment falls.

Again, we see the accumulation of the martyrs who are recognized before God. The bond servants of God are acknowledged as those who have come alive in Him in the first resurrection. All who are "in Him" and recognized as those baptized in Him have come alive in the first resurrection, "having been buried with Him in baptism, in which you were also raised up with Him through faith in the working of God, who raised Him from the dead" (Colossians 2:12). This is the first resurrection, the fruit of Jesus' resurrection.

> Therefore we have been buried with Him through baptism into death, so that as Christ was raised from the dead through the glory of the Father, so we too might walk in newness of life. (Romans 6:4)

Following the release of Satan is the all-consuming judgment described as the final war. This includes all nations. All that have opposed the Kingdom of God will come to their end in this final judgment. This is the end of the enmity of the serpent.

> And the devil who deceived them was thrown into the lake of fire and brimstone, where the beast and the false prophet are also; and they will be tormented day and night forever and ever. (Revelation 20:10)

The Great White Throne is Jesus recognized place of authority as King and Judge. The books are a representation of His justice in considering all things. He is the ultimate end of all things, and all things must pass through His view. The saints of God have already been judged in the blood of the King on the throne. Their works and words will also pass through His gaze, and only that which is built on Him will survive. All else is consumed in His holiness.

> According to the grace of God which was given to me, like a wise master builder I laid a foundation, and another is building on it. But each man must be careful how he builds on it. For no man can lay a foundation other than the one which is laid, which is Jesus Christ. Now if any man builds on the foundation with gold, silver, precious stones, wood, hay, straw, each man's work will become evident; for the day will show it because it is to be revealed with fire, and the fire itself will test the quality of each man's work. If any man's work which he has built on it remains, he will receive a reward. If any man's work is burned up, he will suffer loss; but he himself will be saved, yet so as through fire. (1 Corinthians 3:10–15)

Failure to survive this judgment is called the second death, the final judgment.

> And if anyone's name was not found written in the book of life, he was thrown into the lake of fire. (Revelation 20:15)

Conclusion

These seven judgments announced in God's unveiling are the overwhelming interest of a fearful and guilty world, like those waiting for a case to be tried. The guilty party has been identified, the accusations have been documented and supported, and the verdict is pronounced with accompanying sentence. After what seems to be a very long wait, the sentence is pronounced and judgment is swiftly meted out, like someone heading for a cliff, continuously moving forward, until a sudden and calamitous conclusion! This is why the sixth key is the most obvious, Judgment: The Result of The Revelation!

The historical novelist and insightful writer of the recent past, Leon Uris, detailed the current and dominant concern for future cataclysm. His novel reflects one of the great atrocities of the twentieth century and warns of future tribulation. His main character is an author who has collected his research and has come to a depressing conclusion. He clearly and prophetically describes the eschatological mind-set of today. He concludes his novel *QB VII* with this following thought:

> In order to fall into a state of depression these days one only had to think about the massive disintegration of the earth and air and water and the moral rot, the greed, and corruption and that endless list of human failures that we were suddenly being made keenly aware of.
>
> Man the predator, the plunderer, the destroyer was coming face to face with the thousands of sins and crimes and there would be an Armageddon in this century. It was all rushing to a terrifying climax.
>
> If we were to catalogue and make charges of the abuses of the human race, if we were to calculate what man had taken and what he owed, then he would have had to declare bankruptcy.
>
> We were now faced with the frightening question of whether or not we were coming to the end of our purpose to live any longer. The old gods and wisdoms failed to provide the answers. And a horrible sense of futility and desperation invaded the upcoming generation.
>
> Great and grand wars were now a thing of the past. There were two super powers in the world, each capable of raining total destruction. Therefore, future wars would have to be fought in compact limited boundaries and under stringent rules.
>
> Now that a great war was out of the question, man seem to need something to replace war. The crux of the problem is that there

exists a basic flaw in the human race and that is man's inevitable drive toward self-extinction.

Instead of war, he has replaced war with things as deadly. He intends to destroy himself by contaminating the air he breaths, by burning and rioting and pillaging, by making a shambles of the institutions and rules of sanity, by mindless extermination of breeds of animals and the gifts of the soil and the sea, by poisoning himself into a slow lethargic death through drugs and dope.

The formal and declared wars have given way to a war directed against himself and his fellow man that is doing the job faster than it was ever done on a battlefield.

Young people have brushed aside and trampled down many old mores and ethical codes. In many cases it was overdue that our society be stripped of hypocrisy and racism and false sexual values. But in their rampage to ring out the old, the young have also brought down the great values and wisdoms and failed to replace them.[7]

He concludes with this poignant statement: "After all, the only thing that is going to save mankind is if enough people live their lives for something or someone other than themselves."

This bleak, cynical outlook pervades the postmodern view of the Western twenty-first-century mind. The absence of Divine revelation leaves a great gaping hole in man's thinking and produces hopelessness in this life. Judgment is inevitable for those whose witnesses against them are creation and conscience. Only in Jesus Christ is that judgment averted, as He has taken it all upon Himself.

Key # 7

RESTORATION: THE PROMISE OF THE REVELATION

> And He who sits on the throne said, "Behold, I am making all things new." And He said, "Write, for these words are faithful and true."
>
> —Revelation 21:5

This final key to opening The Revelation is reflected in the simple statement made by many who find it all too complicated to follow: "We win in the end!" This is true in that our victory is found in Jesus. It is all for His glory and our benefit. The promise from the beginning was one of fellowship with God and life in His creation. The Scriptures reveal to us that it began in a garden, the Garden of Eden—paradise—and all will end in another garden, the dwelling of God with man.

> Now I saw a new heaven and a new earth, for the first heaven and the first earth had passed away. Also there was no more sea. Then I, John, saw the holy city, New Jerusalem, coming down out of heaven from God, prepared as a bride adorned for her husband. And I heard a loud voice from heaven saying, "Behold, the tabernacle of God is with men, and He will dwell with them, and they shall be His people. God Himself will be with them and be their God. And God will wipe away every tear from their eyes; there shall be no more death, nor sorrow, nor crying. There shall be no more pain, for the former things

> have passed away."... Then he showed me a river of the water of life, clear as crystal, coming from the throne of God and of the Lamb, in the middle of its street. On either side of the river was the tree of life, bearing twelve kinds of fruit, yielding its fruit every month; and the leaves of the tree were for the healing of the nations. (Revelation 21:1–4; 22:1–2)

This picture of the regenerative process originally intended in the Garden of Eden is displayed in this description of paradise. God created the human body and it is "fearfully and wonderfully made" with the ability to heal and restore. His provision is seen here as eternal in His eternal Kingdom.

Jesus reveals His intention, His Good News! God has fulfilled His promise. We can choose to live by faith and receive Him and His promise, or we can live in ignorance and fear. The response of the believer is a heart of faith, a willingness to obey and to persevere in this life to its end. His promise is for us. We are brought into the loop—given this insight—so we might live in hope, a life of confident expectation for good. God has revealed His plan and purpose, and in Him we are included.

> But you are a chosen generation, a royal priesthood, a holy nation, His own special people, that you may proclaim the praises of Him who called you out of darkness into His marvelous light; who once were not a people but are now the people of God, who had not obtained mercy but now have obtained mercy. (1 Peter 2:9–10)

Throughout Scripture, God has clearly revealed His twofold purpose to redeem and to restore. Jesus is the "Lamb of God slain from the foundations of the earth" (Revelation 13:8) who has redeemed us from our separation from God, His life, His love, and His purpose. He has restored His delegated authority, the King and His Kingdom, in His creation for His good. The entire Bible is a telling of His story to accomplish this for our benefit, that He might have a people of promise, people who choose Him by love in faith.

This reality is revealed in the first two chapters of Genesis and the last two chapters of Revelation. These Scripture portions serve as the bookends of the Bible to enclose the intention and salvation of God, the restoration of all things, in Him. All the remaining chapters and books tell the story of God winning a people of choice, people of faith, His bond servants. This is God's mission, and we are invited to participate with Him to its conclusion.

The church exists in an inaugurated eschatology: the Kingdom is here, but not yet. Those who are His in the earth have become new in Him, not overhauled or refurbished but brand-new, in the first resurrection (Romans 6:4–5).

> Therefore if anyone is in Christ, he is a *new* creature; the old things passed away; behold, *new* things have come. (2 Corinthians 5:17, emphasis added)

The "new" creation has already begun! This is our realized eschatology. This same Greek word used to describe "new creatures" is the same word used by Jesus to describe His announcement in His Revelation.

> And He who sits on the throne said, "Behold, I am making all things *new*." And He said, "Write, for these words are faithful and true." (Revelation 21:5, emphasis added)

This is the conclusion of the Unveiling. The *three main components of all apocalyptic literature* are amplified in this disclosure: The Revelation concludes with God's *judgment of the wicked* and promises the *reward for the righteous* with an ultimate and complete *restoration*. We are immediately encouraged with the hope of restoration at the introduction of Jesus' Unveiling. His promise is proclaimed in our inclusion and His expression that His servants know.

The description of the glorified Christ is our initial revelation. The pronouncement of blessing is our hopeful expectation. We are assured that the sovereign God is on the throne. He is not reacting to the actions of any other being; rather, He is unfolding His plan.

The *first vision* of the glorified Christ assures His own of the hope of restoration in His promises to them if they continue in Him, and the *second vision* includes the glorified church.

> John to the seven churches that are in Asia: Grace to you and peace, from Him who is and who was and who is to come, and from the seven Spirits who are before His throne, and from Jesus Christ, the faithful witness, the firstborn of the dead, and the ruler of the kings of the earth. To Him who loves us and released us from our sins by His blood—and He has made us to be a kingdom, priests to His God and Father—to Him be the glory and the dominion forever and ever. Amen. (Revelation 1:4-6)

The promises of restoration are included as a confident expectation for those who continue in Him. We have the confidence that we are granted to eat of the Tree of Life in the paradise of God. We will not to be hurt by the second death. The promise of intimacy is expressed in the expectation of receiving some hidden manna, a white stone and a new name. Our purpose is expressed in the promise that we will rule with Him and receive authority over the nations and the morning star. The omniscience of God is expressed in our favor with the promise that we shall be clothed in white garments, our names are written in the Book of Life, and will be confessed before God and the angels. His promise is an eternal one in that He will make us pillars in the temple of God and will write God's Name upon us. Finally, we will sit down with Jesus on His throne.

The restoration, His finished work, is proclaimed in the *second vision* from the throne room of God. He reiterates His promise and intention by announcing for the second time that He has made us to be a kingdom, priests to His God and Father. The second vision adds the disclosure

THE UNVEILING

that we, as creatures of time and creation, will rule and reign in that new creation forever.

> And they sang a new song, saying, "Worthy are You to take the book and to break its seals; for You were slain, and purchased for God with Your blood men from every tribe and tongue and people and nation. You have made them to be a kingdom and priests to our God; and they will reign upon the earth." ... After these things I looked, and behold, a great multitude which no one could count, from every nation and all tribes and peoples and tongues, standing before the throne and before the Lamb, clothed in white robes, and palm branches were in their hands; and they cry out with a loud voice, saying, "Salvation to our God who sits on the throne, and to the Lamb." (Revelation 5:9–10; 7:9–10)

At the conclusion of this second vision, we are encouraged with the promise of consummation, the final conclusion and fulfillment. All heaven announces that God's purpose is complete.

> But in the days of the voice of the seventh angel, when he is about to sound, then the mystery of God is finished, as He preached to His servants the prophets... Then the seventh angel sounded; and there were loud voices in heaven, saying, "The kingdom of the world has become the kingdom of our Lord and of His Christ; and He will reign forever and ever." And the twenty-four elders, who sit on their thrones before God, fell on their faces and worshiped God, saying, "We give You thanks, O Lord God, the Almighty, who are and who were, because You have taken Your great power and have begun to reign." (Revelation 10:7; 11:15–17)

The *third vision* describes the seven signs from the heavenly perspective announcing God's planned purpose of the unfolding drama. The symbols revealed in these characters disclose the challenges and consequences of the volition of God's creatures in broad strokes. The vision concludes with the seventh sign of the victorious Lamb and those He has purchased among men, those who have made themselves pure by His cleansing blood. He comforts those in the midst of this temporary battle with the hope of rest and restoration.

> And I heard a voice from heaven, saying, "Write, 'Blessed are the dead who die in the Lord from now on!'" "Yes," says the Spirit, "so that they may rest from their labors, for their deeds follow with them." (Revelation 14:13)

The *fourth vision* gives a conclusive justification for the final expectation of judgment in the seven bowls of the wrath of God. The early *type* of justice and deliverance of the people of Israel from Egypt is called the "Song of Moses" and is remembered at the end of days.

> And they sang the song of Moses, the bond-servant of God, and the song of the Lamb, saying, "Great and marvelous are Your works, O Lord God, the Almighty; Righteous and true are Your ways, King of the nations! Who will not fear, O Lord, and glorify Your name? For You alone are holy; For all the nations will come and worship before You, for Your righteous acts have been revealed." (Revelation 15:3–4)

The *fifth vision* of the doom of Babylon details the end of the enemies of God and the corrupt governments of man. The victory of the Lamb is concluded with the defeat of the demonically empowered empires of the world that reject the rule of God and threaten His saints.

> These will wage war against the Lamb, and the Lamb will overcome them, because He is Lord of lords and King of kings, and those who are with Him are the called and chosen and faithful. (Revelation 17:14)

The Revelation proclaims a reminder from the psalmist that sees the conclusion of the judgment.

> Rejoice over her, O heaven, and you saints and apostles and prophets, because God has pronounced judgment for you against her. (Revelation 18:20)

> The righteous will rejoice when he sees the vengeance; He will wash his feet in the blood of the wicked. And men will say, "Surely there is a reward for the righteous; Surely there is a God who judges on earth!" (Psalm 58:10–11)

The *sixth vision* discloses the celebration of a great multitude with the fourfold hallelujahs. Praise is shouted, announcing the salvation of God, and worship is expressed by the hosts of heaven. The announcement of the consummation of the marriage of the Lamb as the bride has made herself ready. This is the expectation of those who are His. The restoration of relationship is seen as a marriage. The beginning of the new age is like the honeymoon of the couple with nothing but a hopeful future ahead.

> Then he said to me, "Write, 'Blessed are those who are invited to the marriage supper of the Lamb.'" And he said to me, "These are true words of God." (Revelation 19:9)

This vision gives the overall ministry of the Lamb in the affairs of the earth. He is the King of kings Whose robe is dipped in His own blood. He is the Word of God, and from His mouth comes the sword of His justice. This vision concludes with the fulfillment of His promise for those in His omniscience who have found their life in Him, and their names are written in His Book of Life.

The *seventh vision* is the complete unveiling of His restoration. We anticipate this new heaven and new earth without the chaos of rebellious humanity: "there is no longer any sea." The New Jerusalem is the tabernacle of God and man. The ancient city Jerusalem, named the City of Peace, was a *type* of God dwelling with man in His creation. The New Jerusalem is the fulfillment of that type and requires no temple in that God dwells among His bride.

> And I saw the holy city, new Jerusalem, coming down out of heaven from God, made ready as a bride adorned for her husband. And I heard a loud voice from the throne, saying, "Behold, the tabernacle of God is among men, and He will dwell among them, and they shall be His people, and God Himself will be among them." (Revelation 21:2–3)

The New Jerusalem, the holy city, is seen as coming down out of heaven from God (Revelation 21:10). The glory of God is her glory, and her description reflects the people of God. The number *twelve* is the descriptive number of God's delegated authority in His creation. This is another restoration of the primary and cultural mandate.

> God blessed them; and God said to them, "Be fruitful and multiply, and fill the earth, and subdue it; and rule over the fish of the sea and over the birds of the sky and over every living thing that moves on the earth." (Genesis 1:28)

The use of the symbol of the number *twelve* amplifies the all-encompassing conclusion that describes God's finished work and the restoration of all things. The place of the dwelling of God and man is described as a city with *twelve* gates and *twelve* foundations. It will be *twelve* thousand stadia by *twelve* thousand stadia in dimension. The number *twelve* in *thousands* and squared, as referenced in the *twelve* tribes in *thousands* and squared, infers the complete number of fulfillment. All throughout the city, the number *twelve* is describing the heavenly dwelling of God by the people of God. Jesus is the center; He is the source. His water of life continually flows from the throne of God, and the *twelve* trees of healing and life bear fruit through the *twelve* months of the year for the people of God for eternal life. He restores all things.

> For the kingdom of God is not eating and drinking, but righteousness and peace and joy in the Holy Spirit. (Romans 14:17)

This is the promise of The Revelation. This is our confident expectation. This is the substance of our faith that brings the reality of eternal life into the present. This was the intention of The Unveiling from the first century, disclosed in and by Jesus for His bond servants for this age. The earthly ministry of Jesus Christ is initiated in this proclamation of the presence of the Kingdom of God "in our midst" (Luke 17:21). He was introduced by John the Baptist as the One Who was promised, the One Who brings the Kingdom.

> Now in those days John the Baptist came, preaching in the wilderness of Judea, saying, "Repent, for the kingdom of heaven is at hand." For this is the one referred to by Isaiah the prophet when he said, "The voice of one crying in the wilderness, make ready the way of the Lord, make His paths straight!" (Matthew 3:1–3)

Jesus lays out the foundation of His Kingdom with the descriptions of the eight blessings (beatitudes) of those who pursue it, the very constitution of the Kingdom. *Eight* is the number of new beginnings.

> Blessed are the poor in spirit, for theirs is the kingdom of heaven. Blessed are those who mourn, for they shall be comforted. Blessed are the gentle, for they shall inherit the earth. Blessed are those who hunger and thirst for righteousness, for they shall be satisfied. Blessed are the merciful, for they shall receive mercy. Blessed are the pure in heart, for they shall see God. Blessed are the peacemakers, for they shall be called sons of God. Blessed are those who have been persecuted for the sake of righteousness, for theirs is the kingdom of heaven. Blessed are you when people insult you and persecute you, and falsely say all kinds of evil against you because of Me. Rejoice and be glad, for your reward in heaven is great; for in the same way they persecuted the prophets who were before you. (Matthew 5:3–12)

The restoration of all things results in the inheritance of the saints, the comfort of all those who mourn the losses of the rebellious world. Gentleness will rule rather than violence. Complete satisfaction will finally be realized in being in right standing with God. Mercy is granted and received. Holiness is the way of life and existence in the presence of God. The restoration is filled with peace and the peacemakers. The end of all suffering, tribulations, and persecution is realized, and God will award those who have sown into this eternity. Jesus' invitation is realized in His rest.

> Come to Me, all who are weary and heavy-laden, and I will give you rest. Take My yoke upon you and learn from Me, for I am gentle and humble in heart, and you will find rest for your souls for My yoke is easy and My burden is light. (Matthew 11:28–30)

> So there remains a Sabbath rest for the people of God. For the one who has entered His rest has himself also rested from his works, as God did from His. (Hebrews 4:9–10)

Jesus unveils the promise of this restoration.

> There will no longer be any curse; and the throne of God and of the Lamb will be in it, and His bond-servants will serve Him; they will see His face, and His name *will be* on their foreheads. And there will no longer be *any* night; and they will not have need of the light of a lamp nor the light of the sun, because the Lord God will illumine them; and they will reign forever and ever. (Revelation 22:3–5)

PART 3

CONSIDERATIONS

EARLY CHURCH EXPECTATIONS

The expectations of the early church did
not line up with their experience.

And as they were gazing intently into the sky while He was going, behold, two men in white clothing stood beside them. They also said, "Men of Galilee, why do you stand looking into the sky? This Jesus, who has been taken up from you into heaven, will come in just the same way as you have watched Him go into heaven."

—Acts 1:10–11

The early church had a great expectation and a simple eschatology. They expected the local and immediate return of Christ in their day. They expected an earthly kingdom with Jesus reigning as King in Jerusalem. Their assumptions and the experience at Christ's ascension on the Mount of Olives gave them a practical, immediate, and personal identification with that expectation. Their comprehension of His eternal Kingdom was still limited to their current experience and their history of centuries of subjugation to the temporal empires of the known world as they were currently dominated by Rome. They had only known the tribulations revealed by Daniel the prophet and they expected, like Daniel, deliverance and victory with their promised Messiah. They expected the restoration of the glory of the nation of Israel as it existed during the days of the kings David and Solomon. The ministry of Jesus the Messiah and His Kingdom were still a mystery to them. So forty days after the resurrection, Jesus stood with His disciples on the Mount of Olives just prior to His ascension, and they still had a question of what to expect.

> So when they had come together, they were asking Him, saying, "Lord, is it at this time You are restoring the kingdom to Israel?" (Acts 1:6)

They had missed the point! Jesus explained that the key issue is the mission, not their understanding of their timing of the end of the age. This is still the key issue today. His resurrection and ascension is our access and source to accomplish His mission. This immediate expectation was deepened and broadened with greater understanding just ten days later on Pentecost with the outpouring of the Holy Spirit. His ministry, through the disciples, inspired the teaching that opened the Scriptures to the church. As a result, God's plan of redemption through His Son became increasingly clear. The New Testament reveals the opening of the mystery of the church and the salvation of God through His Son.

> I have many more things to say to you, but you cannot bear them now. But when He, the Spirit of truth, comes, He will guide you into all the truth; for He will not speak on His own initiative, but whatever He hears, He will speak; and He will disclose to you what is to come. He will glorify Me, for He will take of Mine and will disclose it to you. All things that the Father has are Mine; therefore I said that He takes of Mine and will disclose it to you. (John 16:12–15)

The early church perspective of Jesus' ultimate return was taught by Jesus Himself and reinforced by the apostles Peter and Paul. However, it became obvious that both Peter and Paul responded to their expectations with clarification. Paul served them as an apostle and a teacher. He modeled and taught a lifestyle of expectation and obedience with the awareness of the brevity of life. He also taught that we should practice an individual and corporate life with the expectation of coming face to face with the Living Lord. His teaching to the Thessalonian church was a word of encouragement in the midst of their confusion and loss. He intended to help them process the grief of their loss of loved ones and their failed expectation of the timing of the return of Christ.

> But we do not want you to be uninformed, brethren, about those who are asleep, so that you will not grieve as do the rest who have no hope. For if we believe that Jesus died and rose again, even so God will bring with Him those who have fallen asleep in Jesus. For this we say to you by the word of the Lord, that we who are alive and remain until the coming of the Lord, will not precede those who have fallen asleep. For the Lord Himself will descend from heaven with a shout, with the voice of the archangel and with the trumpet of God, and the dead in Christ will rise first. Then we who are alive and remain will be caught up together with them in the clouds to meet the Lord in the air, and so we shall always be with the Lord. Therefore comfort one another with these words. (1 Thessalonians 4:13–18)

The expectations of the early church did not line up with their experience. The comments, questions, and expectations that are documented in the days immediately following the ascension and through the next few decades expose the process of opening, or the unfolding, of God's revelation to His church. The mystery of the church and the mysteries of His Kingdom are unveiled to the churches through the Gospels and the epistles. Jesus announced to His disciples this promise of disclosure.

> Jesus answered them, "To you it has been granted to know the mysteries of the kingdom of heaven, but to them it has not been granted. For whoever has, to him more shall be given, and he will have an abundance; but whoever does not have, even what he has shall be taken away from him." (Matthew 13:11–12)

The Hebrew eschatology disclosed throughout the Old Testament is realized in the New Testament. This study of "end things" throughout Scripture included three basic components: the judgment of the wicked, a reward for the righteous, and the restoration of all things. These components are more specifically defined in each eschatological narrative, or lens. The unique perspectives are fleshed out with very descriptive and detailed explanations in retrospect or in a projected future. However, the early church clearly expected God to judge the enemies of the church, to rescue His people and raise the righteous dead in their generation. They expected this inauguration of the new age of life and peace in the Spirit of God under the immediate rule of Jesus by the will of the Father in Jerusalem and now! They had been introduced to the fulfillment of Messianic prophecy in Jesus, and they expected their understanding of this reality to be concluded immediately.

This study of "end things" throughout Scripture included three basic components: the judgment of the wicked, a reward for the righteous, and the restoration of all things.

There was the beginning of awareness, an inkling of realization of the conclusion of the old age. Jesus had prophesied the end of the physical earthly temple and the sacrificial system. He had introduced the New Covenant in His blood. The message of the cross, the fulfillment of the atonement types introduced throughout Biblical history, and the definition and hope for salvation were only beginning to dawn on Jesus' followers. God's judgment of the four kingdoms prophesied in Daniel, of Babylon, Medo-Persia, Greece, and Rome had been historically realized leading up to their current day of Roman occupation. The prophetic purpose of those nations were coming to a conclusion in the realization of the prophetic fulfillment of Daniel's prophecy.

> Then after the sixty-two weeks the Messiah will be cut off and have nothing, and the people of the prince who is to come will destroy the city and the sanctuary. And its end will come with a flood; even to the end there will be war; desolations are determined. (Daniel 9:26)

Their Messiah had indeed been "cut off," and the anticipation of Jesus' prophecy concerning the city of Jerusalem and the Temple that "not one stone here will be left upon another" still perplexed those early disciples. They would not become clear until AD 70.

> And He said to them, "Do you not see all these things? Truly I say to you, not one stone here will be left upon another, which will not be torn down." (Matthew 24:2)

They had experienced some of these realities but did not comprehend them. The recent history of the Maccabean Revolt and the rise of "last days" movements in Israel leading to Messiah were now to be realized in Jesus' death, burial, and resurrection. They believed they were living at the end of an era, an old age dominated by forces in opposition to the Kingdom of God. Their world was inundated with pagan gods and political rulers that seemed to hold all things in their grip. The people of Israel were the focus of constant affliction as they proved to be a constant irritant to the Roman Empire. There were numerous expressions of this cry for deliverance. The early church was influenced by Pharisees, Sadducees, Herodians, Essenes and zealots. Pious Israelites cried out for deliverance. They expected God to break in again and bring judgment on this wicked world. The Messiah's imminent return was expected by all. The first-century church saw the fulfillment in Jesus but was left confused and disappointed in its false expectation of an earthly kingdom.

Of course, after centuries of study and the passing of time, all of these conclusions are now clearer than they were to the early church. However, the church today is still enamored with the idea of an earthly kingdom. Jesus was very clear in His response to Pilate about the nature of His Kingdom.

> Jesus answered, "My kingdom is not of this world. If My kingdom were of this world, then My servants would be fighting so that I would not be handed over to the Jews; but as it is, My kingdom is not of this realm." (John 18:36)

The mystery of the Messiah and His suffering was only then being opened to those early Christians. The response of the early church in Jerusalem is exposed in the book of Acts as they considered the Scripture in a new light. When Peter preached the Pentecost message, they began to acknowledge that they had rejected Jesus and had therefore participated in putting Him to death. This meant that they were included with the pagans as God's enemies. The result was their cry for mercy. They, along with all humanity, had been pronounced guilty!

> Now when they heard this, they were pierced to the heart, and said to Peter and the rest of the apostles, "Brethren, what shall we do?" Peter said to them, "Repent, and each of you be baptized in the name of Jesus Christ for the forgiveness of your sins; and you will receive the gift of the Holy Spirit. For the promise is for you and your children and for all who are far off, as many as the Lord our God will call to Himself." (Acts 2:37-39)

The apostle Paul is credited with the majority of teaching clarifying salvation and Jesus' earthly ministry and ultimate sacrifice. God prepared him very specifically for this task with his understanding of the Hebrew Torah, the Wisdom writings, and the prophets. Jesus called him into ministry for this purpose as His apostle to the Gentiles. Paul's greatest resistance came from the Judaizers, who insisted that the Gentiles live like Jews with a combination of God's grace and human effort. These were those who would not receive the fulfilling work of Jesus or they intended to pervert His finished work with the imposition of the sacrificial system.

> But when I saw that they were not straightforward about the truth of the gospel, I said to Cephas in the presence of all, "If you, being a Jew, live like the Gentiles and not like the Jews, how is it that you compel the Gentiles to live like Jews?" (Galatians 2:14)

The eschatology of the New Testament proclaims that Jesus is the Lamb of God Who takes away the sin of the world. But it is obvious that those who were with Jesus in His earthly ministry were not clear about His intentions: His mission. He was continually questioned about His kingdom and its manifestation. John the Baptist is included with those who expressed this confusion and doubt. Just prior to his martyrdom, he sent his disciples to Jesus to question Him about the Kingdom and His purpose. All Israel looked for their promised Messiah King even as Simeon was recorded as "looking for the consolation of Israel" (Luke 2:25).

The Jewish expectation was for an earthly king, a victorious warrior to sit on David's throne. They wanted a leader who would vanquish the heavy Roman hand and elevate the people of Israel to the glory days of David and Solomon. So the early disciples, almost all Jewish, also had similar expectations. This explains why they were not able to comprehend Jesus' words about His death in Jerusalem. It did not sink in because of their preconceived ideas. Their eschatological perspective blinded them to God's intention that was revealed by His prophets and in Jesus' own earthly ministry and teaching. This same problem is evident in the church today. Many are blinded by preconceived ideas and distracted by their eschatological expectations.

> **Their eschatological perspective blinded them to God's intention that was revealed by His prophets and in Jesus' own earthly ministry and teaching.**

The Messiah, instead of coming as a victorious warrior as they expected, appeared as a suffering servant. Jesus' death, though announced, was unexpected. His resurrection, though prophesied, was even more unexpected. However, all judgment had fallen on Him, and He has paid the price of redemption for all who receive Him. He made the way for all those who have placed their hope in God and His promised remedy for man's sin. Jesus proclaimed in the introduction of His earthly ministry that He did not come to judge the world, for it was already under judgment (John 12:47).

> For God so loved the world, that He gave His only begotten Son, that whosoever believes in Him should not perish, but have eternal life. (John 3:16)

The prophet Isaiah speaks for God in his description of the suffering servant receiving this judgment in chapter 53. Jesus now sits victorious over sin and Satan at the right hand of the Father. He has made a display of the enemy as the apostle Paul proclaimed to the Colossian church.

> When He had disarmed the rulers and authorities, He made a public display of them, having triumphed over them through Him. (Colossians 2:15)

So the three components of Biblical eschatology are realized in Jesus and opened to the church. The first component, concerning *judgment*, is fulfilled in the judgment of all sin, as it was laid on Jesus for those who call on Him. The judgment of sin was already in the world, resulting in suffering, death, and destruction. It would be manifested in its fullness and completion at the end of the age. God's ultimate judgment falls on those who do not accept His remedy, the substitutionary sacrifice that ransoms man from the consequences of his sin. This does not replace or remove the conclusion of judgment at the end of the age; rather it is salvation from judgment for all who will receive Him.

The three components of Biblical eschatology are realized in Jesus and opened to the church.

Concerning *reward*, all who call on the Lord have the reward of the righteous in that they are raised up with Him in the newness of life and the hope of eternal life. This is their rescue that results in full restoration, "Behold, I am making all things new" (Revelation 21:5). They have been reconciled with God and have been made alive by the Spirit of God. This is the first resurrection!

> Having been buried with Him in baptism, in which you were also raised up with Him through faith in the working of God, who raised Him from the dead. (Colossians 2:12)

THE UNVEILING

> Therefore we have been buried with Him through baptism into death, so that as Christ was raised from the dead through the glory of the Father, so we too might walk in newness of life. For if we have become united with Him in the likeness of His death, certainly we shall also be in the likeness of His resurrection, knowing this, that our old self was crucified with Him, in order that our body of sin might be done away with, so that we would no longer be slaves to sin; for he who has died is freed from sin. (Romans 6:4–7)

We can now walk in newness of life in Christ Jesus. The early church discovered that the anticipated resurrection of the righteous dead had *already* occurred in Christ! Jesus is the first fruits of the harvest.

> But now Christ has been raised from the dead, the first fruits of those who are asleep. For since by a man came death, by a man also came the resurrection of the dead. For as in Adam all die, so also in Christ all will be made alive. But each in his own order: Christ the first fruits, after that those who are Christ's at His coming, then comes the end, when He hands over the kingdom to the God and Father, when He has abolished all rule and all authority and power. For He must reign until He has put all His enemies under His feet. The last enemy that will be abolished is death. (1 Corinthians 15:20–26)

Finally, concerning *restoration*, the seventh key that opens The Revelation, this is the promise of God's unveiling for His people. The restoration of all things has begun in Jesus' resurrection. This new life "in Christ" introduced the church to this new age of grace and expectation. Hope is now realized in the Words of Christ and defines our way of life. This hope, this confident expectation, is the very substance of this new life in Christ. We do not have to wait until death to realize this. Christianity is not something that happens to you when you die!

> Now faith is the assurance of things hoped for, the conviction of things not seen. (Hebrews 11:1)

Therefore there is now no condemnation for those who are in Christ Jesus. For the law of the Spirit of life in Christ Jesus has set you free from the law of sin and of death... For I consider that the sufferings of this present time are not worthy to be compared with the glory that is to be revealed to us. For the anxious longing of the creation waits eagerly for the revealing of the sons of God. (Romans 8:1–2; 18–19)

The Christians of the first century were continually unfolding the revelation of the work of Christ and applying this truth to their lives that resulted in turning the world upside down. The testimony of their resolve is revealed in their sacrificial lives of service and obedience. The enemy had been defeated and the process, the beginning of the end, had already begun.

HISTORY AND IMPACT

The four kingdoms prophesied in Daniel and their pagan domination of God's people were coming to an end. The comprehension of this fulfillment was progressively opened to the church. I suggest that the argument of silence can be very persuasive. The New Testament's silence of the fulfillment of Jesus' Mount of Olives discourse announcing the destruction of the temple indicates the possibility that all New Testament documents were written before this event occurred. The common knowledge of the Jewish Wars and Titus's destruction of Jerusalem in AD 70 had not yet concluded. The old adage that "bad news circles the globe while good news is tying its shoes" probably applies to the first-century destruction of Jerusalem. Since news traveled on foot and horseback, it would still take quite awhile for all the disbursed Jews and the early church to hear of this tragedy. This "bad news" would have served as a Scriptural affirmation and another "convincing proof" of Jesus' authenticity (Acts 1:3). The assumption that all Jesus spoke of in this discourse was only a proclamation for a far future realization ignores the historical and Biblical reality of this event.

The early church then continued to live in an atmosphere charged with expectation of the end of the age and the restoration of all things. They lived and died with a sense of victory, a realization of the triumph of Jesus Christ that proclaimed "the Kingdom of God is in our midst." They lived with a vibrant hope, an expectation of His continued and consummated Kingdom. They continued to struggle with the yet unregenerate world and the demonically inspired systems that oppose God. However, they did so in faith by powerfully confronting the sin and suffering of this present age. They were convinced that life in the Spirit of God was possible, and they walked it out.

R. JEFF COLLENE

The known and reported histories of the early church, of the temple and the city of Jerusalem, and of the dispersion and deaths of the early disciples all indicate first-century dates. The writings of the New Testament appear to have occurred within the generation immediately following Christ's earthly ministry and His ascension. In fact, this was a requirement of the early church fathers for the canon (*rule*) of New Testament Scriptures. It is possible that some Scriptures were completed after the dispersion of the sixties and seventies, but there appears to be no clear documentation or acknowledgment in the early church fathers' writings to corroborate this. Our access to documentation of the demise of the disciples and writers of the New Testament is limited.

As mentioned, the church fathers have recorded some of these facts in the second, third, and fourth centuries. We would really like to have the certainty of chronicled historical events of those early years like we have today in our documentaries, but this was not possible and is not available. The accessibility of documentation was limited to a very few. The expense of handwritten documents was out of reach for common people. It would be another fifteen hundred years before such accessibility. The legends that have been handed down give some sketchy detail of those early disciples and writers of the New Testament—who was martyred and how and when. These traditions help to establish a timeline for the early church and their realized tribulations. They also reinforce the reality of their faith in the testimony of their lives.

The New Testament only mentions the deaths of two apostles. First, Judas's suicide is documented in the passion of Christ, and second, Herod Agrippa put James to death in AD 44. There is no historical record or tradition of the death of the apostle John the Beloved. This does not hinder the legends from continuing through the ages. Early church historians documented the deaths of remaining apostles. There are many good books that narrate these traditions, detailing that eight of the apostles died as martyrs. The traditional explanations are drawn from three sources: New Testament Scripture, early church historians, and legends handed down through the church.

THE UNVEILING

There are conflicting traditions, but the general chronological list of apostles and contributors to the New Testament are as follows:

Judas Iscariot died by suicide in AD 33. The Scripture reports that he hanged himself at Hakeldama (Field of Blood) on the southern slope of the valley of Hinnom near Jerusalem. There are two possibilities that explain how he hung himself that would give insight to these Scriptural reports. Either he hung himself by the typical rope from an edifice or he hung himself on his sword.

> Then when Judas, who had betrayed Him, saw that He had been condemned, he felt remorse and returned the thirty pieces of silver to the chief priests and elders, saying, "I have sinned by betraying innocent blood." But they said, "What is that to us? See to that yourself!" And he threw the pieces of silver into the temple sanctuary and departed; and he went away and hanged himself. The chief priests took the pieces of silver and said, "It is not lawful to put them into the temple treasury, since it is the price of blood." And they conferred together and with the money bought the Potter's Field as a burial place for strangers. For this reason that field has been called the Field of Blood to this day. Then that which was spoken through Jeremiah the prophet was fulfilled: "And they took the thirty pieces of silver, the price of one whose price had been set by the sons of Israel; and they gave them for the Potter's field, as the Lord directed me." (Matthew 27:3–10)

Brethren, the Scripture had to be fulfilled, which the Holy Spirit foretold by the mouth of David concerning Judas, who became a guide to those who arrested Jesus. For he was counted among us and received his share in this ministry. (Now this man acquired a field with the price of his wickedness, and falling headlong, he burst open in the middle and all his intestines gushed out. And it became known to all who were living in Jerusalem; so that in their own language that field was called Hakeldama, that is, Field of Blood.) (Acts 1:16–19)

James, the son of Zebedee, was put to death by Herod Agrippa I prior to the Passover in AD 44–45.

> Now about that time Herod the king laid hands on some who belonged to the church in order to mistreat them. And he had James the brother of John put to death with a sword. (Acts 12:1–2)

The apostle *Philip*, according to tradition, preached in Phrygia and died at Hierapolis in AD 54. This tradition has been recently substantiated with reports of an archaeological discovery of his tomb that has been uncovered in that city. Tradition says that he was tortured and crucified by hostile Jews.

The apostle *Matthew*, also called Levi, the son of Alpheus, was a despised tax collector prior to his calling to Christ. He is reported to have been sent to proclaim the gospel in Ethiopia after writing the Gospel of Matthew. The reports handed down relate that he was effective in ministry until the death of a sympathetic king, Aeglippus. This king's successor, Hytacus, an unbeliever, is reported to have persecuted Matthew and then had him nailed to the ground and beheaded in Nad-Devar, the capitol of Ethiopia in AD 60–70.

James, son of Alphaeus the Less, is reported to have been martyred in Jerusalem about the time of the Passover in AD 62. These reports are documented by the historian Josephus in the first century. They are also mentioned much later by Eusebius and his son Jerome in the fourth and fifth centuries. It is reported that the high priest commanded James to speak against Jesus and he refused. He was then throne down from the temple wall and stoned. Both of these assaults failed, and he was clubbed to death.

Peter is reported as being martyred in AD 64. Simon Peter died thirty-three to thirty-four years after Christ at the beginning of the persecutions of Nero. These persecutions reached their zenith in AD 67–68. All stories of his death report that he was crucified. The early church father Origen wrote that Peter felt himself unworthy to die in the same manner

THE UNVEILING

as his Master, and was, therefore, at his request, crucified with his head downward. Jesus had been very revealing to Peter in His conversation of restoration prior to the ascension.

> Truly, truly, I say to you, when you were younger, you used to gird yourself and walk wherever you wished; but when you grow old, you will stretch out your hands and someone else will gird you, and bring you where you do not wish to go. Now this He said, signifying by what kind of death he would glorify God. And when He had spoken this, He said to him, "Follow Me!" (John 21:18–19)

Judas Thaddeus and *Simon the Zealot* were both reported to have been martyred in Beirut in the Roman province of Syria in 65 AD.

The apostle Paul is clearly documented by his own writings to have been persecuted for his faith. The New Testament epistles are filled with these reports, concluding in his death in Rome in AD 67.

> And he was talking and arguing with the Hellenistic Jews; but they were attempting to put him to death. But when the brethren learned of it, they brought him down to Caesarea and sent him away to Tarsus. (Acts 9:29–30)

There are thirteen additional verses that are mentioned in the book of Acts and the letters to the Corinthian Church as well as Paul's second letter to his protégé, Timothy. Tradition says that he was ultimately beheaded in Rome at the command of Emperor Nero.

Andrew, Peter's brother, is reported to have been crucified around AD 70. Reports are that he preached in Scythia (Greece), in Asia Minor (Turkey), and Thrace. Hippolytus wrote that he was hanged on an olive tree at Patrae, a town of Achaia.

Thomas was also reported to have been martyred around AD 70. It is reported that he preached in India. Legends say that he was thrust through with a lance or pine spears, burned with red-hot plates, and then burned alive.

Nathanael (Bartholomew) is reported to have been martyred around AD 70. Tradition has recorded that he was skinned alive and beheaded at Derbent near the Caspian Sea. Many stories and relics of this apostle have multiplied through the years, including the areas of Iraq, Iran, Turkey, Armenia, and India.

Also around AD 70, *Matthias* was reported to have been martyred. The fourth-century church father Eusebius wrote that Matthias preached in Ethiopia and was later stoned while hanging on a cross.

Finally, the apostle *John* and assumed author of The Revelation, is the longest living of the apostles. The date of his death is unknown and varied dates are between AD 89 and 120. The Gospel of John records a conversation between Jesus and Peter in the forty days of Jesus' appearances prior to His ascension.

> Peter, turning around, saw the disciple whom Jesus loved following them; the one who also had leaned back on His bosom at the supper and said, "Lord, who is the one who betrays You?" So Peter seeing him said to Jesus, "Lord, and what about this man?" Jesus said to him, "If I want him to remain until I come, what is that to you? You follow Me!" Therefore this saying went out among the brethren that that disciple would not die; yet Jesus did not say to him that he would not die, but only, "If I want him to remain until I come, what is that to you?" This is the disciple who is testifying to these things and wrote these things, and we know that his testimony is true. (John 21:20–24)

Tradition states that John was the only surviving apostle toward the end of the first century. He was considered the bishop over the church of Asia. During the persecutions of the Imperial Cult, he was apprehended at Ephesus and sent as a prisoner to Rome. Emperor Domitian condemned him to death by casting him into a cauldron of boiling oil at the Latin

Gate of Rome. He is reported to have miraculously survived this ordeal. His ultimate demise is not recorded.

All these early stories indicate the reality of faith in the face of tribulation. These early church stories strengthen the eschatological expectation that were walked out in the first century. The Revelation of Jesus Christ is a strong exhortation for His church to trust Him in this life and be faithful to persevere until the end. The stories, churches, reports of relics, documented histories, and archeological finds have only resulted in a greater witness and affirmation of the testimony of the church and the truth of the gospel.

The early church endured the leaven of the Judaizers, the persecutions of Rome, and the influential philosophies of Hellenism. It endured in faithfulness to its Savior and service to others, so the church today is to continue in faith. We are to endure as the writer of The Unveiling has testified: persevering until our end.

> I, John, your brother and fellow partaker in the tribulation and kingdom and perseverance which are in Jesus, was on the island called Patmos because of the word of God and the testimony of Jesus. (Revelation 1:9)

LENSES: DEFINING PERSPECTIVES

> "Behold, He is coming with the clouds, and every eye will see Him, even those who pierced Him; and all the tribes of the earth will mourn over Him. So it is to be. Amen." "I am the Alpha and the Omega," says the Lord God, "who is and who was and who is to come, the Almighty."
>
> —Revelation 1:7–8

This introductory statement in the seventh verse of the first chapter introduces the challenge of our chronological view of the past, present, and future in our consideration of The Revelation. I have addressed this specific verse in depth in the Keys of Part 2, Heaven; The Perspective of The Revelation and Judgment: The Result of The Revelation. The initiation of God's disclosure introduces the Divine perspective that is applied to the flow of His revelation. This timeless perception also introduces the varied perspectives that have developed in church history.

There have been many books written on the last days of the earth. There are many scholarly commentaries on the apocalyptic portions of the Old and New Testaments and especially The Revelation of Jesus Christ. I've read and appreciated numerous commentaries. They were sometimes helpful and always insightful. Some even come with a formulae for divining the end of days based on their specific assumptions. I am always challenged by the conflicting views of godly students and their teachers. Therefore, I am motivated to pray and read The Revelation with the pursuit of a fresh starting point of faith. I trust in the sovereignty of God in the formation and purpose of His Scripture through His church, the canon. The pursuit of God's revelation has always been an act of faith.

The canon of Scripture has proven to be just that, God's revelation, and it has been affirmed and reinforced by literary, historical, archeological, and practical discoveries in our modern era.

This is my justification for yet another book on The Revelation. I have personally found many complicated, conflicting, and troubling explanations within current commentaries. Most are well thought out and seemingly complete (from the perspective of the author). Some authors just skip over difficult passages. Others appear to lack an intellectual integrity in their disregard for the Scriptural library that precedes The Revelation. Others seem to have an inconsistent and arbitrary application of symbols, signs, and literal explanations. Others still include blind assumptions or presuppositions that are applied as an overlay that then direct their commentaries and conclusions. Unfortunately, there are also many commentaries and explanations that undermine the veracity of The Revelation based on their critical view of its inclusion in the canon of Scripture. Still others have a discounting historical view that reduces the visions to the hyperbole of a political cartoon directed toward and limited to the destruction of the Roman Empire.

In studying the primary views that have coalesced since the second century, an interesting pattern of dominant perspectives has developed. However, I've noticed that the personal perspective of most commentators are rarely stated or even acknowledged. This reveals either an ignorance of or a disregard for the existence of differing perspectives. A limited study within any of these defining perspectives or eschatological systems may be a result of a lack of awareness of any other view. It appears that some students are so entrenched in their approach to the apocalyptic literature that is being explained that they are unable to see the apparent conflicts and shortcomings of their perspective.

These issues result in a diminishing of Scripture, sometimes making excuses for the language used or discounting it as exaggeration within The Revelation. I have found that most commentaries are slim in their explanations unless they are established in one of the two dominant perspectives of preterism (already fulfilled prophecy) or futurism (prophecy as history in advance). These perspectives can be dogmatic. They both have variations but are defined with rigid assumptions and a black-and-white approach to interpretation. My personal experience of pursuing understanding in any of the four systems has left me with many unanswered questions and some conflicting explanations, or no explanation at all. This is the motivation for these past seven years of study and the discovery of the simple keys that open The Revelation.

In general, Christian eschatology, the study of end things, has developed and branched out into four dominant viewpoints or schools of thought. The preterist view is considered already fulfilled as we look behind. The historicist interpretation is referenced as unfolding in a look back. The futurist system is a look forward, and the idealist application is a general look around. Each perspective has multiple variations and nuanced explanations. The dominant interpretive systems are described, for the most part, as an unfolding chronological and sequential narrative of events.

I find that the process of considering a new perspective can be unsettling. When I was introduced to a new system of interpretation in my studies, I felt insecure in my ignorance. So if the ideas I've introduced in The Unveiling have produced this reaction, maybe the explanation of the following interpretive systems will help. When we become dependent on these systems of interpretation, we can feel threatened by a new thought. I pray that our presuppositions will be subject only to the Holy Spirit and our hearts open to new insights.

The four perspectives I've experienced serve as defining lenses and are described as preterism, historicism, idealism, and futurism.

Preterism

This school of thought basically looks back at The Revelation as practically applied to the early church, the persecution endured, the fulfilment of Jesus' prophecy of the Temple, and the destruction of the

Roman Empire. The term is drawn from the Latin *praeteritus*, meaning, "gone by," and is applied to apocalyptic Scriptures as being fulfilled in the past.

The *preterist* view of already-fulfilled prophecy includes the Messianic prophesies throughout the Old Testament, such as Genesis 3 protoprophecy; the covenant promises of Abraham, Moses, and David; and all that refer to Jesus' first coming and His ministry as the suffering servant. Preterism is the key interpretive tool of Daniel's prophecies of the four Gentile kingdoms that ruled over the nation of Israel from the Babylonian dispersion until the arrival of Messiah and the destruction of the sacrificial system. The four world empires listed in Daniel (Babylon, Medo-Persia, Greece, and Rome) were literally listed and have been historically realized as God's hand of judgment on a disobedient people. They also served as His pinions of protection to keep them isolated and identified as His people in the last days of this era to accomplish His Word and His Work. This was originally seen in the ancient kingdom of Egypt during the four centuries of exile leading to Israel's march of fulfillment into Canaan. These prophecies, some of which are apocalyptic, are focused on the end of the age of God's temporal sacrificial system and the initiation of the Kingdom of God on earth.

Since the fulfillment of these prophecies were realized in Jesus' earthly ministry, preterism has been considered, inferred, and referred to by a number of theologians through the years to explain New Testament eschatology. History records that the end of the nineteenth century brought the two dominant and polarizing views, preterism and futurism, into the forefront as the focus at the beginning of the third millennium.

Preterism has settled into two major contemporary variations, full and partial. These views apply their perspectives either radically or moderately. This view generally adheres to the premise that the apocalyptic Scriptures that expressed a future fulfillment of the Kingdom of God were ultimately fulfilled in the earthly ministry of Jesus and the fulfillment of His key prophetic announcement of the destruction of the temple in Jerusalem that was accomplished by the Roman invasion in AD 70. The absence of any mention of the fulfillment of Jesus' prophecy throughout the New Testament, except for The Revelation, is a powerful argument for this perspective and the early date of John's writing of The Revelation.

Both full and partial preterism interpret the Biblical prophecies as events that have already happened. Preterist concepts were introduced in the fourth century by the bishop of Caesarea, Eusebius, and John Chrysostom, the bishop of Antioch and later Archbishop of Constantinople. During the Counter-Reformation, a Jesuit priest, Luis de Alcasar (1554–1613), wrote the first systematic exposition of Biblical prophecy based on the preterist perspective.

That which has come to be defined as full preterism, or the radical expression of this view, was codified in the book *Parousia* in 1878 by J. Stuart Russell, MA, DD. This book is referenced as a key document of the contemporary Preterist Association. He taught that Jesus second coming fully occurred in the first century and was realized in the final judgment on Israel and, more specifically, Jerusalem and the Temple.

The invasion of Israel in the First Jewish Roman War in AD 66 was led by the Roman military commander Vespasian and later completed by his son Titus. The threat on Jerusalem and the temple occurred over a period of conflict that was temporarily halted at the death of Emperor Nero in AD 68. This was followed by a siege and the ultimate destruction of Jerusalem, as prophesied by Jesus and recorded in Matthew 24, Mark 13, and Luke 21.

Titus's achievements in Israel were celebrated by his younger brother, Emperor Domitian. He commemorated the Arch of Titus in Rome in AD 82 depicting the booty of war, including the Jewish Menorah and other temple valuables. He was further honored as Emperor Titus from AD 79 to 81, completing the Colosseum, and giving government relief for the seemingly apocalyptic catastrophes that occurred during his reign. These included the eruption of Mount Vesuvius and a great fire in Rome in AD 80. The first century was beleaguered with many major natural catastrophes that also seriously affected the churches of Asia Minor, including the seven churches addressed in The Revelation.

The moderate expression of preterism holds to a similar view of the fulfillment of The Revelation. This view considers some references of judgment as exaggeration or hyperbolic descriptions of the catastrophes of the first century. It still maintains an expectation of the Second Coming of Christ to occur in the future. There are three Scriptures that most partial preterists believe are yet to be fulfilled.

First, at Jesus' ascension recorded by Luke in the beginning of the books of Acts, two men (God's messengers) appear to the disciples and exhort them concerning the departure of Jesus.

> And as they were gazing intently into the sky while He was going, behold, two men in white clothing stood beside them. They also said, "Men of Galilee, why do you stand looking into the sky? This Jesus, who has been taken up from you into heaven, will come in just the same way as you have watched Him go into heaven." (Acts 1:10–11)

Luke's record reports the messengers' exhortation and information to be applicable to their immediate experience. This is considered a tangible, historical, visible reality yet to be realized in the future.

The second and third Scriptures are the Apostle Paul's responses to the churches. He gives an in-depth description of the resurrection to the Corinthian church that includes a specific correlation with the return of Christ and the resurrection of the dead along with the specific reference to the immediate timing of these two key eschatological events (1 Corinthians 15:20–57). Paul also references this event, commonly called "the rapture of the church," to encourage the disappointed and grieving church of Thessalonica (1 Thessalonians 4:13–18).

Preterism, then, is a system of eschatology that considers prophecies concerning the return of Christ to have already been fulfilled in the judgment of Israel and the collapse of the sacrificial system with the destruction of the temple in Jerusalem. These prophecies are ultimately concluded in the ongoing struggle in the first century with the Roman Empire and its resulting destruction. Full preterism considers the judgment on Jerusalem the Second Coming of Christ.

In the preface of *Parousia*, Russell reflects the frustration and lack of clarity in the application of his interpretation of The Revelation. He considers the prevailing "state of uncertainty and confusion of thought in regard to New Testament prophecy, which to some extent explains, though it may not justify, the consigning of the whole subject to the region of hopelessly obscure and insoluble problems."[8] He did not begin nor conclude his comments on The Revelation with an air of certainty, though many of his explanations are given without any other possible explanation.

The question, then, is whether the eager anticipation and hope of the early church and the anxiety of these last days can be realized by the unveiling of Jesus revelation to John and to His church. If the preterist explanation is accepted, The Revelation is merely a difficult and irrelevant explanation of first century prophesied events. All the following centuries of disciples can only draw spiritual lessons of good and evil and continue in the prevailing "state of uncertainty and confusion of thought in regard to New Testament prophecy." For a relevant yet contextual application there must be another explanation.

Another defining component of preterism to consider is called "amillennialism." This is a derogatory term intended to diminish the preterist perspective by its detractors. The *millennium* is the term used to describe a future period of Jesus' ministry on earth with a literal interpretation of the one thousand-year period of time in Revelation 20:1–6, a specific utopian era on the earth. The preterist explanation of these six verses is varied but generally refers to a symbolic period between Jesus first coming and an end of the age.

Amillennialism and Postmillennialism

Another distinction of the preterist perspective is negatively called amillennialism and a positive title of postmillennialism. Amillennialism is occasionally used as a derogatory term by those that dismiss this perspective. Postmillennialism is a more detailed and hopeful explanation of moderate preterism.

Postmillennialism interprets the Scriptures on the second coming of Christ to be fulfilled after a millennial or golden age in which the church is effective in inculcating her Biblical ethics in the world and thus setting the stage for a triumphant return of Christ. This view holds that Jesus Christ initiated His Kingdom during His earthly ministry and He is establishing His Kingdom on earth through His church by continued preaching and service fulfilling the great Commission (Matthew 28:18-20; Mark 16:15).

> This gospel of the kingdom shall be preached in the whole world as a testimony to all the nations, and then the end will come. (Matthew 24:14)

This view also expects a great "end time" harvest. This would include an awakening of the nations and a revival of the church with many ethnic Jews receiving their Messiah. This revival will reflect the Golden Age of Israel when King David was on the throne and succeeded by his son Solomon. This is a utopian existence where righteousness dwell and peace and prosperity prevail. After this is established then this will usher in the presence of the King. Jesus will dwell in bodily form and the general resurrection will occur and a final judgment will follow.

This view of progressive development was the dominant belief among American Protestants who promoted reform and social justice. This "social gospel" was successful in the abolition of slavery in the western world. It had great hopes of imposing Christian ethics on the nations of the earth. This movement was codified in 1658 with the Savoy Declaration, a modification of the Westminster Confession of Faith of 1646 which was one of the earliest creedal statements of postmillennial eschatology. This view was articulated by men like John Owen in the 17th century, and Jonathon Edwards in the 18th century, and Charles Hodge in the 19th century. The shock and pessimism of the 20th century world wars quelled this ideology with pessimism and disillusionment.

Another point of differentiation is the literal and figurative view of the millennium. The amillennial name was applied to those who held to a figurative interpretation. So in their estimation and expectation, the millennial era has already begun with an indefinite time for Christ's return. These views are creatively named optimillennialists in contrast to pessimilleniasts.

Historicism

The historicist view is the explanation of a prophetic and progressively unfolding of future events into an historical narrative across the years. This system is seen as having been fulfilled in the past yet is continuing its fulfillment even in the present. This is a view that covers the entire church age. As expected, this view can only be affirmed and explained after the fact. It is continually updating its narrative as centuries fly by between the first and second coming of Christ. It is rarely referenced today except for aspects that can serve to support one of the two dominant views.

There are two main expressions of the historicist view, linear and cyclical. The linear view is detailed as a progressive and continuous fulfillment of prophecy that ranges from the first coming until the second coming. Most of the Protestant reformers of the nineteenth century held historicist views, such as Martin Luther, John Calvin, Thomas Cranmer, and others. This view was in contrast to the preterist and futurist positions held during the Counter-Reformation. Many interpreted the prophetic future in condemnation of the Roman papacy. Jesuit commentators of the Counter-Revolution are credited with some of the earliest explanations that today are defined as preterism and futurism.

Through the centuries, many books have been written using the symbols of The Revelation to describe the struggle during the Reformation and the development of Protestantism in conflict with the Roman and Eastern papacies and the responses of the Counter-Reformation. As a result, this view has associated the symbols of The Revelation with historical persons, nations, and events.

The historicist perspective is applied and can reflect the entire course of history between the first and second coming as the prophetic narrative. This system has been criticized for its inconsistencies and the fluidity of its interpretations based on current events. There have been many revised outlines of church history and many volumes written through the years.

This approach has been used in attempts to predict the date of the end of the world. An example in post-Reformation Britain is in the works of Charles Wesley, who predicted that the end of the world would occur in 1794, based on his analysis of the book of Revelation. Adam Clarke, whose commentary was published in 1831, proposed a possible date of 2015 for the end of the papal power.

In nineteenth-century America, William Miller proposed that the end of the world would occur on October 22, 1844, based on a historicist model used with Daniel 8:14 prophecy of the twenty-three hundred evenings and mornings. Miller's historicist approach to the book of Daniel spawned a national movement in the United States known as Millerism. After the "Great Disappointment," the passing of these dates, some of the Millerites eventually organized the Seventh-Day Adventist Church, which continues to maintain a historicist reading of Biblical prophecy as essential to its eschatology. Millerites also formed other Adventist bodies, including the one that spawned the Watch Tower movement, better known as Jehovah's Witnesses, who hold to their own unique historicist interpretations of Biblical prophecy.

Prophetic commentaries in the early church usually interpreted individual passages rather than entire books. The earliest complete commentary on the book of Revelation was carried out by Victorinus of Pettau, considered as one of the earliest historicist commentators, around AD 300. Through the next few centuries, a number of students of Revelation modified and developed their historicist interpretations.

Christian Church history is replete with the stories of Protestant reformers who had a major interest in historicism, with a direct application to their struggle against the papacy. Many prominent leaders and scholars among them, including Martin Luther, John Calvin, Thomas Cranmer, John Thomas, John Knox, and Cotton Mather, identified the Roman papacy as the Antichrist. A group of Lutheran scholars called the Centuriators of Magdeburg was headed by Matthias Flacius, who wrote the twelve-volume *Magdeburg Centuries* to discredit the papacy and identify the pope as the Antichrist.

The second expression of historicism is considered cyclical. This is an expression of multiple repetitions of the prophetic pictures of The Revelation throughout the church age. A more descriptive phrase that describes the repeating cycles was introduced by William Hendriksen as progressive parallelism in his book *More Than Conqueror* (Baker 1940, 1967).

Idealism

The very pliable allegorical or spiritual application is also called a spiritualist application and is based on a nonliteral approach to The Revelation. In this system, eschatological Scriptures are interpreted symbolically with a contemporary application. There is an implied resistance to establishing a time frame to the prophetic symbols and warnings.

This view considers that the prophetic visions refer to the ongoing battle of good and evil with a revelation of the ultimate triumph of good over evil in human history. Therefore, it is a valuable approach for mining complicated symbolic portions of Scripture for contemporary application by creative teachers. This has been applied throughout the centuries of church history as the struggle continues, for we are more than conquerors.

> But in all these things we overwhelmingly conquer through Him who loved us. (Romans 8:37)

Futurism

The most dominant contemporary perspective is the *futurist* system of yet-unfolding events to a conclusive consummation at the end of the age. This view states that the apocalyptic prophecies in the Bible are primarily to be fulfilled during the years immediately prior to the Second Coming of Christ. The years are preceded by a global time of chaos and deception under the demonic leadership of the Antichrist referred to as the Great Tribulation. They are succeeded by a thousand-year earthly reign of Christ, referred to as the Millennium.

While this perspective was originally fueled by the setting of dates, many contemporary futurist teachers now leave the date open for the consummation of the age. This open date usually stretches in to the near future; that is to say that its fulfillment, by their estimation, will most likely and conveniently occur toward the end of their own lives and ministries. This system is expanded to include four separate expressions of a future revolving around interpretations of three key issues, the rapture, the great tribulation, and the millennium.

The specific timing expected within these views produce four variations of this perspective. The complexity of these four sequential narratives requires an elementary explanation for identification. Briefly noted here, the rapture, or being "caught up" as the apostle Paul states in his encouragement to the Thessalonian church, has differing expectations based on other presumptions. This is in response to the concerns of the church and in reference to the return of Christ.

> Then we who are alive and remain will be *caught up* together with them in the clouds to meet the Lord in the air, and so we

shall always be with the Lord. (1 Thessalonians 4:17, emphasis added)

The different systems reflect the various understandings and implication of this event. With this understanding, the rapture event precedes the literal expectation of the *millennium,* or the one-thousand year earthly reign of Jesus between global catastrophic judgments on sin and the enemies of the Kingdom of God.

> Then I saw thrones, and they sat on them, and judgment was given to them. And I saw the souls of those who had been beheaded because of their testimony of Jesus and because of the word of God, and those who had not worshiped the beast or his image, and had not received the mark on their forehead and on their hand; and they came to life and reigned with Christ for a thousand years. (Revelation 20:4)

The four variations of the futurist perspective are described as dispensational premillennialism, historic premillennialism, postmillennialism, and amillennialism. It is obvious that a literal interpretation of Revelation 20:1-6 is the central eschatological component defining these systems. They each have developed a sequential narrative of events drawn from apocalyptic prophecies. Each one projects a one thousand-year earthly reign of Christ followed by yet another great tribulation of demonic activity and judgment. This expectation was previously defined as *Chiliasm* (Greek for "one thousand years"), the defined Christian hope of an earthly kingdom as expected by the early disciples.

A brief explanation of these narrations is as follows:

The Dispensational Premillennialist Sequential Narrative

This system is recently founded in eschatological schemes based on a number of assumptions, primarily on the Biblical interpretation of two ongoing and simultaneous covenants operating among God's people.

I addressed this issue in the second key concerning the bond servants of God. This view considers both the initial covenant that is entered into and limited to ethnic Israel and contemporary Jews and the New Covenant of the early Jewish believers and, more dominantly, for Gentile believers in Jesus.

This system considers that the Kingdom of God is here but not yet, an initial inauguration of eschatology. However, it is not considered a present reality on the earth but has been postponed to the next dispensation of God, the next age. This narrative waits an unknown period of time while prophecies focused on the end times are fulfilled. These include a rebuilding of the third temple in Jerusalem with a reinitiated sacrificial system and a reformed and revived Roman Empire from which the Antichrist arises.

The inauguration of these events is preceded by ever-defined "signs of the times" leading to a sudden and secret rapture of qualified saints called "true Christians." This will then initiate the beginning of the concluding seven-year period of Daniel's yet-to-be-realized "seventieth week." This is defined as the Great Tribulation that falls on the remaining humanity who is "left behind."

The raptured believers expect to immediately receive their resurrected glorified physical bodies. As referenced in Thessalonians, those who have died before this event will be resurrected from their graves and reunited with their souls prior to the living raptured souls. The events listed in The Revelation will then begin to unfold in a global catastrophic domino effect with the rise of the ungodly trinity of the Antichrist and his false prophet under the power of Satan to usher in a temporary false global political and religious peace. This is referred to as the Great Tribulation. The cataclysmic judgments released by the breaking of seals and the blowing of trumpets and the pouring of bowls of wrath are drawn from the descriptions listed in The Revelation. The global catastrophe results in billions dead and much of the earth devastated from physical and spiritual calamities.

During this seven-year period of testing and temptation many people left behind will come to faith in Jesus and be severely persecuted. There is also the expectation of a Jewish revival of tens of thousands converting and witnessing for Jesus.

At the conclusion of this seven-year period, Jesus will return in bodily form as the Lord of Hosts. His angel armies and the contingent of raptured and glorified saints will accompany Him as He overcomes His enemies in the expected battle of Armageddon. At this time, the Antichrist will be defeated along with the false prophet. Jesus will finally establish His earthly, visible kingdom in Jerusalem. It is expected that He will revive the sacrificial system in the new temple and reign on the earth for one thousand years.

During this millennium, Satan will be bound and the glorified, raptured believers will rule with Christ in a new hierarchy of delegated authority. The remaining survivors on earth will live under this governmental system and inhabit and repopulate the earth. They are expected to live elongated, blessed lives under a heavenly theocratic government.

At the end of this millennial reign, the futurist perspective of The Revelation introduces one final test of loyalty. Satan will be released from his prison and stir up a rebellion and final war against Christ's kingdom that will be quickly won by the sword of Jesus Word. A final judgment will follow on all remaining evil. Satan and his demons will be cast into the lake of fire, and the bodies of the unbelieving dead will be raised from their graves, reunited with their souls for their ultimate judgment, and also cast into the lake of fire. A new heaven and a new earth will initiate the eternal life of God's people.

The Historic Premillennial Sequential Narrative

This narrative recognizes that God has only one fulfilled new covenant with His people through Jesus Christ. Jesus fulfilled God's original covenant with Abraham, and it includes and applies equally to all ethnic Jews and Gentiles who put their faith in Jesus as the Messiah. The

Kingdom of God was inaugurated and is present on earth through the First Coming of Jesus. It is primarily invisible in nature and will not be substantially manifested in the visible world until the Second Coming of Christ and the thousand-year millennial reign of Christ is established in Jerusalem.

These beliefs distinguish this second view as a quite different system of eschatology than the first. There will not be a rapture of believers until Christ returns at the end of the seven-year great tribulation, during which the warfare and Divine judgments of the book of Revelation take place; the rest of the "last days" beliefs about the two resurrections, the nature of the millennium, the unbinding of Satan, and the final war and judgment significantly mirror the Dispensational view above (usually minus the temple sacrifices during the millennium). This view was referred to in the early centuries of church history by some church leaders and movements; hence the "historic" tag.

Francisco Ribera in 1590 was one of the first to develop a form of futurism as a reaction to the historicists interpretations accusing the Roman church and her papacy as the antichrist system of a degenerate church. He began writing his commentary on the book of Revelation in 1585, proposing that the first chapters of The Revelation apply to ancient pagan Rome and the rest is limited to a yet future three and one half-year period immediately prior to the Second Coming of Christ. Then he proposed that the Antichrist was a single individual who would persecute and blaspheme the saints of God, rebuild the temple in Jerusalem, abolish the Christian religion, deny Jesus Christ, destroy Rome, be received by the Jews, pretend to be God, kill the two witnesses of God, and conquer the world. To accomplish this, Ribera proposed that the 1,260 days, and the 42 months and 3½ times, times, and half a time referenced in The Revelation were not 1,260 years as based on the year-day principle (Numbers 14:34 and Ezekiel 4:6), but a literal three and one-half years, hence preventing the arrival of the deduction of the 1,260 years that had passed.

Conclusion

The four schools of thought that have developed in the past 1,500 years have become more polarized and descriptive as the years pass. The criticism that each holds for the other is divisive and confusing for the disciple who wants to read the book of Revelation and receive the blessing. I hope that the considerations of this book will provide a framework for comprehension and application. I also hope to dissuade the developing cultic followings of their unique applications of the prophetic view that generate an elitist segregation and grandiose ministry expectation.

THE RAPTURE OF THE CHURCH

The "Blessed Hope" is not our going but His coming!

But I do not want you to be ignorant, brethren, concerning those who have fallen asleep, lest you sorrow as others who have no hope. For if we believe that Jesus died and rose again, even so God will bring with Him those who sleep in Jesus. For this we say to you by the word of the Lord, that we who are alive and remain until the coming of the Lord will by no means precede those who are asleep. For the Lord Himself will descend from heaven with a shout, with the voice of an archangel, and with the trumpet of God. And the dead in Christ will rise first. *Then we who are alive and remain shall be caught up together with them in the clouds to meet the Lord in the air.* And thus we shall always be with the Lord. Therefore comfort one another with these words.
—1 Thessalonians 4:13–18, emphasis added

For almost two centuries, the church has been introduced to, and then fixated on, a secret rapture, a great escape. This is based on the ancient promise that those who are alive and remain shall be caught up (raptured) together with those who have already gone on to the Lord "to be caught up together with them in the clouds to meet the Lord in the air." The recent teachings that have been introduced, in the past two centuries, are based in the futuristic perspective of eschatology with the prophetic additions of application. They are looking for "signs of His coming" and anticipating this "catching away" prior to the final judgment in order to steel their souls against fear.

The anticipation of this "escape" has resulted in many false expectations and has produced great disillusionment in the church. There have been many disappointed believers since its introduction due to the failed prognostications of well-meaning teachers. The promise is true, but the expectation has been misconstrued. Jesus has made us promises, and we can be sure that He will not fail.

> And if I go and prepare a place for you, I will come again and receive you to Myself; that where I am, there you may be also. (John 13:3)

> And while they looked steadfastly toward heaven as He went up, behold, two men stood by them in white apparel, who also said, "Men of Galilee, why do you stand gazing up into heaven? This same Jesus, who was taken up from you into heaven, will so come in like manner as you saw Him go into heaven." (Acts 1:10–11)

The apostle Paul has revealed his insight to us and many teachers have attempted to fill in the blanks. The Western mind has been formed with the expectation of interpreted revelation from a rational, chronological, literal, and empirical approach to Scripture. However, God's revelation is a fruit of relationship. This does not exclude intellect and reason, but like Jesus' parables, His truth is aimed at the heart rather than the head.

> But blessed are your eyes, because they see; and your ears, because they hear. For truly I say to you that many prophets and righteous men desired to see what you see, and did not see it, and to hear what you hear, and did not hear it. (Matthew 13:16–17)

Eternal truth is revealed to all the saints by the Holy Spirit for all time. The contemporary philosophy of presentism has produced an approach to The Revelation that has attempted to literally discern the future by reading and interpreting prophetic and apocalyptic Scripture as history written in advance. I do not discount the accuracy of the fulfilled prophecy; however, I do question the myopic application of The Revelation. The historical and chronological attempts at literal, sequential, and contemporary approaches have resulted in many failed and false projections. The great disappointments of these failures have generated even more confusion as interpreters tried to explain, justify, and adjust their anticipated future.

> Know this first of all, that in the last days mockers will come with their mocking, following after their own lusts, and saying, "Where is the promise of His coming? For ever since the fathers fell asleep, all continues just as it was from the beginning of creation." (2 Peter 3:3–4)

This is the cry heard again today: "What happened to the promise that Jesus is coming again?"

> For the grace of God has appeared, bringing salvation to all men, instructing us to deny ungodliness and worldly desires and to live sensibly, righteously and godly in the present age, looking for the blessed hope and the appearing of the glory of our great God and Savior, Christ Jesus, who gave Himself for us to redeem us from every lawless deed, and to purify for Himself a people for His own possession, zealous for good deeds. (Titus 2:11–14)

The "Blessed Hope" is not our going but His coming!

We have a blessed hope and this hope does not disappoint (Romans 5:5). Recent church history is replete with missed dates and great disappointments of the anticipated rapture event. Attempts to puzzle out literal applications, mathematical formulae for past historical events, and lunar calendar comparisons—along with watching for celestial and contemporary historical events—has resulted in a frenzy of "last days" projections. When these projected dates pass by, the "end times" teachers reevaluate and try again with spiritualized explanations of their miscalculations.

The Biblical basis for this ultimate expectation is revealed by the apostle Paul in his letters to the Thessalonian and Corinthian churches. The Greek word *harpazō* is translated "caught up." This Greek word was translated first into Latin, *rapio,* and has been transliterated into the English word *rapture.* The apostle Paul was describing the forceful, sovereign act of God to pluck, pull, or take by force His own at the end of the age "at the last trumpet."

The rapture, then, is the catching up of believers by Christ at the time of His return. Living believers are said to be "caught up" to meet the Lord at His coming. The question is not if, but when.

> Now I say this, brethren, that flesh and blood cannot inherit the kingdom of God; nor does the perishable inherit the imperishable. Behold, I tell you a mystery; we will not all sleep, but we will all be changed, in a moment, in the twinkling of an eye, at the last trumpet; for the trumpet will sound, and the dead will be raised imperishable, and we will be changed. For this perishable must put on the imperishable, and this mortal must put on immortality. But when this perishable will have put on the imperishable, and this mortal will have put on immortality, then will come about the saying that is written, "DEATH IS SWALLOWED UP in victory. O DEATH, WHERE IS YOUR VICTORY? O DEATH, WHERE IS YOUR STING?" (1 Corinthians 15:50–55)

The Novel Idea

This relatively new doctrine of a secret rapture divides the return of Christ into a second and third coming. According to the *Encyclopedia of Biblical Prophecy* by J. Barton Payne, there are about 700 prophecies in the Bible and about 150 remain to be fulfilled. These remaining prophetic words refer to the consummation of the age, the great tribulation, and the final judgment. The doctrine of a secret rapture of the saints is directed at the escape from this cataclysmic period and the final conflict.

Eschatological history described in church writings makes no mention of a secret rapture. The Scriptures referred to for this idea are, unfortunately, drawn from the prophecy that clearly defines the terrible destruction of Jerusalem. However, if there is not an understanding of the separation of prophetic consummation of the two ages, from Adam to the cross and from the cross to Christ's return, these events are not recognized in His prophetic announcement. The two tracks of apocalyptic events appear to be the only clear explanation for Jesus' Olivet discourse and The Revelation.

So there is no question as to the rapture occurring at the end of the age. The origination of this notion of a secret rapture is well recorded, and many good books have detailed the historical development of the doctrine. In short, it is recorded that a prophetic word given by Margaret MacDonald in Port Glasgow, Scotland, in the early nineteenth century is the source of the developing teaching. There have been many books detailing the history of this event and the unfolding process that has resulted in this very unique and detailed perspective. Rev. Edward Irvine is reported to have left the Church of Scotland to found the now-defunct Catholic Apostolic Church. It is reported that he hosted prophetic conferences in the library at Dr. Henry Drummond's Albury Court. These conferences were attended by the Rev. John Nelson Darby, who left the Anglican Church to found the Brethren. He crossed the Atlantic Ocean and is known as the teacher who persuaded a lawyer, C. I. Scofield, to adopt this concept, which he incorporated in his study notes of the *Scofield Reference Bible*. He is credited with producing one of the initial study Bibles and included Darby's teaching as the lens by which The Revelation should be read and interpreted.

This teaching has since multiplied into a number of scenarios. As described in the previous chapter, there are four main lenses by which prophecy is viewed. The unique views of the futuristic perspective have developed into a number of rapture possibilities. Also described previously, the two topics of rapture and millennium are the most varied. However, it is within the premillennial view that the teaching of a rapture finds major emphasis.

The secret rapture, then, is explained as the "catching away" of the living saints on earth prior to Jesus' second coming. It expects a seven-year tribulation period as an explanation for Daniel's seventieth week; therefore, discounting the fall of Jerusalem and the destruction of the temple. This view sees a tribulation period occurring immediately before the Second Coming of Christ.

Again, there are three main positions including this expectation and the rapture. The first are called pretribulationists, who see the rapture occurring prior to a seven-year tribulation. This view places the church in heaven during the time of tribulation on earth. Second is the mid-tribulationists, placing the rapture at the mid-point of a seven-year tribulation period. This view places the church on earth for the first half of the tribulation but escapes the last half, which is seen to be the time of intense or great tribulation. This view, along with the previous one, sees the Second Coming of Christ in two phases. The first phase is taught as a secret coming in clouds to rapture the church. The second phase is His final return with His church to begin a thousand-year reign on earth. The third view teaches that His second coming and the beginning of His earthly reign will occur simultaneously. This posttribulationists view holds that the church will remain on earth during the tribulation period. It teaches that this time will be one of wrath upon the world system. However, the church will be protected from Divine wrath although experiencing tribulation. This view avoids dividing the return of Christ into two phases.

The apostle Peter encourages the church with his explanation in the third chapter of his second letter. He addresses the disappointment of many concerning their understanding of the "end of days" and the return of Christ. He states the ultimate conclusion resulting in a new heaven and a new earth as is revealed in the last vision of The Revelation at the time of the great white throne judgment, or judgment seat of Christ.

> But of that day and hour no one knows, not even the angels of heaven, nor the Son, but the Father alone. (Matthew 24:36)

THE UNVEILING

Jesus is very clear concerning this reality. The inner counsel of the Lord is for those who fear Him, and Jesus promises to disclose Himself to us. This is our desire, satisfaction, hope, and joy.

> The secret of the Lord is with those who fear Him, And He will show them His covenant. (Psalm 25:14)

We are servants of Jesus Christ and stewards of His mysteries. Mysteries are things to be revealed, not necessarily explained. Mysteries are always unsettling. The overwhelming process of God pouring His ocean of revelation into our teacup of understanding is our eternal prospect.

> Jesus answered them, "To you it has been granted to know the mysteries of the kingdom of heaven, but to them it has not been granted. For whoever has, to him more shall be given, and he will have an abundance; but whoever does not have, even what he has shall be taken away from him." (Matthew 13:11–12)

> Let a man so consider us, as servants of Christ and stewards of the mysteries of God. (1 Corinthians 4:1)

Peter exhorts us to keep the main thing the main thing. We are to keep our eyes on Jesus.

> Since all these things are to be destroyed in this way, what sort of people ought you to be in holy conduct and godliness, looking for and hastening the coming of the day of God, because of which the heavens will be destroyed by burning, and the elements will melt with intense heat! But according to His promise we are looking for new heavens and a new earth, in which righteousness dwells. (2 Peter 3:11–13)

Let's purpose to live as faithful witnesses and hasten the day of His return with our ministries of intercession and evangelism.

CONCLUSION

After reading The Revelation through many dozens of times with the desire to experience what John experienced in his recorded vision, I believe I am slightly further along in comprehending this unveiled truth than I was before. As with all Scriptural revelation, we are studying the eternal Word of God. His Word is not something to be mastered but received and consumed. The more we study and meditate on His Word, the greater the glimpse of His glory.

One of the initial observations of John's writing is the unique structure of this book. It is a report, a dictation of experiences. Unlike other Scripture, this book appears to have been written down quickly, forcibly captured like a student in a lecture hall listening to the speaker, absorbing, processing, and trying to record and document in his own mind and onto paper the many experiences, sights, and sounds and their associated new thoughts. The sequence of seven powerful visions separated by transitional experiences and instructions is overwhelming. If John were not inspired by the Holy Spirit to accomplish this task, he would not have succeeded on his own.

I've noted many times in this book that one of the greatest hurdles to reading and receiving from The Revelation is the accumulation of preconceived ideas. I've attempted to read what the Word says without the running commentary of what others say it says. The fit-over lenses of many systems of interpretation are not easily discarded or discounted. I have honestly been perplexed for many years with this book. I've heard many good teachers from many different streams describe the book in their words, assign meaning to each image or event, and then come to a conclusion about the purpose and its application. But I would not stay satisfied for very long. I found these explanations wanting but could not completely refute their opinion or explain why. Each author used the tools of language and history to substantiate his or her explanation. Some used simple explanations with an Andy Griffith aw-shucks simplicity while others boggled the mind with dozens of Scriptures, obscure news clippings, and scientific revelations to prove their assumed conclusions.

There were two key considerations that I found missing from most commentaries and have come to believe are critical to understanding The Revelation. I have incorporated both of them in my reading and explanation of The Revelation. The common threads of the timelessness of God and the promise of seed of the woman are woven throughout the Scriptures. From the Genesis account of creation to the final reveal of the Apocalypse, the fact that God is not bound by time but is the Creator of time is understood and that Scripture is His story. These facts are key to our perspective of God's revealed truth.

Apocalyptic Scripture is the very disclosure of God from His perspective. However, all the commentaries I have read and all the teachers I have received from all seem to attempt discernment from the human perspective, from the sequential and chronological unfolding of John's seven visions. This approach from the outset ignores the transitions and separations and links the visions in an order that does not appear to be cohesive but redundant. We must see God's great disclosure from God's perspective.

The second consideration has been a divisive separation of the ethnic people of Israel and the Church. The age of the Law and the prophets was realized by weak men and weak blood and has come to its conclusion and fulfillment in Jesus Christ. He has fulfilled all that was required in the Law and introduced the New Covenant in His blood. The conclusion of this age is seen in His life, death, burial, and resurrection. The exclamation mark of His ministry of fulfillment was realized within the generation of His earthly ministry. This was prophesied by Daniel and realized in the final blow of Jesus' prophetic announcement to

Jerusalem and the destruction of the temple. This catastrophic event is the focus of the preterist perspective within the human chronological viewpoint. However, I suggest that their timeline based on the human chronological perspective is a limiting factor in the application of the big picture. This results in a diminishing of Scripture by discounting what has been revealed.

The futurist perspective has developed a sequence of radical expectations to fulfill these prophetic announcements. The statements by the patriarchs of God's fulfilled promises concerning the Promised Land are not accepted, and a future earthly kingdom is expected. The prophetic pictures from Daniel and Jesus' discourse on the Mount of Olives have been thrust into the always-near future. The cataclysmic reality of the demise of Jerusalem and the Temple is relegated to a historical fact that is not tied into God's "end of age" warnings and promises. I believe that these truths are pertinent to the reading and application of The Revelation.

As our world appears to race toward oblivion, The Revelation becomes more relevant to this busy world. The inundation of fearful daily reports reveals that the world is headed for catastrophe. It seems to be spinning out of control, approaching a threshold of lethality. We cannot continue in this direction and maintain this momentum without sure disaster. The globalization of economies and technologies is shrinking our world at a pace that overwhelms our sensibilities. We are so interconnected and interdependent that the destructive trends developing in major population centers are reaching the remotest parts of the earth even to the remotest cultures.

I am reminded of a scene just a few years ago in the remote area of northern Kenya. A thin, scantily dressed middle-aged man was standing on his rudely made oxcart with a small whip shouting at his beast of burden and furiously swishing the whip back and forth. I thought he looked odd from a distance, as his head was bent precariously to one side. As we approached him on the road, it became obvious that he had a mobile phone wedged between his shoulder and his ear and was carrying on his lively conversation while driving his cart through the traffic. The nations and cultures that were left behind technologically for many years are now leap-frogging ahead of the cultures that have been developing new tech daily. As with technology, so also with the fears, controls, and manipulations of man to his own destruction.

As a Christian I take it for granted that human history will someday end; and I am offering Omniscience no advice as to the best date for that consummation.

—C. S. Lewis[9]

NOTES

1. Cell and Molecular Biology by Eugene Rosenberg, p. 199, 1971.

2. J. Stuart Russell, The Parousia (IPA–International Preterist Association pages 366-367)

3. Allen Menzies, ed., *The Writing of the Fathers Down to AD32*, vol. 3 *Latin Christianity: Its Founder, Tertullian* (Grand Rapids, MI: William B. Eerdmans, 2009), 101, Christian Classics Ethereal Library, http://www.ccel.org/ccel/schaff/anf03.i.html

4. The Works of Flavius Josephus—The Wars Of The Jews Or The History Of The Destruction Of Jerusalem Book V

5. Book Five (1-13) of The Histories by Tacitus

6. http://www.bible.ca/pre-destruction70AD-george-holford-1805AD.htm

7. Leon Uris *QB VII*—Part 2 Chapter 18 (page 191))

8. *The Parousi*a Preface pg xxviii IPA

9. C.S. Lewis, "Is Progress Possible?" *God In The Dock: Essays On Theology and Ethics* (Grand Rapids, MI: Eerdmans, 1970), page 312